MAKE YOUR
STORY A MOVIE

ALSO BY JOHN ROBERT MARLOW

NANO

MAKE YOUR STORY A MOVIE

ADAPTING YOUR BOOK OR IDEA FOR HOLLYWOOD

JOHN ROBERT MARLOW

ST. MARTIN'S GRIFFIN ☙ NEW YORK

MAKE YOUR STORY A MOVIE: ADAPTING YOUR BOOK OR IDEA FOR HOLLYWOOD. Copyright © 2012 by John Robert Marlow. All rights reserved. Printed in the United States of America. For information, address St. Martin's Press, 175 Fifth Avenue, New York, N.Y. 10010.

www.stmartins.com

Design by Omar Chapa

Library of Congress Cataloging-in-Publication Data

Marlow, John Robert.
    Make your story a movie : adapting your book or idea for Hollywood / John Robert Marlow.—First St. Martin's Griffin edition.
        pages cm
    ISBN 978-1-250-00183-2 (trade pbk.)
    ISBN 978-1-250-01787-1 (e-book)
    1. Film adaptations.   2. Motion picture authorship.   I. Title.
    PN1997.85.M275 2013
    808.2'3—dc23

                                                              2012036199

First Edition: December 2012

10   9   8   7   6   5   4   3   2   1

For Jacqueline Radley,
for shining a light where I could not see

CONTENTS

ACKNOWLEDGMENTS

Many people contributed generously of their time to help this project become a reality. Unlike some of them, who've had to remember who to thank while facing a billion-member audience, I have the luxury of calmly searching my memory. So if I've left anyone out, I can't blame it on the ticking clock or the music coming up.

I would like to express my gratitude to my agent, Andy Ross (of the Andy Ross Agency), who offered to represent me without my even having to ask—and also to my editor at Macmillan/St. Martin's Griffin, Daniela Rapp, who very quickly decided she wanted the book, made a number of helpful suggestions, and pretty much let me do my thing. I'd like to acknowledge as well the assistance of Sarah Jae-Jones and Helen Chin at the copyediting stage. Thanks also to Chris Lockhart for teaching me much of what I know about loglines and story structure; to Ken Atchity and Chi-Li Wong for their continued passion for *War Gods*; to Michael A. Simpson for educating me about the world of independent finance; to Matt Galsor, Hillary Bibicoff, and Alexander Plitt of Greenberg Glusker for their legal counsel; and to Julie Richardson for hiring a private detective (two, actually) to find me when I couldn't find myself.

And, of course, thanks to the interviewees whose words and wisdom appear in these pages—some of whom I already knew, and some of whom I came to know while writing this book: Alan Glynn, Barry Levine, Bill Marsilii, Bonnie Eskenazi, Cathleen Blackburn, Christopher Lockhart, Ed Solomon, Ehren Kruger, Evan Daugherty, Gail Lyon, Gale Anne Hurd, Isa Dick Hackett, Jay Simpson, John August, Jonathan Hensleigh, Leslie Dixon, Michael Nozik, Mike Richardson, Pamela DuMond, Paul Haggis, Rex Pickett, Ryan Condal, Steve Niles, Susannah Grant, Terry Rossio (who also granted kind permission to excerpt from some of his own writings), Vikas Swarup, and Walter Kirn.

Thanks as well to those who helped in reaching out to others, including Ann Garretson, Bonnie Eskenazi, Caitlin Meares, Daniela Rapp, Drew McWeeny, Gale Anne Hurd, Gian Sardar, Greg Beal, Harry Knowles, Matt Misetich, Michael Nozik, Perry Sachs, Sharline Liu, Stuart Friedel, and Susannah Grant.

INTRODUCTION
THE POWER OF HOLLYWOOD

"Looking back," says Rex Pickett, author of the novel *Sideways,* "I wish I hadn't taken the measly $5,000 advance from the publisher. Had I waited until the film was released, I'm told the book would have sold for $1,000,000."

Rex divides his life into before-and-after episodes. "Before the movie, I was nobody. My life was complete shit. The day the movie went into production, I made $300,000. Suddenly everybody wanted something, and I had four agents working for me."

The *Sideways* film cost $16 million, made $109 million at the box office, supercharged the California wine industry (with the notable exception of merlot, which it nearly destroyed), and drew five Academy Award nominations, including Best Picture and Best Adapted Screenplay (winning the latter). Among Pickett's follow-up projects: a sequel to the *Sideways* novel, called *Vertical,* and a play based on the first book.

Walter Kirn is a self-described eccentric author. "To be frank," he says, "I'm not a guy who sold a lot of books, or even managed to project a coherent image of himself and his art. All of my books have weird little publishing histories, and each has been quite different from the others and often eccentric. It's hard for a writer like me to keep doing the kinds of things he wants to do, in a world where the big question is, 'Hey man, how many hundreds of thousands of units have you sold for me lately?' That I can go on doing this at all is probably a credit to the movie.

"Really quite specifically, I think it saved my ass. When the movie came along, not much was happening in Walter World. I felt like one of those disaster victims lying out on a football field somewhere, about to expire, and they've only got so many syringes filled with adrenaline. And someone just happened to stick one into me."

The film based on Kirn's book, *Up in the Air,* was made for $25 million, starred George Clooney, earned over $160 million at the box office, was nominated for six Academy Awards (Best Picture and Best Adapted Screenplay among them) and, in Kirn's words, "sold a hell of a lot of books." True to form, he has since published several more books—none of which bear much resemblance to any other.

Alan Glynn's novel *The Dark Fields* had been out of print for years. Despite glowing reviews from *The New York Times* and *Publishers Weekly,* he found himself teaching English as a second language. "I was fairly miserable and losing hope of ever being published again," he recalls. Then came the movie based on his novel: *Limitless.*

"It brought my book back from the dead. It was re-released under the film title. Suddenly I'm watching a TV spot for the *Limitless* movie, playing during the Super Bowl. And the movie definitely sends people out to bookstores." *Limitless* earned over $150 million in theaters.

Alan now has two more books out—*Bloodland* and *Winterland*—with another, *Graveland,* slated for 2013. He writes full time, in a house with a paid-off mortgage.

Even writers whose works are already selling briskly benefit from movies. "A great example is Frank Miller," says Dark Horse Comics founder Mike Richardson. "He's probably the premier creator in comics, and his sales were already stellar. Every book he does is an event.

"But when a movie like *300* comes out and hits, it adds new heat. People see the movie and want the book, even those who may not have been comic or graphic novel readers before that. We put out a new hardcover edition priced at thirty-five dollars, which is certainly at the high end for a graphic novel, and sold hundreds of thousands of copies while the movie was playing."

This in an industry where, says comic writer Steve Niles, "most comics are selling around 20,000 to 30,000 copies, independents are surviving on 5,000 to 10,000, and anything that sells 100,000 is a smash hit."

When *Slumdog Millionaire* hit theaters, says author Vikas Swarup, "*Q&A* [the novel on which the film is based] had already been translated into thirty-six languages. But the film catapulted it to a different level altogether. It created a totally new following, composed of people who came to know about the book because of the movie. The American book sales zoomed up once the movie came out, and the book entered the *New York Times* Best Seller List."

The film, made for $15 million, grossed nearly $400 million at the box office, winning eight of the ten Academy Awards for which it was nominated, including Best Picture and Best Adapted Screenplay. Hollywood can be very good to authors.

Still, the rewards awaiting those with screenplays to sell are even greater. "Though my earnings from the movie deal were high, and I'm not complaining for a second," Glynn notes, "it's still peanuts compared to what other major players involved in the movie get. There would be no movie without the book and yet, relatively speaking, they don't have to pay that much to acquire the book— mainly because most writers are poor, and happy to accept the first offer that comes along."

If you have a script (screenplay) to sell, the equation shifts in your favor. Ryan Condal, an advertising executive, adapted the Arthurian legend into a screenplay. *Galahad* was his first sale, fetching $500,000. Though the film has yet to be produced, he's already been hired by studios to adapt several comic books for the screen— including *Hercules: The Thracian Wars.*

Evan Daugherty adapted the Snow White faery tale into a screenplay called *Snow White and the Huntsman*—which sold for $3.2 million in 2010, was released in theaters June of 2012 and made over $100 million in its first ten days. Bill Marsilii, who has since adapted comics, novels, children's books and more, earlier teamed up with veteran screenwriter Terry Rossio (*Pirates of the Caribbean, Shrek,* and *Zorro* adaptation franchises) to write *Déjà Vu*—which sold for $5 million. It was Bill's first sale.

In the book world, you have to be a J. K. Rowling, a Stephen King, or a John Grisham to pull advances like that. In Hollywood, today's hot writer can be—and often is—yesterday's nobody.

Clearly, these are best-case scenarios, and not every screenplay adaptation sells for $3 million. In fact, most screenplays—like most books—never sell at all. ("I take a Han Solo approach," says Marsilii. "Never tell me the odds. A more healthy outlook is to recognize what the odds are, and go do it anyway.")

On the other hand, an average spec screenplay (one written "on speculation," rather than on assignment) sells for $300,000 to $600,000, whereas the average book advance is more like $10,000 to $20,000, and film rights options (employed when there is no screenplay) can be as low as $1.

Even so, you're better off with a book (or other source material) *and* a screenplay. Consider: you have two properties to sell instead of one (and to completely different markets at that); the sale of either will increase the price of the other; the success of either will bring you more money from both; the movie may take years to make (if it's made at all); you control the content of your book or other story; and—despite the comparatively vast sums paid to most screenwriters—no pure screenwriter has ever been paid what a top-end author receives. Not even close.

Nevertheless, those top-end authors would not receive the gargantuan paydays they do—and often would not be household names—if not for the movies based on their books. So if you're going for the gold, you really need both.

And while it's true that there are very few writers capable of creating good books (or comic books, plays, short stories, blogs, magazine articles, games, musicals, etc.) *and* good screenplays—you don't have to be one of them to make your mark in Hollywood. Because you can team up with a screenwriter who specializes in adaptations.

Whichever path you choose, this book will lay down the ground rules, explaining what Hollywood looks for in source material and in screenplays, what's involved in creating a good—or great—adaptation, and how to find help, or strike out on your own. You'll also find hard-won creative and business advice from authors, publishers, producers, screenwriters, directors, and others whose projects have become household names, won Academy Awards, and earned tens of billions of dollars from box office and DVD sales alone.

Creators, authors, screenwriters, producers, agents and managers interested in adaptations—this book is for you.

John Robert Marlow
Los Angeles

ADAPTATION CODES USED IN THIS BOOK

The following shorthand codes are used throughout this book to indicate the type of source material on which adapted films are based. Note that the definition of adaptation used here is broader than that used by the Academy of Motion Picture Arts and Sciences—which does not, for example, consider screenplays based on true stories or historical events to be adaptations. Also as used in this book, re-makes are considered to be adaptations (of the films on which they're based). Sequels are not counted as adaptations unless the first movie was itself an adaptation.

ART	Article in magazine, newspaper, etc.	**NOV**	Novel/children's book
		PLY	Play
BLG	Blog	**RAD**	Radio program
COM	Comic book/graphic novel	**SCR**	Screenplay (for a different movie)
GAM	Game or toy	**SNG**	Song
HIS	Historic event	**STO**	Short story, novella, etc.
MLF	Myth/legend/faery tale	**THM**	Theme park/theme park ride
MOV	Movie (remake)	**TRU**	True-life story
NFB	Nonfiction book	**TVS**	Television series

PART I

ADAPT OR DIE

What can an adaptation do for you and your story? Are there things that can't or shouldn't be adapted? Should you really go to the trouble of adapting your story before selling it——and if so, why? The following three chapters answer these questions——along with several others you probably haven't thought to ask . . .

CHAPTER 1
WHY ADAPT?

Audience, Money, Synergy

Humans have always been storytellers. Whether gathered around a campfire, painting on cave walls, writing words on dead trees or computer screens—it's in our blood. Books and other storytelling formats can be noble undertakings, capable of reaching hundreds of thousands of readers.

But movies are the global campfires of our time.

GLOBAL AUDIENCE

Filmed entertainment routinely reaches millions, sometimes hundreds of millions of people, all over the world. On those occasions where book sales reach this level, they do so with the aid of movies based on the books. Aside from religious texts with thousands of years to build an audience, there are no exceptions to this rule.

It makes no difference whether a story is little known and personal (*Monster, Erin Brockovich,* both TRU*), or a household name on

---

*See page 7 for list of adaptation codes used in this book and on the companion Web site.

multiple continents (*Harry Potter, Twilight,* both NOV), *Batman, Spider-Man* (both COM)—a movie can expand the audience exponentially. There are a number of reasons for this, the most obvious being that people who don't—and people who can't—read books still watch movies. But there are other reasons as well. . . .

THE FUTURE IS DIGITAL

A recent Associated Press–Ipsos poll found that only one in four American adults claimed to have read a book during the previous year. Those who did read reported going through an average of nine books—in an entire year. Reasons cited by the poll include competition from other media, and a mature publishing industry with "limited opportunities for expansion."

One poll respondent summed things up succinctly: "If I'm going to get a story, I'll get a movie." The AP's article on the study referred to book sales as "flat in recent years" and "expected to stay that way indefinitely."

As it turns out, this may be optimistic: a report released in 2010 by the Association of American Publishers shows an overall decline in actual book sales compared with the previous year. The print figures for 2011 are below those for 2010: adult hardcovers down 17.5 percent; trade paperbacks down by 15.6 percent; and mass market paperbacks down by 35.9 percent. Even a sharp increase in e-book sales could not reverse this downward trend, Borders is now bankrupt, and Penguin announced that first-half operating profits had fallen by 50 percent in 2012.

Movies, on the other hand, are doing better than ever, and pollsters would be hard-pressed to find any first world resident—adult or juvenile—who has viewed a paltry nine movies over the course of any recent year. According to the Motion Picture Association of America, Hollywood's worldwide box office receipts grew by 10 percent in 2009, to $29.9 billion. In 2010, they grew another 8 percent, to $31.8 billion. In 2011, another 3 percent, to $32.6 billion. Overall, revenues have climbed 35 percent in five years. (For the latest stats, visit http://makeyourstoryamovie.com/bookbonus .html.) DVD sales alone easily triple or quadruple this figure, even without merchandising and other revenue streams, which can in some cases outperform the movies themselves.

Likewise, the film industry's "opportunities for expansion" are plentiful. The first large-scale 3D film—*Avatar*—raked in nearly $3 billion at the box office, annihilating the previous record set by *Titanic* (HIS) over ten years before. A typical hit film earns three to four times the box office revenues in DVD sales, which brings *Avatar*'s total to an absolute minimum of $12 billion to $15 billion, exclusive of merchandising and other rights.

That's nearly double the total of all trade book (nontextbook) book sales from U.S. publishers for the entire preceding year. *For a single film.* (Sequels are planned for 2014 and 2015.) If *Avatar*'s earnings (again excluding merchandising) were gross domestic product, the film would rank just outside the top-100 national economies in the world for its year of release.

Equipment created to shoot *Avatar* seems poised to revolutionize other aspects of the film and television industries as well. Recent developments include the rollout of 3D televisions, a new process to upconvert 2D films to 3D, online streaming of theatrical releases and television episodes, the coming digital distribution of theatrical films—everywhere you look, movies are breaking new ground, and showing us things no human eye has ever seen before. Strictly speaking, it's not even film anymore; *Avatar* and many other movies are now entirely digital.

While the persistent rumors of print's death remain highly exaggerated, it is undeniable that movies are evolving in a way that print is not. And whether we like it or not, the writing (so to speak) is on the wall (or screen): in an increasingly digital culture, entertainment becomes increasingly digitized. And there is, in the end, only so much we can do with printed, even digitized words.

But while books and other storytelling media still live, movies—and the screenplays on which they're based—can be used to amplify their impact, and the bank accounts of their authors or rights-holders.

MONEY

The film industry operates on its own financial plain, which is not really comparable to any other storytelling medium. Expenses run high, and so do paychecks. A typical midlist hardcover book release might cost the publisher $80,000, all told. An extremely low-budget film might cost $1 million to produce and release; $30 million to $50 million is more typical, $100 million increasingly common, and $400 million to $500 million (*Avatar*'s budget) the current top end.

The typical advance for a first novel is in the neighborhood of $10,000 to $20,000, and—as any book agent will tell you—advances have actually declined in recent years. The typical selling price of a screenplay by a first-time writer hovers between $300,000 and $600,000, with some first scripts soaring well beyond the $1 million mark. (This is not true of adaptation rights alone, when there is no screenplay; for more on this, see Chapter 3.)

Novels run 250 to 500 pages. Screenplays run 100 to 120 pages. So even on the low end, a book (at 500 pages and $10,000) pays $20 a page, while a screenplay (120 pages and $300,000) pays $2,500 per page—with fewer words on each page.

Before deciding to give up books and start writing screenplays, though, be aware that screenplay earnings are generally capped; regardless of how successful the film or television series may be, you will be paid the purchase price, bonuses, residuals, and so on—and that's all. After that, the well runs dry—for you. Producers, directors, and actors can sometimes cut themselves a better deal, while the studio (of course) makes money forever.

The book world imposes no such ceiling: every copy sold puts more money in your pocket. If the book does insanely well, you make an insane amount of money. This is why there are no pure screenwriters on the *Forbes* list of the world's highest-earning writers.

But keep in mind: there are no book authors without film involvement, either. That's because of . . .

SYNERGY

Having two properties instead of one opens up new possibilities. Let's use a book as an example—starting with an unpublished manuscript. And let's say you "go out" with (offer for sale) the manuscript and the adapted screenplay at the same time—one to New York publishers, the other to Hollywood. Mere interest in either is almost certain to increase interest in the other. If a publisher bites on the book, you make that known to Hollywood, because that makes the script seem more worthy of their attention—and vice versa.

The actual sale of either book or screenplay will make it easier to get the other seen by the right people, and will make sale of the other more likely because someone else—a professional in the book or film industry—has already placed a bet on you. In the best of all possible worlds, one or both of the properties generates "heat," and a savvy agent (or two) can play studio interest against publisher interest and elevate the price of book and screenplay to ridiculous heights.

If the book sells high, or is published and succeeds, the screenplay (if unsold) is far more likely to be purchased, and (if already sold) far more likely to be produced, because a successful book creates a built-in audience for the film and reduces film investor risk. If the book doesn't sell, but the screenplay does, publishers will suddenly become interested in the book.

The reverse is also true: a successful movie will resurrect sluggish book sales, put out-of-print titles (like Alan Glynn's *The Dark Fields/Limitless* novel) back on store shelves, and push brisk sales even higher. Because of the cap on screen-side earnings, a hit film can cause your book to make you far more money—in rare cases, millions more—than the screenplay ever will.

But you need the screenplay to make it happen. That's synergy.

"When the *Sideways* novel came out," says author Rex Pickett, "my publisher did no publicity. Nothing. After the movie, things improved dramatically. The film's success raised my profile as a writer, and suddenly everyone wanted something from me. They wanted me to write TV—which I'm now doing. They wanted me to write another novel, to do adaptations, even a TV show. Everyone wanted something they could capitalize on."

Author Vikas Swarup recalls his *Slumdog Millionaire* experience. "The film became a global product," he relates. "The song 'Jai-Ho' became a global anthem. I heard it at a Milan catwalk, in American shopping malls, South African plazas. *Slumdog Millionaire* became a brand, so to speak. And while I did get money from the movie as well, after the initial payment, much of it really has come from increased book sales." This from an author whose book was already selling briskly in 36 languages before the movie came out.

TIMING

There has never been a better time to adapt for film. "Adaptations are superhot right now," says Christopher Lockhart, sole story editor at reigning Hollywood superagency WME (previously called William Morris Endeavor). His job is to read and consult on scripts for household-name, top-end clients, which have included Nicolas Cage, Russell Crowe, Robert Downey Jr., Richard Gere, Mel Gibson, Jennifer Lopez, Steve Martin, Matthew McConaughey, Liam Neeson, Ed Norton, Michelle Pfeiffer, Winona Ryder, Sylvester Stallone, Sharon Stone and Denzel Washington, among many others. He's also a producer: his first documentary, *Most Valuable Players,* was selected by Oprah for her Documentary Film Club, and aired on the Oprah Winfrey Network. An earlier work, *The Inside Pitch,* was nominated for an L.A. Area Emmy Award. He also produces the Collector franchise. Before moving to WME, Lockhart was sole story editor at ICM.

"It's all about the underlying property right now," he continues. "A script based on source material is good. One based on source material that's been bought for some other medium—book, video game, and so on—is better, because it shows someone else has confidence in the work and thinks it will be successful. And if you're fortunate enough to have something that already has an audience of some kind, that's ideal because now you've got an existing fan base for the studio to build on."

Ryan Condal, who recently sold his first script *Galahad* (MLF) for $500,000, feels the same. "The thirst for original material is not what it was," he says. "Probably 99 percent of the active projects in Hollywood are adaptations of one kind or another."

Screenwriter John August's credits include *Charlie's Angels* and *Charlie's Angels: Full Throttle* (both TVS), *Charlie and the Chocolate Factory* (NOV), *Big Fish* (NOV), *Corpse Bride, Titan A.E., Dark Shadows* (TVS), *Tarzan* (NOV), *Frankenweenie,* and *Preacher* (COM)—the last two not yet released as of this writing. He directed *The Nines,* and produced *Prince of Persia: The Sands of Time* (GAM) and the *D.C.* television series, and worked (uncredited) on *Iron Man* (COM), *Minority Report* (STO), *Hancock,* and *Jurassic Park 3* (NOV). His first adaptation was a children's book with the unlikely title *How to Eat Fried Worms* (NOV). "My favorite genre," he says, "is movies that get made. And increasingly, movies that get made are adaptations of some preexisting thing. Those are the projects that studios are willing to spend the money to try to make into big, expensive movies. So the bulk of movies I've written that got made were based on something that came before me."

The preference for adaptations has progressed to the point where several first-time screenwriters have been advised to adapt their screenplays into books or comic books—and then offer the original screenplays as adaptations based on the books or comic books. Adaptations of the latter are particularly sought-after right now. Screenwriter Jonathan Hensleigh's credits include *Armageddon, Die Hard with a Vengeance* (NOV/SCR), *Jumanji* (NOV), *The Punisher* (COM), *The Saint* (NOVs/TVS), and *Kill the Irishman* (TRU). "The studios' desire to do high-concept projects that are a reflection of the world of graphic novels," he says, "is higher than it's ever been. If you're a screenwriter, know it's there, respect it, be willing to work within it."

At the time of this writing, seven of the top ten, and twenty of the top twenty five highest-grossing films of all time are adaptations—of books (12), comics (3), historical events (1), toys (1), even amusement park rides (3); the top thirty moneymakers are listed in the next chapter.

Six of the nine films nominated for Best Picture in 2011 were also adaptations—of novels (5) and nonfiction books/true stories (1). (For updated figures, film titles, and box office earnings, visit http://makeyourstoryamovie.com/bookbonus.html)

Given the number of adaptations currently being purchased, those slated for production, and those already underway, these figures seem unlikely to change any time soon. When the studios find something that works, they stick with it—and for the foreseeable future, that means adaptations.

CHAPTER 2
WHAT CAN (AND CAN'T) BE ADAPTED?

Get the Rights, or Get Out

Once upon a time, Hollywood adaptations were limited to films based on what might be termed "traditional" sources—books, plays, historical events, the occasional true-life story. No longer. Today, almost anything can be—and currently is being—adapted by Hollywood. Though novels still lead the pack in terms of overall box office success, script purchases and worldwide grosses reflect a broadening of categories.

What follows is a list of the top 30 highest-grossing adaptations, as of the time of this writing (figures rounded to the nearest million). Remember that DVD sales alone are likely triple or quadruple the figures shown below—and that neither figure accounts for merchandising and other rights exploitation.

- *Titanic* (HIS), $2,185,000,000
- *Marvel's The Avengers* (COM), $1,461,000,000
- *Harry Potter and the Deathly Hallows, Part 2* (NOV), $1,328,000,000
- *Transformers: Dark of the Moon* (GAM), $1,124,000,000

- *The Lord of the Rings: The Return of the King* (NOV), $1,120,000,000
- *Pirates of the Caribbean: Dead Man's Chest* (THM), $1,066,000,000
- *Pirates of the Caribbean: On Stranger Tides* (THM), $1,044,000,000
- *Alice in Wonderland* (NOVs), $1,024,000,000
- *The Dark Knight* (COM), $1,002,000,000
- *Harry Potter and the Sorcerer's Stone* (NOV), $975,000,000
- *Pirates of the Caribbean: At World's End* (THM), $963,000,000
- *Harry Potter and the Deathly Hallows, Part 1* (NOV), $956,000,000
- *Harry Potter and the Order of the Phoenix* (NOV), $940,000,000
- *Harry Potter and the Half-Blood Prince* (NOV), $934,000,000
- *The Lord of the Rings: The Two Towers* (NOV), $926,000,000
- *Shrek 2* (NOV), $920,000,000
- *Jurassic Park* (NOV), $915,000,000
- *Harry Potter and the Goblet of Fire* (NOV), $897,000,000
- *Spider-Man 3* (COM), $891,000,000
- *Harry Potter and the Chamber of Secrets* (NOV), $879,000,000
- *The Lord of the Rings: The Fellowship of the Ring* (NOV), $872,000,000
- *Transformers: Revenge of the Fallen* (GAM), $836,000,000
- *Spider-Man* (COM), $822,000,000
- *Shrek the Third* (NOV), $799,000,000
- *Harry Potter and the Prisoner of Azkaban* (NOV), $797,000,000
- *Spider-Man 2* (COM), $784,000,000
- *The Da Vinci Code* (NOV), $758,000,000

- *Shrek Forever After* (NOV), $753,000,000
- *The Chronicles of Narnia: The Lion, the Witch, and the Wardrobe* (NOV), $745,000,000
- *The Dark Knight Rises* (COM), $733,000,000
- *The Twilight Saga: New Moon* (NOV), $710,000,000
- *Transformers* (GAM), $710,000,000

For a complete and current list of all adaptations ranking among the top 100 highest-grossing films, and of all film adaptations nominated for Oscars (Best Picture or Best Screenplay) since 2000, visit http://makeyourstoryamovie.com/bookbonus.html.

Given that it has become possible to film almost anything the human mind can imagine, the only real questions left for those considering adaptations would seem to be these:

- Is the source material cinematic (or can it be rendered cinematic)?
- Can this material be adapted while remaining true to the heart of the original?
- Can I get the rights?

THE NO-FLY LIST

Given sufficient imagination, it might seem that any existing work can be successfully adapted, and to a very large extent that's true. *The Hobbit* and *The Lord of the Rings* books total nearly 1,500 pages; the *Snow White* faery tale, as related by the Brothers Grimm, a mere six pages; while toys like the *Transformers* have zero pages.

There are, however, two things that simply cannot be successfully adapted. These are no-fly projects:

- Works to which you do not hold the rights
- Works to which you do hold the rights, but whose owners insist on retaining control of the adaptations

If you own the rights because it's your story and you wrote it, and you understand that Hollywood is free to alter your work after buying it, then you're set. If you *hold* (as opposed to *own*) the rights— because (for example) you've optioned them from the owner (see Chapter 31)—and your agreement with the owner makes it clear that Hollywood is free to alter the work after buying it, you're also set. But if neither is the case, you must realize that both of the no-fly situations mentioned above are hopeless.

If you don't control the appropriate rights in the underlying property, you obviously can't sell the project. It would be like stealing someone else's car engine, sticking it in your own car—and then selling your car. Not cool, to say the least. (Prison time, to say the most.)

This isn't as simple as it might appear; screenwriter Bill Marsi-lii, with the best of intentions, once sold a book adaptation to a studio (that is, the studio agreed to buy it)—only to find out later that he and his producers (Ted Elliott and Terry Rossio) didn't control the rights yet because the author they were dealing with, who thought he controlled the film rights, actually didn't. Fortunately, things were straightened out and the deal went through.

Oscar-winning screenwriter Paul Haggis ran into the opposite problem. "A studio came to me," he relates, "to adapt a series of books they'd recently optioned. I read four or five of the books, pitched them my take, we made a deal and I got started. They said they were still tidying up the author's long-form contract, and my deal was of course contingent on them closing the rights deal, but this type of thing takes months and is almost always about haggling over the fine print. Everything substantive is negotiated in the short-form deal.

"I was really excited about these books, so I jumped in and spent several months developing it, coming up with a story and characters that would work to launch the series and creating a detailed outline—only to discover that, to their chagrin, the studio couldn't close the deal with the author. The whole thing fell apart.

The studio executives were mortified and very apologetic, but in truth it was my own foolishness for doing all that work before someone else's deal was nailed down. But writing is about passion, and I am quite sure, after learning this lesson, that I would make the exact same mistake again."

Of course, you could always do the adaptation with no paper (contract), hoping the source material's owner will, in a fit of awestruck gratitude, hand you a free option—but you can't count on that. "You're taking a huge risk adapting it without controlling the rights," says Bill Marsilii. "You're basically renovating somebody else's house and trusting that after you do that, they'll say thank you and let you take possession instead of saying never mind, forget about it."

Confirms Haggis: "When dealing with a spec project, you have to get control of the source material, legally, before you put months into writing a screenplay. Don't do it otherwise, as the rights-holder can turn around and sell it to someone else, or refuse to sell at all—and then you've done all that work for nothing."

It might even be that the original author no longer holds the rights—so they couldn't make a deal with you if they wanted to. Leslie Dixon is one of Hollywood's few A-list female screenwriters. Her credits include *Limitless* (NOV), *Mrs. Doubtfire* (NOV), *Freaky Friday* (2003; MOV/NOV), *The Thomas Crown Affair* (MOV), *Outrageous Fortune* and *Limitless* (NOV)—which she also produced—and other films. "For a writer or producer," she says, "the most important thing is to really know for certain who has the rights. That's really, really critical, before you even think about anything else. You don't want to start writing something and then find out that someone else has the rights locked up for years and your script's never going to see the light of day."

If you don't own the *exclusive* film rights, or cannot lock them up with an option or purchase (see Chapters 3 and 31 for more on this)—walk away.

Controlling rights-owners are equally fatal to the deal-making process. Simply put, Hollywood demands the right to make whatever changes it likes, at any time it likes, for any reason at all, or for no reason whatsoever. Absent huge, raging success on the order of, say, J. K. Rowling, this is nonnegotiable.

Rights-owners who insist on control of any aspect of the movie doom the project from the start. If you're planning to adapt someone else's work, do not grant them contractual control early on and hope they'll change their minds later, because if they don't, the project is dead and your time has been wasted. Unless you can finance the film yourself, and so have no one else to please, this is another walkaway. Even if you can finance it yourself, consider: what happens if a studio wants to pick up the film—but insists on making a few changes before release? If you are unable to authorize those changes, the deal disappears.

It's fine and in fact desirable for an adapting writer or producer to work with the story's owner to create an adaptation that everyone is happy with—but the original owner must understand that once the screenplay finds a buyer, that buyer will control the nature of the final product.

Michael Nozik has produced over two dozen movies, including *The Next Three Days* (MOV), *Love in the Time of Cholera* (NOV), *Syriana* (NFB), *The Motorcycle Diaries* (NFBs/TRU), The *Legend of Bagger Vance* (NOV), and *Quiz Show* (NFB/HIS). "I've been involved in several situations," he says, "where the owner of the source material wanted to create restrictions on what the buyer could do with the adaptation, what kinds of changes they could make—but ultimately you can't work that way. Those deals usually fall apart and the movies never get made."

PUBLIC DOMAIN WORKS

A third category of source material—works in the public domain—is often problematic. Here, the same thing that allows you to adapt such works—the lack of any enforceable ownership rights—also allows anyone (or everyone) else to do the same. Look at it from the buyer's perspective.

Let's say you're retelling the Arthurian legend of the Knights of the Round Table. Why should I (as a buyer) pay you for that? Not only can I hire someone else to write it, cheaper—but what would be the point? I've heard and seen that story a hundred times before, and (worse) so has everyone else.

True enough. But what if, in your story, King Arthur is an aging coward, Guinevere a murderous bitch who covets his throne, Galahad the only honorable knight at the table, and Lancelot a near-invincible warrior torn between honor and his queen—who chooses him as her champion when Galahad accuses her of murdering the king?

Now you've got a story that resonates with the power of legend, but is also unique—and therefore protectable. This is exactly what Ryan Condal did with *Galahad* (MLF).

"There's something primal about those old myths and faery tales," says Evan Daugherty, whose first script sale—*Snow White and the Huntsman* (MLF)—fetched $3.2 million in a studio bidding war. "But at the same time, they were originally meant for people of a different time and culture. So in some ways they're relevant to us now, and in other ways not. I looked backward, and tried to figure out how I might update Snow White and make it a little more relevant to a modern reader or audience."

By looking backward, Daugherty wound up ahead of the curve. "The interesting thing about *Snow White and the Huntsman* is that at this juncture in Hollywood, adapting these old public domain folk tales or faery tales and spinning them around in some kind of revisionist way has become very of-the-moment—but I wrote the first draft of this screenplay years ago."

If you're going to tackle something in the public domain, you must—as Ryan did with *Galahad* and Evan did with *Snow White and the Huntsman*—make it your own in some way that renders it both unique and protectable. Other examples include *Titanic* (HIS), *Braveheart* (HIS), and *300* (COM/HIS)—all of which retell historical events with largely (or entirely) fictionalized characters.

THE ONE RULE

If you don't own or control the rights Hollywood demands, do not adapt. (For more on this, see Chapter 31.)

CHAPTER 3
ADAPTING VS. SELLING FILM RIGHTS

There's a Difference

Most books and other properties are not movies. Some never will be. Many, however—including most books—*could* be movies, if skillfully adapted. And therein lies the rub: When Hollywood people (agents, managers, producers, directors, actors, studio execs and investors) look at a book, even a very good book, they see . . . a book. And the business of Hollywood is making movies, not books. As Paul Haggis says, "You need to be able to picture the film."

"SHOW ME THE MOVIE"
The purpose of a book is to be a book, to be enjoyed and appreciated for what it is. There is no next step, except perhaps to read the author's next book. The purpose of a screenplay is to roll a movie in the reader's head, and get them to take the next step: to help turn that screenplay into the movie they saw as they read it. The script's mission is to be a blueprint. "The screenplay isn't the final version of anything," says screenwriter John August. "It's a plan for making a movie."

Christopher Lockhart of WME explains. "When someone in this town reads a story," he says, "they ask themselves one question:

Is this a movie? Agents, managers, producers—that's all they want to know in the beginning: Is this a movie? If they can't see the movie in their heads, they're not interested. And the way you roll a movie in someone's head—when the movie doesn't yet exist—is with a screenplay."

Producer Michael Nozik echoes this sentiment. "Hollywood's always looking for the easiest, quickest path to the end zone. One of the first things I ask, and I'm sure every other producer who looks at a piece of material asks, is this: Is this thing a movie, or is this not a movie? And if it is, what kind of movie is it? And is it a movie that can ever get made? Sometimes I'll look at source material and think, this could be great, but I have no idea how to make it work as a movie, the story's just too difficult to translate.

"Probably for the same reason, studios are less willing to consider source material than finished screenplays based on the same material, and they're willing to spend more when they can see it well executed, because you're helping them get to the end zone—a finished film—quicker." Christopher Lockhart continues. "The only time you approach someone without a screenplay is when you: (a) don't have one, and (b) can't get one. Or (c) your work is already so enormously well-known and successful and obviously cinematic that you don't need one to sell the project."

Lesli Linka Glatter drew an Oscar nomination for her first film, *Tales of Meeting and Parting,* which she both wrote and directed, based on a series of true stories. She has since directed feature films, TV movies, and dozens of series episodes. She recently won the Director's Guild Award for Best Director of Dramatic Series (Night), and currently has several adaptations in development. "If I read something and I see the movie," she says, "I know immediately I'm the right person to direct it. If I don't see the movie, it's probably better that someone else does it, because the project deserves someone who's that passionate about it."

Of adaptations, she says, "If you've actually got the adapted screenplay and it's a good screenplay, I think you have a better chance of getting it made. Because someone can look at it and say, 'Wow, this is great.' And that's a big step closer to a movie. Whether you're raising money independently or going through the studios, you don't have anything without the screenplay."

Producer Gail Lyon, whose credits include *Erin Brockovich* (TRU), *Gattaca, Edge of Darkness* (TVS) and *Stuart Little 2* (NOV), recalls her experience with the Erin Brockovich story. "Nobody in town wanted to buy it, everybody passed and I don't blame them, because until an idea like that is executed as smartly and surprisingly as [screenwriter] Susannah Grant did it, it sounds like a TV movie.

"Susannah was much more of an emerging writer at the time, not as established as she is now by any means, but she was always very talented with great instincts. Once she wrote the script and hit it out of the park, people saw the story differently, and they saw the value in it."

Screenwriter/producer Leslie Dixon offers this advice: "Having a completed script is really the most likely way to sell. If you've written a great script based on great source material, then the studios can do what they prefer to do and in fact do best: look for money to get the project made. They're not really interested in making development deals anymore; they're looking for things that are ready to go."

Paul Haggis concurs. "I've had more success just writing the whole screenplay. It's easier for buyers to see the movie if they have the script in front of them. To do that, you have to be willing to put in the work to get the script done, without knowing whether someone will buy it. That's what I did with *Million Dollar Baby*. I wrote it, they read it, and they never even looked at the source material. They should, it's brilliant, but that's not what interests them, because the movie will be based on the script."

BOOK QUESTIONS

Books raise questions screenplays don't: "Will this work onscreen? How do we squeeze five hundred pages into two hours? Half the book takes place inside the hero's head; how do we fix that? This would cost $300 million to shoot—can we make it less expensive? Can we tell this story in three acts, streamline the plot, strengthen the character arcs? If we buy the rights, who do we hire for the adaptation? How much is that going to cost? And, at the end of all that—will this be a movie?"

The adaptation process can be time consuming and expensive, particularly for buyers who may be juggling a dozen (or a hundred) other projects and paying industry rates to everyone involved for what may be years on end, hoping to get it right.

By going in with a screenplay instead of the source material, you avoid such complications and potential objections, allowing the prospective buyer to focus on that one, all-important question: Is this a movie?

To be fair, there are those who feel that going in with a completed script locks the reader into a single interpretation of the source material when there may be other, perhaps better ways to adapt the story. But the same could be said of original screenplays as well. You choose what seems the best way to tell the story—and you take your best shot. You tell that story. And while there may be some truth to the "locked-in" argument, it's also true that there's a huge difference when it comes to . . .

SELLING PRICE: RIGHTS VS. SCRIPT

Lastly (or perhaps firstly), there's the matter of price. As we've seen, screenplays are movie blueprints. A book or other source material serves as a starting point for an adaptation that might—or might not—make a good movie. Without the screenplay, it's hard to tell. Once the source material's rights are acquired, a good deal of work remains to be done before the project can be offered for sale to others.

The portion of this work that is paid for—the writing of the screenplay itself, for example—is often paid for at industry rates. Which means that, if you've sold rights only and the project moves ahead with a WGA (Writers Guild of America) signatory company, someone is going to get paid between $50,000 and $1 million to write the adapted screenplay. That someone will not be you, nor will they be splitting the money with you.

So unless you're selling the rights to something that's already massively successful on its own terms (bestselling book, comic book, video or other game, toy, etc.) and will therefore fetch a high price, you're making a bit of a trade-off on the financial side. You're also more likely to wind up with an option (described in Chapter 31) than with an outright and immediate purchase, because the other party is going to need some serious time to work out the details of the adaptation and construct a pitch or commission, review, and sell an adapted screenplay.

During the option period (typically one to three years), you will be unable to sell the rights to anyone else, and there will be no point to doing a screenplay, because you no longer control the screen rights, and no one's obligated to use your script even if they do buy the rights.

If you are somehow hired to write a first draft, it won't belong to you because you will at that point be an employee. (More on this in Chapter 31.) As Leslie Dixon points out, "If you're getting paid to write the script, they own it and they can do anything they want with it, including fire you." Or stick it in a drawer for the next twenty years. If the script is yours and things don't work out, you're free to take it elsewhere.

Typical rights option prices range from one dollar to thousands, with a final purchase price (if the option is "exercised") of perhaps $10,000 to $100,000—the latter figure being for a book that's already sold in the neighborhood of a million copies. More successful properties—*Harry Potter,* for example—may command far higher prices.

Screenplays can be optioned as well, but they can also be sold outright. So the strategy here is to go for the sale and, if that doesn't work out, settle for an option. By going for a sale, you're bypassing many of the people who would option the rights, and directly approaching many of the same people they would approach themselves after putting together a pitch pack (covered in the Bonus Chapter The Pitch Pack: Pitching the Screenplay—Without the Screenplay) or commissioning a screenplay. In a way, you're cutting out the middleman (or woman).

And while it's true that you'll most likely ally yourself with another sort of middleman—an agent or manager—to help you with this, your potential upside is far greater. As mentioned earlier, spec screenplays sell for an average of $300,000 to $600,000, with occasional forays past the $1 million mark. If you (the rights owner) wrote or commissioned the screenplay yourself, much of that money will be yours, even if the buyer puts the script on a shelf and never looks at it again.

Your agent gets 10 percent; if you use a manager instead, he'll get 10 percent—but if your manager is also a producer, you may get your entire commission back when the movie gets made. (He's not working for free; he's getting paid even more by the studio or other buyer to produce, so he kicks you back the commission—provided you know enough to ask for this in your agreement with him, and he goes along.)

If the script doesn't sell, you can regroup and package ("attach" a major producer, director, star or investor, most likely with the help of your agent or manager) and try again. This technique recently scored several major sales for scripts that had gone out a year or two earlier and found no buyer. (More on this in Chapter 27.)

Or you can go for an option—but even here you're better off than you would be with rights alone. That's because you're now optioning a script, and if the option is exercised, you will be paid for the screenplay and not just the rights. So now you're back in the $300,000 to $600,000+ club, even if the "underlying property" (book, game, whatever) is unpublished and completely unknown.

In every case, you are—assuming there's a purchase at the end of the rainbow—better off selling a screenplay with rights than rights alone. Unless you dwell in *Potter*land, in which case you can pretty much write your own ticket either way.

Writing or commissioning the screenplay yourself also has another advantage: the story presented will be the story you want to tell, rather than the unpredictable interpretation of an unknown writer, producer, or studio executive, who may not "get" what you really mean to say. And while there's no guarantee this won't happen anyway in rewrites (this is Hollywood, after all)—your own vision will at the very least be seen and considered, because it's the first thing the buyer will look at.

PART II

WHAT HOLLYWOOD WANTS (AND WHY)

Most authors would like to see their work adapted for the big (or small) screen, but the path from here to there is, at best, unfamiliar—and can seem incomprehensible. Some bestsellers are made into movies, others ignored. Obscure books, short stories, and magazine articles are blessed by Hollywood's magic, while thousands of screenplays are turned away. What sense does that make? Is there no rhyme or reason here?

Well, yes, actually. But it's hard to make out when—like most writers— you're on the outside looking in. The twelve chapters that follow will take you through the looking glass and make some sense of the enigma that is the Hollywood adaptation process. More importantly, it will explain why some books are made into movies while others are not, and what you can do to make your story more attractive to filmmakers.

CHAPTER 4
TWELVE THINGS HOLLYWOOD WANTS

The Buyer's Checklist

As Sylvester Stallone once pointed out, "There's a reason they call it show business, not show art." The business of filmmaking is something that can only be learned by doing, or by heeding the advice of those who've been there before you, and lived to tell the tale.

Ehren Kruger's screenwriting credits include *Transformers 2, 3,* and *4* (GAM), *The Ring 1* and *2* (NOV), *God is a Bullet* (NOV), *The Talisman* TV series (NOV), and *Arlington Road*—a script that won him a prestigious Nicholl Fellowships* award and kicked off his professional career. "There are writers," he says, "and certainly I was one of them, with an unrealistically optimistic opinion of the salability of stories that they themselves have fallen in love with simply because they want to tell those particular stories. This is fine for novelists, because at least in that industry you have the last resort option to self-publish. For screenwriters, it's different.

"Studios are running a business. And you have to make your

---

*The Nicholl Fellowships in Screenwriting Program of the Academy of Motion Picture Arts and Sciences. (For more on this competition, see Chapter 24.)

peace with that. They're looking for a return on their investment, and they need to be making movies that put people in seats. That holds true whether the project is something you can make for a million dollars and auction at Sundance, or something you can only make for a hundred million dollars.

"Looking back to the beginning of my career, I wish I could have known better which stories not to write. That I could have put a more objective and realistic business eye on some of the ideas and stories I started to tell—things that, in hindsight, I look at now and recognize, 'That one really never stood a chance.'

"When you start any project, you need to ask yourself some questions and figure out what elements will make it an attractive investment and get other people excited about it, so it has a chance of getting made. These are not questions I thought to ask when I was starting out." Thanks to the hard-won experience of Ehren and others, we can ask those questions now.

Indeed, experience has led film studios and the production companies that team with them to look for a number of very specific things in the projects they choose to adapt. Says Jonathan Hensleigh: "The moving target that a screenwriter has to hit to satisfy the commercial requirements of the studios has gotten smaller and is now moving faster, so it's harder to hit. They want very specific elements, and the reason for that is because the fear factor in Hollywood is worse now owing to the cost of the films and the cost of marketing."

Some of these "specific elements" mean little or nothing to publishers, which is one of the reasons why many good books are never adapted—and also why those that are adapted often undergo significant changes before hitting the screen.

The most important of these things are covered in the next eleven chapters, and form a sort of buyer-friendly checklist of questions you should ask yourself about your own projects. Briefly summarized, they are . . .

- Pitchable Concept: A cinematic story concept that can be conveyed in ten seconds or less.
- A Relatable Hero or one with whom the reader/viewer can sympathize or empathize (or at least find compelling); if people don't care about your characters and what happens to them, Hollywood doesn't care about your story.
- An Emotionally Compelling Story because, in the end, a relatable hero is not enough; the most engaging character in the world will soon turn boring if he or she has nothing emotionally meaningful to do. The hero must "have skin in the game," must have something at stake.
- A "Ticking Clock" to add immediacy to the story; no ticking clock means no hurry, no urgency to get anything done—and that, in turn, makes for a boring story or (worse) no story at all.
- Strong Visual Potential: A story whose main events can be engagingly depicted onscreen; if the camera can't see it, it's not a movie.
- Classical (Three-Act) Structure: With something like 90 percent of all commercially successful films adhering to this structure, Hollywood is inclined to play the odds—and you should be, too.
- An Actor-Friendly Lead role that appeals to bankable actors; for the most part, studio greenlights hinge on actor (and sometimes director) participation. No actor interest means no studio (or other buyer) interest.
- Average Length: 105 to 120 minutes or thereabouts; time is money, and first-timers do not warrant exceptions.
- Reasonable Budget: You are not James Cameron, and your film cannot cost half a billion dollars. (Cameron's first movie—*The Terminator*—cost a mere $6.5 million,

$4 million of which reportedly went to star Arnold
Schwarzenegger.
- Low-Fat Story: Everything in the story must be there for
  a reason—other than being one of the writer's favorite
  scenes.
- Franchise Potential: Sequels to successful films are less
  risky investments than original films, making this a big
  advantage—particularly at higher budget levels. Not
  always required, but nice to have.
- Four-Quadrant Appeal: A story that appeals to
  everyone—young and older males and females (the four
  quadrants). This is where James Cameron lives and
  breathes, and the reason his films can cost what they do.
  Not required at all levels, but increasingly important as
  budget rises.
- Merchandising Potential: The more stuff the studio can
  sell, the happier they are; irrelevant at lower budget
  levels, critical for many summer blockbusters—which
  often generate more income from merchandising than
  from theatrical release.

Okay, that's thirteen things—but "Twelve Things Hollywood
Wants" sounds better. Point being, the more of these things your
project has, the greater your chances of moving it along. If, on the
other hand, your current story is missing one or more of the first
ten qualities, you may find yourself in Ehren's never-really-stood-
a-chance category. But that doesn't mean you can't change things—or
at least change them in the adaptation, which is what matters to
Hollywood.

So let's take a closer look at each. . . .

CHAPTER 5
PITCHABLE CONCEPT

This Is Your Ten Seconds

When it comes to selling in Hollywood, concept is king. A pitchable concept is like oxygen: without it, you're dead. Still, there is one significant difference: you'll last longer—much longer—without oxygen. Terry Rossio is probably the highest-grossing screenwriter of all time. His credits include the *Pirates of the Caribbean* (THM), *Shrek* (NOV), *Zorro* (TVS/NOV), *Men in Black* (COM), and *National Treasure* franchises, *Godzilla* (MOV), *Aladdin* (MFL), the record-breaking *Déjà Vu* spec sale ($5.6 million, including producer fees), and other projects literally too numerous to mention. His *Lightspeed* project (cowritten with Bill Marsilii), sold for $3.5 million.

"Most aspiring screenwriters simply don't spend enough time choosing their concept," he counsels. "It's by far the most common mistake I see in spec scripts. The writer has lost the race right from the gate. Months—sometimes years—are lost trying to elevate a film idea that by its nature probably had no hope of ever becoming a movie."

WHY "PITCHABLE" CONCEPT?

Before delving into what makes a concept pitchable, it's important to understand why a pitchable concept is needed in the first place. The answer can be boiled down to two words: *time* and *marketing*. Let's tackle time first.

Agents, managers, producers and film executives are among the busiest people on earth. "To their credit," says screenwriter Evan Daugherty, "these guys are insanely busy, and they're getting these scripts all the time, and probably really want to find that magical script in the pile. But there are so many scripts it's just crazy."

Christopher Lockhart, executive story editor at WME, is one of those insanely busy guys. "For any writer trying to break into the business," he says, "it's ultimately about concept. Most new writers don't have the concept. Writer-driven scripts have to be carried by the writing alone—and that's a tougher sell.

"*Juno* is like that. If you pitch that script to me, and you say it's about a pregnant teen who struggles to find the perfect parents to adopt her baby, I'm like, 'Okay, whatever.' Because the charm and the magic of *Juno* is in the writing—the character and the humor—and not in the concept itself. But how do you pitch the writing when the writer is unknown? You can't.

"Whereas with something like *Liar Liar,* the magic and the charm are first and foremost in the concept: it's about a lawyer who has to tell the truth for twenty-four hours, during the biggest case of his career. That sounds exciting. There's a lot more clarity, a lot more conflict, and you can really see the potential just from that description.

"Fine, maybe you wrote a great script—but if you can't get the concept across, who the hell is going to read it? You have to understand: everybody writes a great script. It's like being in prison: everybody's innocent."

The prison analogy is a good one—except in this case, everyone's trying to break *in*. And you might be surprised by the numbers. The WGA (Writers Guild of America) registers some 50,000 new screenplays each year. Many writers copyright their scripts instead of registering them (copyright offers greater protections; see the Bonus Chapter, Copyright: Who Needs It? for more on this), and an even larger number don't bother doing either—so we can conservatively say that 100,000 new scripts enter the marketplace every year. Add these to last year's scripts, and those from previous years (which often continue to circulate as their authors keep revising them and sending them out), and you begin to see the problem.

There's simply not enough time to read every script and adaptable property that comes along—the vast majority of which will, as every industry pro knows from bitter experience, turn out to be poorly written, plotted, or executed (if not all three).

Of those stories which are not one or more of the above, many will be in some way inappropriate for the person or company being contacted: too expensive, too narrowly (or broadly) focused, wrong genre, or simply not a good match for their current needs.

"I can't read every script out there," says Lockhart. "I just can't do it. No one can." And so no one tries. "With hundreds of thousands of scripts from new writers circulating around town," he confirms, "there has to be some kind of vetting process. And concept is the quickest and easiest way to vet. If you don't have representation or a solid recommendation, concept is the best way to catch someone's attention—and in all cases, it's helpful. Concept, concept, concept."

Keeping the above in mind, put yourself in the shoes of the person you hope to impress. In the next three hours, you can read one script—or you can review well over a thousand concepts. Put another way: if you were to read the thousand scripts instead of the concepts, and you did nothing but read those scripts for ten hours a day, every day, it would take you 324 days to read them all. (And more like two to three years if you were reading books instead of screenplays.)

Now let's look at this the other way around: if you were to look at concepts only, for 324 days, for only *one* hour a day—you'd have reviewed just under 350,000 potential projects. If you did this for ten hours a day, the total number of concepts reviewed would approach 3.5 million. Which technique do you think your competitors are using?

So, are you going to spend your time trying to read everything that comes your way—or are you going to vet the concepts first, and then follow up on and read only those that seem both promising and appropriate?

Welcome to Hollywood.

Your agent, manager, or producer will also use the logline to catch the interest of potential buyers. "It's hard to overstate the importance of having a story that you can articulate efficiently and clearly to someone else," says screenwriter Ehren Kruger. "Because that's what a junior studio executive will use when speaking to a senior studio executive, who then speaks to the head of the studio, who ultimately says yes, buy that thing, or no, don't buy that thing."

The other consideration is marketing. "You want to be able to get the concept down to something that makes the reader or listener see the movie poster," screenwriter John August advises. "That seems really gross and wrong, but at the same time, many of the most challenging projects, the ones that are hardest to get going, are that way because it's hard for the buyer to understand how they're going to market it: what the poster feels like, what the trailer feels like. The studio has to know it can promote the movie in those formats."

Ehren Kruger agrees. "At the other end of the process," he says, "you can't market a movie to audiences based on 'Trust us, it's good.' Studio executives need to know what the concept is, so it can be related to the potential audience."

Indeed, with limited exceptions (mostly smaller, independent projects), there is little industry interest in stories whose central concepts and conflicts cannot be plainly and dramatically stated in one to three sentences. Why? Because the finished film will be marketed with "trailers" (those short, coming-attractions previews) as short as 30 to 60 seconds. Experience proves that films which cannot be effectively marketed in this way tend to do poorly at the box office. Which, in turn, makes it difficult if not impossible to find investors. So the very first thing you want to do is take your story and boil it down to trailer-friendly, pitchable basics.

WHAT MAKES A CONCEPT PITCHABLE?

A pitchable concept should be brief, clear, original, and commercial. "The concept also has to be intriguing, compelling, attractive," says Terry Rossio. "I would add, specifically, that the story has to have a compelling main relationship (which all great movies have) and that the concept for the film should exist in the public consciousness in some fashion, yet hasn't been done yet.

"There should be some element that is so inventive, so alluring, it has people in Hollywood kicking themselves for not thinking of it first. Kicking themselves so hard, in fact, that they're willing to give you lots of money because you did think of it first."

In addition, it should contain the three most basic elements of your story: *who* it's about, *what* their goal is, and the nature of the *obstacle* that must be overcome before that goal can be reached.

First up: brevity. Grab a stopwatch, real or virtual. Imagine yourself face-to-face with a Hollywood producer, who asks you the inevitable question: "What's your story about?"

Now start that stopwatch ticking, and answer the question out loud. Stop the clock when you're done. If your answer took more than ten seconds, it's too long. Impossible, you say? Not so—as we'll see in a moment.

On to clarity. When it comes to pitching, clarity is crucial, confusion lethal. Again, put yourself in the other guy's shoes. Someone comes to you with a concept—a mere sentence or two, written or spoken. If they can't manage to pull that off without confusing you, what are the chances they can pull off the whole two-hour story? Probably zip. And while such an assessment may be unfair because writing two-hour stories and ten-second pitches are entirely separate skills . . . once again, welcome to Hollywood.

As Napoleon once said of military orders, "they must be impossible to misunderstand." That's what you're aiming for here: not only does every word count, every phrase or sentence—as well as the overall pitch—must have only one meaning. (The rare exception being an intentional double entendre.)

SAMPLE CONCEPTS

Within the industry, the ten-second, concept-based pitches referred to in this chapter are called *loglines*. Here are four examples of loglines I wrote (after the fact) for successful films you've probably seen on the big (or small) screen. See if you can identify the movies they pitch.

A fugitive doctor wrongly convicted of killing his wife struggles to prove his innocence while pursued by a relentless U.S. Marshal.

In a society where criminals are arrested before their crimes are committed, a cop convicted of a future murder goes on the run to prove his innocence.

An emotionally shuttered Wall Street tycoon hires a vivacious hooker for the week, falls in love, and struggles to forge his first meaningful relationship.

A family struggles to escape a remote island park whose main attractions—genetically restored dinosaurs—have been set loose by a power failure.

If you haven't already guessed, here are the movies to go with those loglines: *The Fugitive* (TVS); *Minority Report* (STO); *Pretty Woman*; and *Jurassic Park* (NOV). Note that each logline is brief, clear, original, and commercial—while at the same time conveying the central who, goal, and obstacle of the story. All in ten seconds or less—even for a relatively complex concept like *Minority Report*.

For more on developing and refining concepts, see Chapter 17; for more on loglines, see Chapter 25.

CHAPTER 6
RELATABLE HERO

Why Do We Care?

Your main character needs to be someone the audience can sympathize or empathize with, or at the very least find compelling. In most cases, that means they like him—but there are exceptions.

WHO GIVES A DAMN?

Important as concept is, it's not enough. Because if that concept isn't wrapped around one or more characters who are both engaging and in some way relatable, no one's going to stick around long enough to see how the concept plays out.

Gale Anne Hurd has produced dozens of films, ranging from small and personal—*The Waterdance*, *Safe Passage* (NOV), and *The Wronged Man* (ART/TRU)—to blockbusters like *Armageddon, Aliens,* and *The Terminator,* as well as the *Hulk* and *Punisher* (both COM) franchises. She also produced *The Walking Dead* TV series (COM). "I respond to character-driven material, regardless of its origin," she says. "I fall in love with the characters and generally respond to stories featuring ordinary people who succeed in overcoming extraordinary challenges."

Dark Horse Comics publisher Mike Richardson has been instrumental as a producer in bringing about such adaptations as *300* (COM/HIS), *Sin City* (COM), *The Mask* and *Timecop* (both COM, and both of which he cowrote), the *Hellboy* franchise (COM), and *R.I.P.D.* (COM). All told, he's optioned or sold close to 100 projects, produced twenty-eight films (including TV), has another two dozen in development, and won an Emmy for producing *Mr. Warmth: The Don Rickles Project*. When describing what he looks for in an adaptable comic, his advice is eerily similar to Hurd's.

"We've been very successful creating stories involving regular people who are caught up in unusual or fantastic circumstances. It's a recipe that seems to work. If we can relate to the main character of the story—if we can identify with him or her—then as viewers we end up putting ourselves in that same situation. I think that's a good approach for coming up with an interesting film or book. Of course, it's easy to say and hard to accomplish."

Note that it is the *character* who is (or seems) ordinary. Why? Because an obviously extraordinary character is less relatable to the average reader or viewer, who then has a harder time rooting for—or imagining himself in the same situation as—the hero. In those relatively few instances in which the lead character seems extraordinary from the start, he usually has some kind of relatable flaw or vulnerability: a marriage or career on the rocks, an addiction, a failure or fear or accusation that has run his life off the tracks—making him, because of that, relatable when he (or she) otherwise wouldn't be.

Since selling his first script (*Galahad*), screenwriter Ryan Condal has been hired to adapt several properties written by others. When it comes to adaptations, he says, "what's most often missing in the original work is a compelling protagonist that we want to pay 12, 13, or 18 dollars to see in a movie theater on a Saturday night. That's where I make my reputation and my money as a writer of adaptations: cracking the hero's journey in a given property. The world of the story is usually fairly well thought out in the original work; I have to make sure the main character is someone we give a damn about."

To drive this point home with clients, I often use the following analogy. Imagine reading about a terrible accident. It could be nearby, or half a world away. There's a flicker of sympathy—"Oh, those poor people"—and then you're thinking about your next cheeseburger because, in the final analysis, this sort of thing happens to someone, somewhere, every day, turning the victims into statistics. That doesn't make you insensitive; it's a necessary coping mechanism, without which you'd probably go batso.

Now imagine that, a short time later, you learn that a close friend or relative was in that same accident. Suddenly, you can think of nothing else. Did they survive, were they hurt, will they be okay? Where are they, how can you reach them, what can you do to help? These questions consume you; everything else can and does go to hell until you find the answers.

It's the same exact event—yet its effect on you is totally different. That's not rational, so why does it happen? Because in the second instance, you care deeply about the person involved. This makes you emotionally invested in the outcome. As Ryan might put it: "The main character is someone you give a damn about."

It's the same with a movie (or book or comic or true story, for that matter): when you care about the characters, you become emotionally invested in the story and its outcome. Make no mistake: story is what happens to characters. Events alone, happening in isolation, have no context, no meaning—and no emotion attached to them.

When, on the other hand, they're happening to someone you've come to care about, you *have* to know what happens next. That's what keeps readers reading and audiences watching. It's why the whole world seems to disappear when you're caught up in a great story. It's what makes you stay up late to finish that book. And it is why, in an increasingly repressive and isolated society, people continue to flock to the movies: to experience emotions that are unsafe, less intense, or altogether inaccessible in the real world. (Would you *really* want to be chased by a Terminator—or a tyrannosaur?) After all, if we could find what we get from movies elsewhere, Hollywood would be out of business.

"A relatable hero is generally what they're looking for," notes screenwriter/producer Leslie Dixon. "On the other hand, an antihero can also work. We don't really have a Steve McQueen among our stars right now, but you can definitely make somebody like him and I wouldn't say he's exactly relatable, but you still want to be him if you're a guy. You want to kiss him if you're a woman. Not every hero has to have the relatability of Tom Hanks to be the hero of your movie."

Screenwriter Jonathan Hensleigh also sees the antihero as potentially commercial. "The role of antihero found a niche in commercial filmmaking," he says. "But always the American antihero is someone who is rejected by society for whatever reason, an outcast, maybe morally conflicted—but at the end he always does good."

And here we begin to expand the definition of *relatable*—and even step beyond it. "Actors," says Leslie Dixon, "vastly prefer complex and flawed characters to straight-ahead good guys. If your hero is a saint, you're doing something wrong. Relatability is actually less important than whether the actor will say, 'Yes, I'll do it.' Because your movie will never get made if some actor doesn't say they want to play that part.

"So while the character also has to appeal to the audience, you must always think, if I were an actor or an actress, would I want to play this part? And all of a sudden, you might realize that, geez, my lead character runs an orphanage and volunteers with disabled people on the weekends. She's so goody-goody, I want to slap her teeth out. I don't want to play that part. I'd rather play this drug addict over here, who kills somebody in self-defense. So I would definitely make sure the protagonist is compelling.

"Actors need something they can bite into, and not that many people are writing them really good parts. That is one of the absolute best ways to get in. It's a sideways door into the industry, where you could write some really great role for an actor—something they might win an Oscar for—and somehow get it to their manager or get it to their agent and come in that way."

In the end, a good commercial story must have at least one relatable or sympathetic or empathetic or compelling or root-for-able main character, or hero. Plot is reason; character, emotion. "You need to create characters people care about," confirms screenwriter Ehren Kruger. "You want that propulsive energy: what's going to happen to these people, where are they going to end up? You can't have characters who are just there to serve the function of the plot."

Ryan Condal agrees. "I search for a compelling hero I can build a story around," he says. "It all starts with the hero—who are they, how are they different, and why do we care about them?"

It's also important to remember that heroes do not exist in isolation; the people and things they care about both tell us something about them, and provide another way to draw readers into the tale. "To me," says Terry Rossio, "the relationships between characters need to be defined; those are the moments audiences want to watch, and the actual characters can be adjusted to make the main relationship or relationships the most interesting. That leads to thinking about what kind of character, and character situation, is best to mine the concept, or take best advantage of the concept or story arena."

It's crucial to understand, as well, that the main character need not be likable. But understand, too, that this is a risky path to pursue, and one which—if not trod with the utmost care—will very likely result in failure. The key here is to create a character with whom the audience can still sympathize or empathize, or at the very least find compelling in some way.

"A lot of people are going to tell you that a likable and relatable character is a must," says Paul Haggis. "*In the Valley of Elah* (ART/ TRU) does not have a relatable, likable protagonist; the one I created was much more unlikable and less relatable than the person upon whom it was based, but I think it's a pretty good movie." It is, however, also a movie whose lead character is a man in search of the truth about what happened to his dead son—and who among us cannot sympathize or empathize with that?

The lead character in *Sideways* (NOV)—Miles—is the kind of guy who steals money from his mother's dresser drawer. And yet, somehow, we want the best for him and his "depression, and anxiety, and neg-head downer" messed-up life. Why? Because he's compelling. He's the self-inflicted total loser we want to see make good.

Occupying the far end of the scale is Steven, the main character in *A Perfect Murder* (MOV/PLY), whose efforts to kill his rich wife form the basis of the story. Though charming, he's not likable in a deeper sense, and hopefully not terribly relatable, sympathetic, or empathetic—but the guy is absolutely fascinating to watch. He's so smart, so bad, so determined and darkly compelling that we almost want to see him pull it off. Importantly, he also has an antagonist who is, in some ways, even more reprehensible than he is.

Still, there are limits. Says Jonathan Hensleigh: "Buyers are not going to sit there and say, 'Well maybe the hero is a heroin-addicted cross-dresser who strives for two hours to achieve his goal and then fails miserably, resulting in the deaths of all of his friends. It's not going to happen, that picture's not going to be made, even by an independent production company.'" Why? Because relatability, sympathy, empathy, and a compelling lead are all missing.

In the final analysis, audiences must care about your hero, or Hollywood doesn't care about your story. If concept is king, character is heart—and with few exceptions, a poor hero with heart will draw more viewers than a king without.

CHAPTER 7
EMOTIONALLY COMPELLING STORY

What's at Stake?

Stories—movies in particular—are vicarious experiences. Adventure. Catharsis. If character is the hook that gets readers and viewers involved, story is the line that reels them in. "I look for a story that moves me," says Paul Haggis—who, as a screenwriter, director, and producer, has a broader perspective than most. "And that's hard to find. You need to be able to say, this is a story that, once it's on the screen, will move me in some way. It'll make me laugh, it'll make me cry, break my heart, heal me. Whatever it is, it will touch me. And if it touches me, it will touch others as well. That's probably the most important thing to know."

When considering material, Oscar-nominated producer Michael Nozik asks questions. "Is there a compelling central character? One whose dilemma can sustain the story? And what is that dilemma? Is it one that I care about, that I can relate to; one that I think an audience will relate to? I actually ask if I relate to it first, because if I can't understand it and relate to it, I'm probably not going to be of much use in moving the project forward.

"I've tried a few times with things where I thought, hey, this story seems commercial—but if it doesn't affect me on an emotional level, if it doesn't compel me, I actually can't go the distance with it, can't develop it, can't sell it very well because I'd just be faking it. And I just don't understand or know how to do that." Even the most fascinating character in the world can't save a bad story.

But what, exactly, is a bad story? Christopher Lockhart of WME sums it up nicely: "A bad story is one where what you think is going to happen twenty pages from now, happens twenty pages from now." Predictability is deadly. It's the reason we don't go around picking up rocks and dropping them; we already know what's going to happen. It's boring, and people don't pay money (not intentionally, anyway) to sit in a theater and be bored.

On the other hand, you can't have a hero who wanders around aimlessly, just to be unpredictable. What you—or, more specifically, your lead character—need are *stakes*. Something to gain or lose, or both. Something (a goal) of tremendous importance to the character and, by extension, to the reader/audience—because if we like, root for, or identify with the hero, his struggles become ours.

Remember that the stakes needn't be huge in any objective sense—your hero doesn't have to be saving the world; perhaps (as in *Little Miss Sunshine*) he just needs to get his daughter to a beauty pageant. Whatever the stakes, they do need to be huge and (subjectively, at least) all-consuming for your hero.

But even this, alone, is not enough. Because there's another crucial aspect that must be in play: we must want the hero to succeed. If the entire plot revolves around the hero's struggle to achieve something we don't want to see happen—for example, to save the life of someone we (and the hero, if he knew what we know) would rather see dead, then you've created a situation where the audience actually wants the hero to fail (or would at least be happier if he failed). Which is, of course, the precise opposite of what you're aiming for, and a recipe for disaster.

The stakes must escalate as the story progresses. Think of it like a fireworks show (or like sex, if you prefer): there's a reason the biggest bang comes at the end. If the most impressive thing happens first, all that follows is bound to disappoint because it doesn't measure up. When the biggest thing happens last, everything else is a buildup.

Another element of a compelling story is this: the hero is captain of his fate and, ultimately, his own actions and resourcefulness determine his fate. A lead character can lose control of his destiny; often, this is what triggers the hero's journey: his or her world spinning out of control. The journey itself is the struggle to attain or regain that control. If on the other hand your hero loses control of his own destiny, and never regains it—or regains it only as a result of some other character's actions—then you, your hero, and the story are in deep trouble. In essence, the hero must save his (or her) own bacon.

The absolute worst thing you can possibly do, storywise, is just the opposite: bail your hero out with a *deus ex machina*—literally, "god from the machine"—some outside force that miraculously shows up at just the right time to make everything okay. This technique originated with the ancient Greeks, who would write the heroes of their plays into impossible situations—only to have a god (lowered onto the stage by a crane) save the day, and the hero. Plato ridiculed it then, and it is equally ill advised today; such endings do not grow "organically" out of the story, but are grafted on afterward to cheat the writer out of a jam. They also cheat the audience out of a story that makes sense.

Finally, to be compelling, the stakes in your story must have an emotional component: will the hero win the girl (or guy), overcome the handicap, stop the bad guy (or gal), save his family, the world—or the galaxy? If people care about your hero; if they want what he wants, are chewing their nails wondering whether he'll succeed, will be happy if he does and disappointed if he doesn't—then your story is compelling.

If none of these things are true, it's not.

CHAPTER 8
TICKING CLOCK

Tension, Suspense, Urgency

A "ticking clock" makes things happen now, rather than later. "I feel more comfortable telling a story within a tight time frame," says producer Michael Nozik, "where there's a pressure, an inherent ticking clock. It doesn't have to take place in an afternoon; it can be over a number of months, even years—but you want to be able to keep the inherent pressure of the clock."

Screenwriter Jonathan Hensleigh is best known for big-budget action films like *Armageddon*. "When you're talking about action pictures," he says, "films that are reliant upon a storyline where your hero is trying to achieve something that requires a tremendous amount of physical action, he's put through the inner circles of hell that all involve physical action around him, he's being chased or whatever—it's almost impossible to do one of these pictures without a ticking clock."

Consider this basic premise: Our Hero must find and disarm a bomb that will destroy New York City at midnight. Now think about this one: Our Hero must find and disarm a bomb that will destroy New York City at some point in the future. You see the difference. The first is workable, the second unfilmmable—because the first has a ticking clock, and the second doesn't. What are we going to do, follow the guy around for five years, wondering when—and if—something's going to happen?

The logic is both simple and inescapable: If the bomb goes off at midnight, Our Hero has to hustle. Suddenly there's tension, suspense, and urgency. Every second counts: a traffic jam, a missed bus, a dropped call could be fatal.

If Our Hero's wife/girlfriend/child is also in the city and can't get out before midnight—so much the better. Because now the stakes are personal, and therefore more emotional and compelling. Furthermore, it's now relatable; even viewers who wouldn't miss NYC, still want to see the hero save his loved ones. (When it comes to fiction, better to save one character we care about than a million we don't—and best of all to do both.)

Saw has a literal ticking clock, as does *Back to the Future*. Still, the ticking clock in your story needn't be a literal, clock-based deadline. Stopping the Bad Guy before he [fill in evil deed here] also works. In this case there is no literal clock, but since the audience will see the bad guy in action—we can see how far along he is, and we know how fast the hero must act to stop him—the tension, suspense, and urgency remain.

There are probably an infinite number of plot-specific ticking clocks, but all fall into one of two broad categories: time-based and event-based. The hero must do (or stop) *x* before a specific time, or the hero must do (or stop) *x* before a specific event takes place. In both cases, the purpose is the same: to compress the story into something that can be told in about 120 pages, or two hours of screen time.

Time-based clocks do not change; we and the characters know exactly when the deadline is—and when the clock hits the established time, that's it. Game over, one way or the other. Event-based clocks, on the other hand, lack a specific, set-in-stone timeline; we do not know precisely when the event will take place. They can also change—as when, for example, the hero thwarts the villain's actions, causing him (when he doesn't succeed) to try, try again (creating new event-clocks), or when the hero fails to beat the first clock and later faces another, often worse clock as the villain's actions escalate.

One example of a time-based clock occurs in *Saw,* which features multiple situations where characters must escape gruesome circumstances within a set period of time, or die. Other examples include: evacuating the Na'vi from Hometree in one hour, at which time the site will be demolished (*Avatar*); hitting the wire from the clock tower at the precise instant that lightning strikes the tower, in order to power a time machine (*Back to the Future*); finding and stopping a bomb/bomber before the fixed time at which the bomb will detonate (*Déjà Vu, Source Code, Die Hard with a Vengeance,* MOV/SCR); win the girl's heart before she marries Mr. Wrong (if the wedding date has been set: *Only You*); get a person or thing from Place A to Place B by a specific time (literally scores of movies, including *Midnight Run*).

Event-based clocks include: convince the Na'vi to abandon Hometree before the RDA dozers get there three months from now (*Avatar*); defeat the RDA corporate military force before it destroys the Tree of Souls (*Avatar*); get everyone off a city bus before the speed drops below 50 mph and triggers a bomb (*Speed*); destroy the Terminator before it kills Sarah Connor (*The Terminator*); destroy the Ring of Power before Sauron finds it (*The Lord of the Rings* trilogy, NOV); stop Ducard or The Joker or Bane before he destroys Gotham City (*Batman Begins, The Dark Knight, The Dark Knight Rises,* all COM); escape the island before being eaten by dinosaurs (*Jurassic Park,* NOV); win the girl's heart before she marries someone else (when the wedding date has not been set: *Sleepless in Seattle*; even if the protagonist doesn't know about the impending marriage, the audience does, and so the clock still works); get to a specific place or thing before someone else does (again, scores of movies).

Some time-based clocks seem like event-based clocks, but really aren't. Both *Armageddon* and *Deep Impact,* for instance, involve blowing up/diverting an asteroid before it slams into the earth and destroys civilization. Which would definitely be event-based—but for the fact that, in each story, both we and the characters know the precise instant by which the mission must be accomplished. So it's actually more like: blow up/divert an asteroid before x time—when it will become impossible to prevent it from slamming into the earth and destroying civilization. That makes it clock-based.

Some movies have both time- and event-based clocks; *Avatar,* as noted above. Also *True Lies,* where the hero must first escape (and save his wife) from an uninhabited island before a nuclear weapon detonates at a predetermined time—and then, later, stop a terrorist from detonating a nuclear weapon (and killing the hero's daughter) in downtown Miami. Note how the stakes are personalized in both cases—and how they escalate.

But, as mentioned, ticking clocks aren't just about action. "If you're going to define the ticking clock broadly as something that lends immediacy or urgency," says screenwriter/director Jonathan Hensleigh, "you rope in virtually every single plotline ever presented in any commercial way since Greek drama."

Occasionally, if you look very hard, you will find a movie (usually independent and low-budget) that has no ticking clock of any kind. Generally speaking, the heroes tend to wander, the plots to ramble, and the box office to flatline. That's not a place you want to be.

CHAPTER 9
VISUAL POTENTIAL

The Eyes Have It

James Cameron—writer/director/producer of *The Terminator, Terminator 2, Aliens, True Lies* (MOV), *Titanic* (HIS) and *Avatar,* among others—is to the film industry what Secretariat was to horse racing when he won the final race of the Triple Crown by 31 lengths. No one else operates at his level, or close to it. While most filmmakers would be out-of-their-minds ecstatic to have a movie gross $400 million to $500 million at the box office, Cameron *spent* $400 million to $500 million just to *make* his film *Avatar.* If you ask him what he looks for in source material and scripts (which I have), he'll tell you this: "Unique visual potential."

Screenwriter Terry Rossio notes that "very often films are based on plays, and so can seem 'stagebound' when those stories are filmed. Or short stories or even novels, which, in exploring their ideas, don't concern themselves with an audience's need for visual relief. It makes sense to explore those story concepts without the restraints imposed by the prior medium."

Screenwriter John August cuts to the heart of the matter in dealing with source material: "You look for a story that can be told visually, that doesn't rely on long passages of exposition to get the story told. You want something that can fit into a two-hour window; it's not so epic and sprawling that you're not going to do justice to what the story is by fitting it into a smaller package."

Simply put, film is less flexible than print. A book, whether fiction or nonfiction, can delve inside characters' heads—and stay there—for three hundred pages. Movies can't do that. Or, to be more accurate, can't do it without externalizing the characters' inner experience in a way that makes that experience seem objective (and therefore lensable). Brilliant examples of this technique include *Inception* and the *Matrix* films—all of which are, of course, action-heavy. *Avatar*—also action-heavy—completely blurs the line between internal and external experience. Film is a visual medium, and interesting things must pass before the camera, even if the character is sealed inside a high-tech coffin for half the movie.

No one knows this better than the director, whose job it is to mold the visual experience. Lesli Linka Glatter's directorial and producing debut—*Tales of Meeting and Parting*—was based on a series of true stories and earned an Academy Award nomination. She currently has five feature films in development, three of which are adaptations. "You need to create the kind of experience that people can see taking place on the screen," she advises. "And doing that with an adaptation is hard. You have to strike a delicate balance between being true to the original material and story concept, and translating it into this other, very visual medium. But it can be done."

Still, this is easier with some adaptations than with others. As screenwriter/producer Leslie Dixon points out, "There are some stories that have a great idea in them, but not a single scene that would translate into a cinematic experience. Maybe the story doesn't go where a movie audience would feel fulfilled, or a character behaves in a way that is just too reprehensible and would throw you right out of the movie. And so you have to change it.

"At the other extreme, there are movies waiting to happen: *The Silence of the Lambs,* or *The Girl with the Dragon Tattoo* series. You've got the characters, the story, the scenes are really dramatic, and there's action."

In adapting Alan Glynn's novel *The Dark Fields* into the hit film *Limitless,* Leslie found herself with a dilemma; main character Eddie narrates the book, but never shares his experiences with anyone other than the reader. In a movie, that's boring; events must be shown, and thoughts conveyed through realistic dialogue.

Enter Eddie's new girlfriend Lindy ("new" because she's not in the book). Now Eddie has someone to talk to about what's happening to him—thus informing the audience indirectly, in a way the camera can see. The addition of Lindy's character also serves another purpose: by placing her life in jeopardy, the stakes are raised tremendously. A third purpose is also served by this: conflict when Lindy disapproves (to put it mildly) of what Eddie's doing. This lends the information conveyed a dramatic aspect, which wouldn't be the case if Eddie were simply reciting the facts to a disinterested third party. A fourth purpose: an emotional expansion of the original story, as Eddie's character is both broadened and given more depth by the relationship. A fifth purpose is to add an additional dimension for the viewer: a love relationship between two characters. A possible sixth purpose would be to up the film's appeal to female audiences. All of this boosts the story's cinematic potential—with the addition of a single character not present in the novel.

As you can see, things aren't always lost in translation; sometimes, things are gained. The best adaptation specialists can help prevent the first and ensure the second.

CHAPTER 10
STRUCTURE

Classic Beauty

Successful film stories aren't just thrown on the page; as with any thing of beauty in art or nature, there is an underlying structure—Blake's "fearsome symmetry," if you will. The result itself is seen and appreciated by all. What lies beneath is often less apparent—as it should be: the greater the work, the more seamless and effortless the outward appearance.

When you see a movie, read a book, or visit a museum, you have an innate sense of whether the work is good, mediocre, awful—or transcendent. And that's really all you need to know, if your goal is appreciation.

If, on the other hand, you want to create such works yourself, or explain to a studio head or financier just why it is that they should sink $100 million-plus into creating a movie based on your material—you need something more than "It works for me." You need a deeper understanding. Michelangelo and Leonardo da Vinci are perhaps the greatest artists in all of human history. Neither relied on outward appearances when rendering their works. Instead, to achieve a greater understanding of the structure underlying those appearances, they dissected human bodies.

Likewise, to create a great screenplay or film, it is necessary to turn a more discerning eye on things that are not obvious to the layman. The casual observer sees the effortless performance; we must understand the work that went into it. Part III: Mapping (and Remapping) Your Story (Chapters 16–21) includes an in-depth discussion of screen story structure. For now, be aware of the following. . . .

The overwhelming majority of commercially successful films are classically structured; if you want a studio or production company to buy or finance your *non*classically structured project—and you don't have someone truly massive already firmly attached—playing the lottery might be a better and more profitable use of your time.

Whether most films are classically structured because this structure is inherently superior, or because buyers have created a self-fulfilling prophecy by greenlighting such films to the near-exclusion of all others is irrelevant. As Damon Runyon famously noted, the race is not always to the swift, nor the battle to the strong—but that's the way to bet. And Hollywood, by and large, places its bets on classically structured films. When you see an exception, chances are it was made by a well-established figure with a long track record of successful—and classically structured—projects.

"There is a physics to storytelling," says Christopher Lockhart, executive story editor at Hollywood superagency WME (and, before that, at ICM). "It's pacing, it's momentum; ebb and flow, highs and lows, peaks and valleys. Those are created via the structure, in the same way a roller coaster generates its momentum. If you have too many peaks or too many valleys, the car slows to a stop." Experienced pros can see when things start to go wrong—and that's deadly."

He continues: "Structure is a living, breathing thing that has a life of its own, based on the story. But an archetypal three-act structure is this: we meet the protagonist, and we learn that there's a problem. By the end of the first act, the protagonist has to set out on a mission to solve that problem. If I don't see that happening around page 30 in a 120-page script, I start to think the writer doesn't know structure.

"The second act goes about exponentially increasing the protagonist's problems, while trying to take him closer to finally solving the problem and achieving his goal. The midpoint is typically the no-turning-back point. This is where the character cannot turn away from the problem. At the end of the second act, he hits a low point, which means the character is about as far away from solving his problem as he can possibly be.

"The third act is when the character rises from the dead—his low point—and concocts a new plan. In the climax we learn whether or not he succeeds in attaining his goal. After which there may be a brief resolution or denouement."

More technically speaking (and I know Chris agrees, because he taught me this), classically structured films have three major acts and seven plot points, in the following order: inciting incident; first act turn; midpoint; low point; second act turn; climax; denouement or wrap-up. If your source material doesn't conform to this pattern, that's okay—so long as you have a screenplay that does.

If the screenplay itself does not possess this structure, you're most likely looking at pursuing the project as an indie (nonstudio) production. Which almost always means—among other things— far less money for just about everyone involved, unless the film a) gets made and b) does phenomenally well. (And sometimes even then.)

When it comes to adapting works from other media, much of the effort revolves around fitting the story into the expected format, length, and "classical" structure. And of course, as Gale Anne Hurd points out, "true stories don't follow traditional plotlines." Which is why they're altered to accommodate the three-act structure demanded by Hollywood. This, in turn, is why so many films are said to be "based upon" or "inspired by" (rather than actual and unaltered) true stories. Gail Lyon, one of the producers on the Oscar-nominated film *Erin Brockovich* (TRU) says, "Screenwriter Susannah Grant adjusted the story to fit a filmic structure, and what she wrote is substantially the movie you see today."

Screenwriter/producer/director Jonathan Hensleigh notes that "any study of motion pictures and how they fare with the public over time reveals that there are certain aspects to script construction that need to be honored for a film to be commercial. For the most part; there are exceptions. The people who run studios are not stupid, and they know something about film and finance. They also know that a traditional three-act structure, with a beginning, middle, and end, is vastly more likely to be successful in the marketplace. Whereas something that, for example, just ends abruptly or is unresolved or unsatisfying is not going to be commercial. So those types of projects are rejected.

"I've heard it said that 90 percent of all commercially successful films are classically structured. But I'd say that percentage is too low."

CHAPTER 11
ACTOR-FRIENDLY LEAD

Attracting Talent

When telling a story in most media, you create your own lead character. In film, the literal face of your lead is an actor. Understandably, those in the business of financing films want that face to be familiar or, at the very least, compelling. There are specific actors they're willing to put their money behind, because they believe that their participation in the film will up the box office/DVD sales/etc. "Studio executives," says screenwriter Ehren Kruger, "need to know not just what the concept is, but what the element is that's going to make this project stand out or attract top talent—meaning directors or actors. Because for the most part, it's really stars and filmmakers who determine which movies do and don't get made."

Which, in turn, means you must have a story with one or more strong roles that one or more of these people will find appealing. This is not always as simple as it seems. For example, most of those outside the industry might think that an actor who just played (let's say) a killer cyborg in a hit film might be looking for another, similar role. As producer Michael Nozik puts it, "People think you made *x,* so therefore you'll want to make *x* again. But that's not often the case." In fact, more often than not, it's the last thing on earth anyone wants to do. Why? Because they've already done it. Shortly after *The Terminator,* for instance, Arnold Schwarzenegger complained about being inundated with "killer robot" scripts.

More surprisingly, according to Oscar-winning screenwriter and novelist William Goldman, actors who've come to prominence with franchises often hate the franchise itself, either because it boxes them into a position where most subsequent offers are for similar roles ("typecasting" them), or because they dislike the perception that the franchise is a bigger draw than they are. In both cases, the reaction is the same: they actively seek to prove themselves in very different roles.

Actors, basically, want to show off. That's why they're actors. They want to be challenged, and demonstrate their ability to do things they haven't done before. Even Schwarzenegger branched out from tentpole action into comedy. The biggest challenge of all is to do something that's never been done by anyone—like, say, The Joker in *The Dark Knight* (COM), or Dexter Morgan in the TV series *Dexter* (NOV). A role like that is extraordinarily rare, and can be a real talent magnet.

"You always look for compelling characters," says Michael Nozik, "characters that will ultimately attract cast, that will be exciting enough and rich enough that you can get actors to want to play them. Because that's the actor's criterion: Is this going to be an interesting character to play? Is their dilemma compelling enough?"

The desire to do something compelling and different is so strong that major actors with huge salaries will sometimes take drastic pay cuts to play unusual or risky roles in smaller films whose makers simply could not afford their usual rates—filmmakers who might well be shooting the entire movie for less than the actor's standard fee.

Often, these roles and films turn out to be Oscar contenders. *Batman* (COM) may haul in billions, but it's not likely to be up for Best Actor or Best Picture. *The Fighter* (TRU), on the other hand, was up for Best Picture, Best Supporting Actor, and Best

Supporting Actress (twice)—and brought *Batman* (COM) and *Terminator Salvation* star Christian Bale his first Academy Award.

The point is not that you have to write an Oscar-caliber screenplay to land a bankable star. You don't. The point is that you don't have to write a summer blockbuster, either. What you absolutely must do is create a story with one or more lead roles that good actors will find appealing. Generally speaking, that means characters with depth, purpose, and a range of emotions on display. It also, generally speaking, means "character arc"—a character who is in some way fundamentally changed by his onscreen journey. This doesn't always happen in action films, and villains and minor characters seldom have substantial arcs (the Grinch being a notable exception). But it's something most actors look for.

Obviously, most writers want bankable actors to play their leads, as do most directors, producers, and studios. But there are exceptions to everything, and this is no exception to that. "There's a nice healthy kind of subgenre," says Jonathan Hensleigh, "where the studio executives, producer, director have been shrewd enough to realize, hey, we don't have to pay $20 million to a star here; this movie is going to go just on concept and execution alone. Again it's a subgenre, a small little area of pictures, but *Star Wars* came out of that."

Exception or not, there is one inviolable rule: characters who are there simply and only to fulfill some particular plot function—that is, they're there for the author's reasons and not their own—will fail to attract quality "talent" (as actors are called). Because the actor is not so much interested in your story, as in his or her character's journey.

CHAPTER 12
AVERAGE LENGTH

Where "Average" Is Good

Have you ever noticed that the biggest-selling authors tend to write the longest books? Stephen King's first novel *Carrie* is 272 pages (including author's introduction); *The Stand*—written years later—is nearly 1,200 pages. Line up J. K. Rowling's *Harry Potter* books, or Stephenie Meyer's *Twilight* novels on a shelf: as time goes on, they get fatter and fatter. This is not coincidence.

Name-brand authors have large followings who line up for each new book. They know the author and the quality, and don't mind paying the higher price publishers must charge to cover their increased costs (bigger advances and more advertising, higher printing and distribution outlays, etc.).

A similar dynamic is at work in the film industry—but with higher stakes. "If I pick up a script," says producer Gale Anne Hurd, "and it's not for a TV miniseries, and it's longer than 140 pages—I tend to put it at the bottom of the pile. It often means that story structure is sadly lacking, and the writer doesn't know the basic rules of the craft." Most producers draw the line considerably sooner— at 125 to 130 pages, tops.

John August is currently adapting *Preacher*, a 48-book graphic novel series—which works out to over 1,300 pages in already-condensed comic form. "When there's way too much story, as there is with *Preacher*," he notes, "you have to ask yourself whether the central idea of the overall story can exist in a two-hour universe. Are you going to be able to introduce the characters and the central idea in a way that's going to make sense as a movie. Because that's what you've got: two hours."

And while one can debate the "ideal" story length and the various prominent exceptions, the hard facts are these: A publisher might spend $80,000 on a typical hardcover book. This includes advance, artwork, editing, typesetting, printing, advertising and distribution. For a 300-page book, that works out to $266 per page.

Now let's look at film. A rock-bottom, dirt-cheap (but high-quality) independent feature like *Saw* or *Hard Candy* might be budgeted at $1 million. A major studio, on the other hand, is likely to spend $60 million to $100 million or more on a typical film. At the high end, *The Dark Knight* cost a reported $240 million—and *Avatar*, $450 million.

All told, this works out to about $10,000 per minute on the low end (*Saw* at 103 minutes and $1 million; *Hard Candy* at 104 minutes and $1 million)—to nearly $3 million per minute on the high end (*Avatar*, at 162 minutes and $450 million). Most films fall somewhere in between, at $500,000 to $1 million per on-screen minute.

Note that first-timers and less-established filmmakers are shooting lower-budget, shorter films. Also note that the high-end films with stratospheric budgets are made by seasoned professionals with decades of experience and huge hits behind them. As you might suspect, this, also, is no coincidence.

Film is an extraordinarily expensive medium, and those footing a bill that could run upward of $1 million per minute of screen time don't want to hear that some newcomer thinks his story should run long. For a feature (theatrical, as opposed to TV) script, you want something that runs 105 to 125 pages. Generally speaking, comedies run short, say 105 to 110 pages, while action films often run longer: 115 to 120 or so.

If a story cannot be told in two hours or less (120 script pages), it may be too costly to shoot. Some industry players will read longer screenplays—but even then, there are limits. Theater owners, too, are reluctant to screen movies (other than those from blockbuster filmmakers) that run substantially over two hours—in this case because that means fewer showings (and, hence, lower box office receipts) per day.

James Cameron's first hit—*The Terminator*—runs 107 minutes; *Titanic* and *Avatar* came much later in his career. Don't try to be the exception your first time out.

CHAPTER 13
REASONABLE BUDGET

Keeping It Real

As screenwriter John August notes, "I think we're past reasonable budgets." Few would argue with this in a broader sense. But what we mean here is reasonable by Hollywood standards, where a small picture like *Doubt* (PLY) with, basically, a couple of people talking at an old church for under two hours costs $20 million.

Bringing your script in at 105 to 120 pages does not mean the movie will be affordable, because the content itself affects the budget. In the book world, the publisher's cost-per-page remains the same, whether your characters are playing checkers in the park or blowing up a planet.

This is not true of Hollywood, where shooting two characters playing checkers might cost $200,000, and filming a major action sequence could run $10 million. Too many "money shots" (also called "set pieces") can raise your project's budget to the point where no one can—or is willing to—lens it. Studios have pulled the plug on some of the biggest stars in the world on budget-busting projects; those films will never be made, unless someone finds a way to make them more affordably.

I personally know of a script that a major director very much wanted to do——but no one could figure out how to shoot it for under $300 million. The writers were either unwilling to or incapable of altering it——and so it was never bought. Veteran screenwriting team Terry Rossio and Ted Elliott have so far written four of the top 20 highest-grossing films of all time. Nevertheless, their *Lone Ranger* project (with Johnny Depp——who also starred in Rossio and Elliott's *Pirates of the Caribbean* franchise) was canceled when the budget estimate approached $250 million. Work resumed on condition that the budget could be brought down to the neighborhood of $200 million. This for a story whose hero carries revolvers and rides a horse——which gives you some idea of what it costs a studio to make a big movie these days.

"Studios are still making expensive movies," says Ehren Kruger, "but the more affordable your project's budget, the more options you have with buyers." WME's Christopher Lockhart expands on this: "You can't expect someone to film on a $500 million budget," he says, "just like you can't write an $80 million movie with an eighty-year-old Japanese female protagonist. It's like, dude, who's gonna make that movie? I'm just constantly trying to pound that reality into those who are new at this, to say listen, I understand what you want to do——but if you want to make a movie, then you have to think like you're in a business."

And make no mistake: Hollywood *is* a business. As one studio head told me: "Unfortunately, studios can't make films out of love. We have to make them out of profit." As publicly held companies they are, in fact, legally required to do this.

And so if your story seems prohibitively expensive to film, it will not become a movie unless someone very powerful pushes the project very hard——and maybe not even then. "In terms of the cost of the negative [the cost of making the film, before marketing and distribution]," counsels Jonathan Hensleigh, "you want to be as low as you can possibly get it while still delivering the sort of wow-'em effect for the trailer."

In short, don't make your project something only James Cameron can afford to make——because if he's not interested, it's over.

CHAPTER 14
LOW-FAT STORY

Lean and Mean Is Green

Because of time and budgetary constraints, there's little room for anything not absolutely essential to the onscreen story. A novelist can burn ten pages describing a room, so long as it stays interesting. A screenwriter might do this in a sentence—and going on for more than a paragraph will mark him (or her) as an amateur. "The forte of screenwriting," says John August, "is that ruthless efficiency and sort of making every word count, which lets you tell a lot of story with very few pages. It's incredibly compressed and condensed and specific. You're not responsible for sketching in every little part of the story world. You're just giving enough information to evoke the sense of watching the movie on a big screen."

Likewise, you're only including story elements that are crucial. This kind of storytelling economy is the point of an old Hollywood adage: "If you show a shotgun over the mantel in the first act, you'd better use it in the third." Examples of this can be seen in James Cameron's *Aliens* and *Avatar* movies, where things seen early on reappear—and prove important—later on.

Think of the power loader Ripley uses to load missiles, and then to fight the alien queen—or the AMP suit Col. Quartich uses to practice his boxing moves, and then escape the burning ship to battle Neytiri and the thanator. In fact, consider the thanator itself—seen early on, and then again in the climactic battle. The same goes for the toruk and the legend of Toruk Makto, which comes to life in the third act.

Another way films cut fat is by compressing timelines and multitasking. Instead of fighting *The Terminator* in the Tech Noir bar and then fleeing, and later explaining what the Terminator is and why Reese is there—everything overlaps: Reese attacks, flees with Sarah while fighting off the pursuing Terminator and explaining who he is, why he's there, what the Terminator is and why it's after Sarah. To do this sequentially would waste time—and of course be far less exciting.

In a book, static conversations—even monologues—can go on for a dozen pages or more. The strength of Robert Ludlum's writing in the Jason Bourne novels is found largely in the dialogue. In film, long static conversations are referred to as "talking heads," and it's not a compliment. Nothing should be static; something else is always going on—some kind of tension, action, conflict, etc. Witness the *Bourne* movies which, while containing some of the best action-movie dialogue ever filmed, do not exactly dwell on long conversations.

Perhaps the best way to keep all of this in mind is to consider what I've come to call Vinge's Law, because the advice comes from science fiction author and mathematician Vernor Vinge: Ideally, every scene should accomplish three things: advance the plot, reveal character, and build backstory. Scenes which achieve two of these three aims are acceptable, but could be better; those which accomplish only one, or none—should be revised or deleted.

Again, look at that *Terminator* scene: plot is advanced, character revealed, backstory built—all in a few brief, tension-filled moments. Learn from the masters; their work is right there to be studied. You just have to know what to look for.

CHAPTER 15
FRANCHISE POTENTIAL, FOUR-QUADRANT APPEAL, AND MERCHANDISING

The Big (Budget) Three

Jonathan Hensleigh, known for blockbusters like *Armageddon*, *Die Hard with a Vengeance* (NOV/SCR), and *Jumanji* (NOV), puts it this way: "Right now, in terms of Hollywood action pictures or high-concept pictures they spend a lot of money on, I would say these things are the number-one requirement. The higher the budget, the more you need it to be four-quadrant and so on, because with anything over a certain budget level, the marketing executives come in with their graphs and say, we need all of this stuff because the picture's so big.

"I'd say any time the cost of the negative is over $100 million, those conversations start to occur. These are vehicles that are meant for speed and to make a lot of money; they're not meant to win Academy Awards, and you have to understand that going in."

FRANCHISE POTENTIAL

Can a film based on your story be sequeled and prequeled? If so, that's a big point in your favor. If the first movie hits, it's a safer financial bet to release a sequel to your film than it is to risk vast sums on something new (and, therefore, untested in the marketplace). This is not absolutely essential (look at *Titanic*), but is highly desired—to the point where a *300* prequel is now moving forward.

As I write this, 24 of the top 25 highest-grossing films of all time are sequels, films that spawned sequels or that incorporate sequels. (*Alice in Wonderland* is based on *two* books by Lewis Carroll, at least two *Avatar* sequels are planned, and *Marvel's The Avengers* is sort of a multi-sequel in itself.) This fact is not lost on Hollywood, which is as crazy about sequels as it is about adaptations (20 of the top 25 highest-grossing films being adaptations). In many cases, the adaptations are also sequels, allowing Hollywood to double-down.

As mentioned earlier, sequel- and prequel-ability are not mandatory. On the other hand, they don't hurt. Generally speaking, the bigger the budget, the more important this becomes: of those top 25 films, most of which were horrendously expensive, only one—James Cameron's *Titanic*—stands alone and unsequeled or unprequeled, though there was a sequel to the soundtrack. (Two *Avatar* sequels are currently in preproduction.)

FOUR-QUADRANT APPEAL

For marketing purposes, studios divide the moviegoing public into four large segments, or quadrants: young male, older male, young female, older female. The greater the number of quadrants your project appeals to, the better.

"A great four-quadrant script is rarer than a Republican in Hollywood," says screenwriter Ryan Condal. "Instead of being force-fit to attract as many people as possible, these stories hold an organic appeal for a mass audience. That's why they're so highly prized."

WME executive story editor Christopher Lockhart expands on that. "Successful writers," he says, "call upon ideas, and characters, and themes that fascinate them, but also intrigue the population at large—and people go to see their movies. I still meet people all the time who say, "I don't want to write something like *Titanic*. That's not real life." But that movie made $2 billion worldwide. (And more like $8 billion to $10 billion with DVD sales.)

"You can say whatever the hell you want to say about *Titanic*—you don't even have to like it—but the truth is that millions upon millions of people connected with that movie. And that's what, as a storyteller, you want to do: you want to connect with people. That writer who hates *Titanic* thinks his script about Grandma's earthworm farm is much more interesting and universal. But *Titanic* is a movie. The earthworm farm is a home video. Either you write a home video, or you write a movie."

Again, four-quadrant appeal is not a strict necessity. "The fact that you're only targeting one or two quadrants," says John August, "relates to other decisions about what your budget's going to be, and many other things. Which can be good. Knowing you're only going to hit those two groups of people, you feel free to hit your harder elements harder, because those are going to be particularly rewarding for those groups of people."

Some filmmakers, in fact, have little interest in four-quadrant projects. "It's hard to create a four-quadrant movie," says producer Michael Nozik. "Hard to write, hard to shoot and market, and very expensive. For a new writer to even come up with such a concept, is a needle in a haystack. You generally have to go through the process with experienced people to help flush out all four quadrants.

"If you can find a clearly defined quadrant or two that you know you can nail, I personally think that's as good as a four-quadrant movie. You build that one or two quadrants, which can create momentum. And momentum can build a multiple-quadrant movie. It becomes a must-see thing, because everybody in that quadrant is talking about it to everyone they know. *The Help* (NOV) started out female-driven, then crossed over to older males and wound up with three quadrants. And if your story is contained, budget-wise, it doesn't have to cross over. You can have a very successful movie with only one strong quadrant."

If, however, you—like James Cameron—can draw viewers from eight to eighty, then you too can be king (or queen) of the world.

MERCHANDISING POTENTIAL

"Merchandising potential is always nice," says Nozik, "because it's a point of serious cash for the participants. But it's a tricky thing. I've seen scripts from young writers who don't really know what they're doing. They have all these gadgets and things in the story, and it feels like they're self-consciously trying to create merchandising appeal. But merchandising has to be organic to the story."

When it is, the payoff can be spectacular. Film studios often make more money from film-related merchandising than they do from the films themselves. A lot more. Films with low or no merchandising potential continue to be made, but as budget levels escalate, the tidal wave is moving the other way—favoring projects with strong merchandising appeal.

In fact, things have now progressed to the point where merchandise is being made into movies, which in turn sell more merchandise: witness the *Transformers* series Ehren Kruger has been writing. Generally speaking, big-budget action and animation films are merchandising bonanzas, while dramas, thrillers, and comedies have considerably less merchandising appeal.

Obviously, this hasn't kept studios from making thrillers and comedies (most dramas are now independents)—which are less expensive to film and, therefore, don't require the kind of Herculean merchandising blitz needed to keep a marketing juggernaut like the *Batman* franchise raking in the billions.

George Lucas became a billionaire not for writing, directing, or producing the *Star Wars* films—but because his deal with the studio gave him merchandising rights to the franchise. Once the studios realized just how much movie merchandising could be worth, they immediately altered their contracts to restrict all subsequent writers to 5 percent or less of the (studio-calculated) merchandising profit—ensuring that Lucas' path to fortune will never be duplicated within the studio system.

Still, it's sometimes possible (through powerful alliances) to get a bigger piece of the merchandising pie when the project is an adaptation of an underlying property to which you own or control the rights. Something to keep in mind.

PART III

MAPPING (AND REMAPPING) YOUR CURRENT STORY

As Christopher Columbus learned the hard way, the lack of an accurate map can land you on the wrong continent. And while things may have worked out for him, countless others never landed anywhere—ending their journeys at the bottom of the ocean. There are plenty of ships down there, but that's not the kind of company you want to be keeping.

The next six chapters will explain how to create a story map based on what you have now (even if it exists only in your imagination at this point), and how to modify that map in ways that will help you navigate the sometimes treacherous waters of Hollywood—where those unfortunate souls with inaccurate maps often don't make it to the ocean bottom, because there are too many sharks in the way.

CHAPTER 16
EVALUATING YOUR CURRENT STORY

If you're reading this, more than likely you have something you'd like to adapt. It could be a concept, a 1,500-page novel, or anything in between. For now, it makes no difference whatsoever—because the first step is always the same.

Think of yourself as a traveler in unfamiliar territory: you know where you want to wind up, you have a map and a friendly guide ready to help, and you're eager to get started. Before you can do that, though—before a guide or a map can do you any good— you need to know where you are now. (Technically, it's enough for the guide to know where you are—but since I've not seen your work, I'll have to help you figure that out for yourself.)

The next five chapters will tell you how to evaluate what you have now. They will delve into the DNA of a story, tracing its development from embryonic concept to full-blown screenplay. And they will show you, step by step, how to cultivate your story's cinematic potential by tinkering with things most moviegoers—and many writers—never consciously perceive. Like Leonardo and Michelangelo, we will peel back the surface and learn what lies beneath. . . .

CHAPTER 17
DISTILLING YOUR STORY'S CONCEPT

WHAT'S YOUR STORY ABOUT?

Forget the bells and whistles, clever plot turns, cute turns of phrase, fascinating subplots, secondary characters and stunning prose. Because when it comes to concept, none of this matters. What does matter is the answer to this question: "What's your story about?" Most authors, when faced with this question, begin rambling: "Well, it's about this guy, and he . . ." And already the tale sounds generic. (For a study in how *not* to answer this question, watch Miles telling Maya about his book in *Sideways* (NOV), or Eddie explaining his novel in *Limitless* (NOV).)

What we're interested in here is the very heart of your story, which can be broken down into three distinct elements: the Who, the Goal, and the Obstacle. Who your story is about, what their Goal is, and the nature of the Obstacle that must be overcome if the Goal is to be reached. Nothing more. Later (in Chapter 25), you'll learn how to get this down to a ten-second logline. For now, we just need something you can work with.

THE WHO

Let's start with the Who. This is your main character, protagonist, or hero—and it's not always who you think it is. In nearly all cases, you can identify the hero by answering the following two questions:

- Which character undergoes the greatest change during the course of the story?
- If this story were told in the first person, who would be telling it?—through whose eyes would we see the story?

The vast majority of stories have only one protagonist. *Harry Potter* (NOV) is a sole protagonist. The same goes for *Alice in Wonderland* (NOVs), *Spider-Man* (COM), *The Da Vinci Code* (NOV), *Titanic* (HIS) and most other adaptations.

Even films which seem to have multiple protagonists often turn out to have only one. The hero of the buddy film *Men in Black* (COM), for instance, is Agent J (played by Will Smith); Agent K (Tommy Lee Jones) is a mentor. The main character in *Sideways* (NOV) is Miles (Paul Giamatti); Jack is a friend who remains unchanged throughout. The hero of *Twilight* (NOV) is Bella Swan (Kristen Stewart); Edward is a love interest. In *Pirates of the Caribbean: The Curse of the Black Pearl* (THM), the protagonist is Elizabeth Swann (Keira Knightley) and not, as many have come to believe, Captain Jack Sparrow. (If you don't believe this last example, check out the special edition DVD, where the screenwriters themselves confirm it. Johnny Depp may be a scene stealer, but his character—in this movie—is not the protagonist.)

Luke Skywalker—despite the strong presence of Obi-Wan (another mentor), Princess Leia, and Han Solo—is the hero of *Star Wars,* as evidenced by the story's original title: *Adventures of Luke Starkiller, as taken from the Journal of the Whills, Saga I: The Star Wars.*

Very occasionally—and in the realm of blockbuster films, almost never—there will be true multiple protagonists, sometimes referred to as a dual or (if more than two) ensemble protagonist. *Jurassic Park* (NOV) is the classic example, with main characters Alan, Ellie, Tim and Lex. *The Lord of the Rings* series (NOV) is a bit of an exception to everything, as author J. R. R. Tolkien had a habit of switching protagonists midstream—and pulling it off. Had the *LOTR* films not been based on huge bestsellers, Hollywood would doubtless have made Frodo the lone protagonist, because he is the ring-bearer whose actions alter the fate of the world.

So—figure out who your protagonist is and make sure he/she is relatable or, at the very least, compelling. (If Dexter the serial killer can be made relatable, chances are your character can, too.) If you appear to have more than one protagonist, examine the story more closely to be certain. If you do indeed have multiple protagonists, start thinking about ways in which the story might be altered to change this. Because absent bestseller status or something like it, this is very likely to place your adaptation project squarely in the "independent film" category.

If that's where you want or need to be—you're aiming for a smaller film with, perhaps, a smaller audience—that's one thing (in which case, be sure to read the Bonus Chapter, Going Rogue: Make Your Own Damned Movie). But if you dream of joining the top ten (or top 500) box office hits, this approach puts you behind the eight ball from the start. Multiple protagonists generally make for complicated and nonclassical plotlines, which make for clunky loglines—which means most industry people won't get past your ten-second pitch. Again, don't try to be the exception your first time out.

Remember: if the studio can't pitch your movie to the public in a 30- or 60-second trailer, they have zero interest in buying your project, because it's too hard to sell. Yes, *Jurassic Park* has multiple protagonists—but it also has dinosaurs. And bestseller status. And a single goal for all protagonists (which keeps the plotline simple).

Make no mistake: even if you're looking to sell to an independent production company and not a studio, the companies that distribute films here (which, in fact, usually are studios) and overseas operate using the same criteria. So—outside of very low-budget films—there's really no escaping this pitchability requirement. And even there, it helps.

Now, write a very brief description of your protagonist. If you have more than one, try to come up with a single description that covers all of them. (*Jurassic Park* example: "a family." While not technically accurate, it gets the job done.) Either way, your description should be no more than a sentence. Keep this handy.

Next up . . .

THE GOAL

In the context of this story only—what does your main character want? What is it that drives him or her (or them) forward, propelling the story? At the most basic level, you have a character who's *here* (wherever here is)—and wants to be *there*. He desires something—an object, situation, event or relationship—that does not exist in the world he knows. The hero's efforts to attain this *something*—to move from here to there—comprise the main thrust of your story.

This goal should come immediately to mind, and is (hopefully) external. It's fine to have both an internal and an external goal, but most of what winds up on-screen is necessarily external. Your story may seem to have several external goals but, as with protagonists, this seldom turns out to be the case.

Goals vary wildly. They can be small and personal, like the mouse *Stuart Little* (NOV) longing to be part of a family. Or personal and romantic: finding Mr. Right (*Bridget Jones's Diary*, NOV). Or climbing the corporate ladder: *The Firm* (NOV).

Some goals are (or seem) internal, but also bring the hero into conflict with external forces: *Memento,* the *Bourne* films, and *The Long Kiss Goodnight* (STO, NOV, and original screenplay, respectively) all deal with protagonists trying—literally—to remember who they are and what happened to them, and yet external conflicts abound.

The goal can be a quest for vengeance (*The Crow,* COM); to save a city (*Batman Begins, The Dark Knight, The Dark Knight Rises,* all COM), a world (*Men in Black,* COM), *The Lord of the Rings* trilogy, NOV), or a galaxy (the original *Star Wars* trilogy, which many believe to be a loose adaptation of Akira Kurosawa's 1958 film *The Hidden Fortress*).

Ideally, your main character's goal is—like the protagonist himself—something that readers and audiences can relate to and get behind; something they *want* to see happen. Without this, you wind up in a situation where your hero succeeds and the reader/ audience reaction is "So what?" Or, worse—they'd be happier if he failed.

An arguably worse situation arises when your hero has no goal at all. Tales without clearly defined goals tend to ramble, almost always lack a strong sense of forward motion (because there's nothing in particular the main character is striving to accomplish or move toward), and are of little if any interest to Hollywood—or, for that matter, New York publishers.

One of the most powerful things you can do is pair an internal goal with an external goal—and place them in conflict. This is not easy, but can be done: witness *Minority Report* (STO). Protagonist John Anderton has built his whole life and identity around the infallibility of the Precrime system, which predicts and prevents crimes before they happen. He may soon head the agency as it goes national, achieving his internal goal of protecting others in a way he could not protect his own son.

When the Precrime system accuses him of a future murder, he becomes a fugitive and sets out to prove his innocence by preventing the predicted crime. That's his external goal. If he commits the murder, his external goal cannot be achieved. If he prevents the murder, his internal goal becomes impossible, and Precrime collapses. There's conflict at every turn: external (the Precrime system and the police who are hunting him) and internal (seeking to prove the fallibility of a system he must believe infallible for his life to have meaning).

Keep in mind that Anderton's primary goal is to prove his innocence; this is an action film, and that's the obvious and (importantly) external goal that drives the action. His internal goal—as well as the fact that it conflicts with his external goal—is icing on the cake.

So settle on your main character's *primary* goal, and write it down. If he doesn't have one, think up a goal you can live with and write a sentence about it. If, on the other hand, your main character appears to have several goals, pick the most important one and write that down in one sentence.

We now have the Who and the Goal; all that's left is . . .

THE OBSTACLE

Who (or what) stands in your hero's way, keeping him (or her) from the Goal? There must be an Obstacle, because things are too easy without it. Consider: Bob wants to marry Sarah; he asks her out; they hit it off and get married and live happily ever after. That may be a story, but it's not interesting to anyone except Bob and Sarah. There's no conflict or suspense there, and so nothing to keep an audience on the edge of its seat, wondering if these two will get together in the end. The same goes for an action hero out to save the world: if nothing stands in his way, it's a walk in the park—and that's not heroic.

There must be a struggle that brings out the best, or worst—or both—in your characters. You must have characters pitted against people, or situations, or odds to be overcome. Your protagonist should be an irresistible force meeting an immovable object—or vice versa. It is from this conflict—two opposed characters with irreconcilable goals, or one character facing incredible odds or resistance—that your plot develops.

Your obstacle can be anything from an alien cockroach (*Men in Black,* COM) to a tyrannosaur or, more properly, dinosaurs (*Jurassic Park,* NOV); from the wrong romantic entanglement (Daniel Cleaver in *Bridget Jones's Diary,* NOV) to a talk-show host (*Slumdog Millionaire,* NOV), a prison warden (*The Shawshank Redemption,* STO), or a cursed pirate captain and his crew (the *Pirates of the Caribbean* films, THM).

Perhaps your obstacle is an archetype. There's an evil wizard in *Harry Potter* (NOV), an evil Jedi Knight in *Star Wars*, and a power-mad warrior with dark abilities in *The Lord of the Rings* trilogy (NOV). But when you come right down to it, Voldemort, Vader, and Sauron are all, essentially, evil wizards. The same is true of the evil or mad scientists in *Iron Man* and *Iron Man 2*, and *Spider-Man* and *Spider-Man 2* (all COM). All derive from a single archetype, which has been cleverly modified to suit particular genres and worldviews.

Your obstacle doesn't have to be a character or creature: it might be a force of nature (*The Perfect Storm*, NFB; *The Call of the Wild*, NFB; *The Old Man and the Sea*, NOV; or time itself, *The Curious Case of Benjamin Button*, NOV). And though most movie obstacles are external (better visual potential), it is possible to craft films with internal obstacles: a disease (*Lorenzo's Oil*, TRU), for example, or the protagonist's own mind (*A Beautiful Mind*, NFB/TRU).

Even so, remember that movies are primarily visual. Internal obstacles are often difficult, and sometimes impossible to portray effectively on film. An internal obstacle paired with an internal goal is a recipe for disaster, because there's nothing to point a camera at.

This doesn't mean that you have to change the story you have now, in whatever medium it currently exists; if you've got a book with an internal obstacle *and* an internal goal, that may be fine—for the book. But if you want it to be a movie, start thinking about ways to visualize, personify, or externalize the current obstacle, or to replace it with one that is external.

Inception and the *Matrix* trilogy present stories that take place almost entirely within the characters' minds—and yet both have external goals (return home/free Mankind from the Machines), and obstacles which are (or appear to be) external as well.

It's important that the nature of the obstacle match the nature of the goal; if the hero's primary goal is external, the obstacle we're looking for must also be external.

So, whatever your hero's *primary* obstacle is—right now, in the version of the story you already have—write it down. Again, in one sentence.

PUTTING IT TOGETHER

String your Who, Goal, and Obstacle sentences together. They needn't read smoothly or "flow" at this point; that will come later. What we want now is a brief summary of your story's most basic, most crucial elements: This is my hero; this is what he wants; this is what he must overcome to get it. We'll call this document your concept sheet.

From here, we'll move on to story structure.

CHAPTER 18
FINDING YOUR STORY'S STRUCTURE

The vast majority of commercially successful films—likely more than 90 percent—are classically structured. (For more on this, see Chapter 10.) And in almost all cases, this is what Hollywood wants and expects to see. Your source material may or may not be classically structured—but if you want to see it produced, the adaptation most likely will be.

CLASSICAL STRUCTURE IN A NUTSHELL

Classically structured stories are told in three major acts, with seven primary plot points: inciting incident, first act turn, midpoint, low point, second act turn, climax, and denouement or wrap-up. Write those down on your screen or a piece of paper, leaving several blank lines below each heading.

As you read through the definitions and examples below, try to pick out the corresponding plot points in your current story. At this stage, some may be unclear, out of order, or missing, but we'll fix that later. For now, just write down the ones that are there, along with the page number on which each begins. For those that aren't there, start thinking about ways to add them. If the story only exists in your head at this point, then write the seven elements on a piece of paper, leaving several blank lines between them—and jot down those parts of the story that seem to fit the criteria detailed below.

The seven elements of classical story structure are, in proper story order:

INCITING INCIDENT

This is the proverbial wrench thrown into your character's life—the event that kicks off the story, after which your hero's life will never be the same. For the adaptation itself, the inciting incident will come roughly 10 percent of the way into the story.

Most often, the inciting incident will be obvious (or at least important) to both character and audience; very occasionally, the event's true significance is not immediately apparent. The incident itself can be subtle, drastic—or anything in-between.

Examples include Harry being told he's a wizard and reading the Hogwarts' letter of acceptance in *Harry Potter and the Sorcerer's Stone* (NOV); Rose's suicide attempt being thwarted by Jack in *Titanic* (HIS); Richard Kimble being sentenced to death for the murder of his wife in *The Fugitive* (TVS); Jason discovering a dozen passports, a pile of money, and a gun in his safe deposit box—with no idea how they got there in *The Bourne Identity* (NOV); Tom Stall's diner being hit in *A History of Violence* (COM); Spartan King Leonidas receiving the Persian emmisary's ultimatum in *300* (COM/HIS); Commodore Norrington's proposal, Elizabeth Swann falling into the sea (where the medallion sends out a shockwave), and being rescued—and then taken hostage—by Captain Jack Sparrow in *Pirates of the Caribbean: The Curse of the Black Pearl* (THM); Frankie's best fighter, Willie, leaving him in *Million Dollar Baby* (STO).

Occasionally, a story will have two inciting incidents. *Up in the Air* (NOV), for example, pursues dual storylines with the same protagonist. The inciting incident in Ryan's personal life is meeting and sleeping with Alex; the inciting incident in his business life is

Natalie's presentation, which threatens Ryan's job and lifestyle. In such cases (which are rare), the first inciting incident takes place exactly where it would if there were no second inciting incident—thus preserving the classical structure. Often, the two take place almost simultaneously, again in line with classical structure.

As a side note, when there are dual storylines with the same protagonist, they may end very differently—as they do in *Up in the Air*.

FIRST ACT TURN

This point marks the end of the first act, and the beginning of the second. Here, your hero knows what he must do (the goal), *and* sets out to do it. For the adaptation, this will happen about 25 percent of the way into the story. Note that a mere decision by the protagonist does not make an act turn, because decisions are both passive and internal; rather, it is the hero's decision *coupled with action* (which is both external and visual) that drives the story forward into the second act.

This is the beginning of the hero's journey. The "journey" itself refers to the new path embarked upon by your main character. This is always emotional, and includes physical (and sometimes spiritual) components as well. Very often, the first act turn involves the start of a physical journey.

Examples of first act turns include Harry Potter boarding the train for Hogwarts in *Harry Potter and the Sorcerer's Stone* (NOV); Rose changing her mind and coming back to Jack in *Titanic* (HIS); Richard Kimble jumping off the spillway to avoid capture and continue his search for the one-armed man in *The Fugitive* (TVS); Jason heading for Paris to find out who he is in *The Bourne Identity* (NOV); Tom Stall protecting his family by insisting he's not the "Joey Cusack" Carl Fogarty thinks he is in *A History of Violence* (COM)—a very unusual act turn because the audience (not knowing that Tom really is Joey) has no awareness of this deliberate action or the decision behind it; Leonidas and his 300 Spartans setting out to intercept the Persian army at the Hot Gates, and so save Sparta in *300* (COM/HIS); Elizabeth saving the town by parlaying with Barbossa and trading him the medallion in *Pirates of the Caribbean: The Curse of the Black Pearl* (THM); Frankie changing his mind and training Maggie in *Million Dollar Baby* (STO)—though one could argue he's not fully committed until the ringside moment when he says, "This is my fighter."

The first act turn needn't be a single event; multiple, very closely spaced events sometimes combine to create the act turn, as in *Rocky*—where he accepts Apollo Creed's offer (which, possibly uniquely, happens offscreen), takes Mick as his coach, and begins training for the fight. To the casual observer, the act turn would seem to come when training begins—but it's actually a series of actions that culminate in the most obvious. In such cases, the act turn takes place over a very short span of pages. And the initial actions set up the last, which is also the largest.

MIDPOINT

The midpoint can be one of two things or, occasionally, both: a point of no return, beyond which your hero cannot turn back or cannot undo his actions—or the point at which some as-yet-unsuspected element is revealed to be at work within the story. This happens at or near the halfway mark, about 50 percent of the way through the tale. In those cases where there are two midpoints—a no-turning-back point *and* an unsuspected element revealed—they occur very close together, often just one sequence apart.

Midpoint examples include the discovery of the three-headed dog Fluffy—and the trapdoor it's guarding—in *Harry Potter and the Sorcerer's Stone* (NOV); Rose sleeping with Jack and telling him they'll leave the ship together in *Titanic* (HIS); the revelation (via flashback/dream) that Richard Kimble is innocent in *The Fugitive* (TVS); Jason sleeping with Marie in *The Bourne Identity* (NOV); Tom Stall attacking Fogarty and his men, instantly followed by the revelation that he is in fact Joey Cusack in *A History of Violence* (COM); Leonidas' insulting refusal of Xerxes's offer to make him warlord of Greece in return for Sparta's submission in *300* (COM/HIS); Elizabeth learning of the terrible curse on the Black Pearl's undead crew in *Pirates of the Caribbean: The Curse of the Black Pearl* (THM); Scrap explaining to Maggie that Frankie might not be the one to take her all the way—and why (thus revealing Frankie's hitherto unsuspected backstory) in *Million Dollar Baby* (STO).

LOW POINT

This is where the main character is as far as it seems possible to get from achieving his goal, and all hope seems lost. Put another way: if your main character were going to commit suicide, this would usually be the place. The low point almost invariably occurs in the second half of the second act, between 50 percent and 75 percent of the way in, and is usually placed very close to the second act turn.

Examples include the deduction that Snape means to get past Fluffy and steal the stone for Voldemort, along with the discovery that Dumbledore is not there to stop him (and no one else can see the threat) in *Harry Potter and the Sorcerer's Stone* (NOV); Rose being placed in the lifeboat while Jack stays behind in *Titanic* (HIS); Richard Kimble learning the man he thought responsible for his wife's death is now dead in *The Fugitive* (TVS); Jason learning that he's an assassin, finding the police flyer with their photos, and Marie trying to leave him (a triple low point in the span of three minutes) in *The Bourne Identity* (NOV); Tom in the hospital, admitting his true identity to his wife in *A History of Violence* (COM); the hunchback Ephialtes betraying the Spartans to Xerxes, Theron all but raping Queen Gorgo, and Leonidas learning the Persians have discovered the hidden goat path (another triple low point) in *300* (COM/HIS); the *Intrepid* being blown to pieces with Elizabeth's love Will Turner apparently still on board, after which the pirates attack her and Will arrives to save her—but only by offering to trade his own life for hers, after which she's forced to walk the plank and marooned on a desert island with Jack (a quintuple low point in just a few minutes) in *Pirates of the Caribbean: The Curse of the Black Pearl* (THM); Frankie failing to get the stool out of the way, watching Maggie go down, and seeing her wake up in the hospital in *Million Dollar Baby* (STO).

SECOND ACT TURN

The second act turn is where the protagonist rebounds from the apparent defeat of the low point by coming up with a new plan and putting it into action—again in pursuit of that all-important goal. Very often, it's an attempt by the hero to turn the tables on the primary antagonist or villain. This typically occurs about 75 percent of the way into the story, and propels the plot into the third and final act.

Examples include Harry, Ron, and Hermione setting off to go through the guarded trapdoor themselves in order to thwart Voldemort in *Harry Potter and the Sorcerer's Stone* (NOV); Rose jumping off the lifeboat and back onto the sinking ship to be with Jack in *Titanic* (HIS); Richard Kimble researching the Provasic drug trials to find the man behind his wife's murder in *The Fugitive* (TVS); Jason using his would-be killer's phone to call Conklin and arrange a meeting in *The Bourne Identity* (NOV); Tom/Joey journeying to Philadelphia to make peace with his brother Richie in *A History of Violence* (COM); Leonidas deciding to stand and fight to the death—"Prepare for glory!"—giving his pep talk and sending Dilios and the others away in preparation for the final, suicidal battle in *300* (COM/HIS); Elizabeth burning the island's supplies to signal the British navy, and then offering to marry Commodore Norrington if he'll save Will in *Pirates of the Caribbean: The Curse of the Black Pearl* (THM); Frankie moving Maggie to a new facility so he can help look after her in *Million Dollar Baby* (STO).

The second act turn, like the first, needn't be a single discrete event—but if it's not, the events comprising it will be very closely spaced.

CLIMAX

This is what NASA would call Max-Q; the point of maximum stress. Translated into story terms, it's the point of maximum conflict between hero and obstacle—the make-or-break effort or confrontation that will determine whether the hero succeeds or fails in his quest to achieve his goal. The climax falls in the last 25 percent of the story, and often in the last 10 percent. Exceptionally long films sometimes have exceptionally long climaxes.

Climax examples include Harry going on alone from the chess game and doing battle with Quirrell and Voldemort in *Harry Potter and the Sorcerer's Stone* (NOV); Rose and Jack fleeing her armed fiancé Cal and then struggling to survive the sinking of the *Titanic* (HIS); Richard Kimble facing off against the one-armed man and his former friend Charles Nichols (and saving Gerard's life) in *The Fugitive* (TVS); Jason breaking into the safe house and confronting Conklin in *The Bourne Identity* (NOV); Tom/Joey confronting his past in the form of Richie and fighting for his life when attacked in *A History of Violence* (COM); Xerxes' men closing in on the Spartans, Leonidas' apparent surrender and final attack in *300* (COM/HIS); the final pirate attack (beginning with the underwater march and Elizabeth's escape from *Intrepid,* and ending when the curse is lifted) in *Pirates of the Caribbean: The Curse of the Black Pearl* (THM); Frankie's final visit with Maggie, where he tells her the meaning *of* "Mo chuisle"—and then kills her, in *Million Dollar Baby* (STO).

It's possible (though rare) to have dual climaxes, if you also have dual storylines. Again, *Up in the Air* serves as an example: the first (personal) climax is when Ryan abandons the podium to find Alex, only to learn she's married with children; the second (business) climax takes place when he hits his ten-million-mile goal, Natalie's virtual system is scrapped, and Ryan regains the job and lifestyle he's been struggling to preserve.

Even here, though, note that the twin climaxes are both back-to-back and short, occupying the same position a single climax would otherwise take—yet again preserving the classical three-act structure.

Dual climaxes allow the writer to end the story on both an up and a down note, as the hero can fail at one goal while achieving the other. When you do see this, it tends to be in smaller, character-driven stories with independent sensibilities.

Having said that, though, it can also be pulled off in tentpole movies: witness *Pirates of the Caribbean: The Curse of the Black Pearl* (THM). Here, the lifting of the curse, Barbossa's death and the pirate defeat conclude the climax of the action storyline—but leave the heroine's romantic storyline (and Captain Jack Sparrow's storyline) unresolved. Thus, we find another climax within the wrap-up itself, in which Jack escapes the hangman, Will professes his love for Elizabeth, and she is released from her engagement by an unexpectedly noble Commodore Norrington—leaving her free to marry Will.

WRAP-UP

Also called the denouement, this is where the main character's future path is indicated or suggested; it answers (or suggests the answer to) the question: What lies ahead for this character? There's enough detail to leave the audience feeling satisfied, but not so much that it detracts from the climax-induced high (or low, if the ending is a downer) they should be feeling. It's also the place to tie up any remaining loose ends. In faery tales and comedies, the denouement sometimes comes down to a single line: *And they lived happily ever after.* Some movies come close: the climax of *Rocky* is the fight with Apollo; the wrap-up is Rocky yelling for Adrian and the two of them embracing. That's it: fade out, cue music.

In *Harry Potter and the Sorcerer's Stone* (NOV); the denouement begins with Harry waking up in the infirmary; in *Titanic* (HIS), it starts with older Rose recounting the number of people who went into the water, and the pitifully small number who were saved; in *The Fugitive* (TVS), it begins when Richard Kimble tells Gerard he didn't kill his wife—and Gerard (this time) cares; in *The Bourne Identity* (NOV), the wrap-up starts when we realize it's Conklin who's being hit on Ward's orders—and that Jason escaped; in *A History of Violence* (COM), the denouement begins right after Richie's death, when Tom/Joey goes to the pond to wash off the blood; in *300* (COM/HIS), it begins with Dilios' return to Sparta following Leonidas' death; in *Pirates of the Caribbean: The Curse of the Black Pearl* (THM), the wrap-up begins with Will missing "the opportune moment" just after the battle; in *Million Dollar Baby* (STO), it starts after Frankie walks off into the darkness.

In all cases, the wrap-up is short, and usually takes place in the final 1 percent to 3 percent of the story. When the wrap-up is over, so is the tale. After that comes the "crawl," or end credits.

FINER POINTS

Classically structured films and the screenplays on which they're based do not have exceptions; all of these elements will be present. Acts do not always turn on a dime, and some stories have act turns that take place over a span of several (but never many) pages. As with inciting incidents and act turns, there are occasional double midpoints and low points; when these are present, they typically relate to different aspects of the hero's journey (internal/external, emotional/physical) or to different main characters, and so avoid repetition. They also come very close together, often in consecutive scenes or sequences—and in the same place a single mid- or low point would otherwise be.

It is possible—though seldom advisable—to shift the placement of individual plot points within the story (so long as their order remains the same). This practice often raises red flags in Hollywood, however—the most common (and immediate) perception being that the writer is clueless about structure. (A late first act turn, for example, is a classic tip-off to a structurally unsound script and a beginning writer.)

Industry pros are given some leeway here, but even they tread cautiously. In *Iron Man* (COM), for example, the inciting incident comes in the film's opening sequence. We then jump back in time, entering Tony Stark's life thirty-six hours earlier. Still, as we follow Tony's story forward, the inciting incident reappears right where it should be—about 10 percent of the way in. Hence, it's not really breaking the rule. Significantly, protagonist Tony Stark is incredibly well set-up in the first two minutes—ensuring we get to know and like him before the excrement hits the rotary oscillator.

Note that even those whose projects are acknowledged rule-breakers in other respects—Oscar-winning writer/director/producer Paul Haggis, for example—still tend to tell classically structured stories (see *Million Dollar Baby* examples, above).

CONCLUSION

Again, look for these points in your existing story. Write down the starting page numbers and a brief description of what happens. If specific elements seem absent or misplaced, start thinking about how they might be added or moved. Jot down your ideas—but don't start shuffling scenes around just yet.

We'll call this your structure sheet. Keep it handy; you'll need it as we map your story in the next step. To see an example of how the structural points above were chosen for *Harry Potter and the Sorcerer's Stone,* see the Bonus Chapter, Structure Workshop: *Harry Potter* (Book and Film) and Structure Workshop: *Jurassic Park* (Book and Film). For additional film structure examples, visit http://makeyour storyamovie.com/bookbonus.html.

CHAPTER 19
MAPPING YOUR CURRENT STORY

Creating a Digital Outline of Your Source Material

At this point, you should have your concept fairly well summarized, with at least a partial structure in place. But if your concept seems wobbly, or your story doesn't quite fit the structure detailed in Chapter 10, that's okay—for the moment. You know the basics, and we'll come back to structure and concept later.

What we need to do right now is get the current story down in a way that is both comprehensive and brief, so we (and possibly others) can get a sort of bird's-eye view of the terrain, with the ability to zoom in or out at will. We'll do this by creating a story map, which will then serve as the jumping-off point for the adaptation process.

THE STORY MAP

The story map is a tool that allows you to make your story digital, so that any element can be added, changed, or deleted in seconds. It also allows you to see how proposed changes will affect other parts of the story, without having to search through hundreds of pages or bookmarks for individual scenes. The story map is superior to a formal outline because it's quicker to alter, and doesn't eat up space with multiple indents.

The story map is a bullet-point version of your story, detailing (in proper story order) every significant physical and emotional (and, where relevant, spiritual) event that takes place during the course of your tale. It's meant to be simple, and it is. Each bullet-point should be from one to just a few lines long, and contain only the most essential and closely related events.

What the story map is not, is a collection of atmospheric details, which will quickly bloat the map to unmanageable proportions. We do not, for example, need to know that what the lighting and temperature are like, or what the characters are wearing, unless this information is somehow important to the story. (As when, say, too much sunlight causes main character Bob to sneeze at *Sanfermines* in Spain, attracting the attention of a nearby bull who aims for Bob's bright red shirt, but slips on ice in unseasonably cold weather and slides into Bob's friend Emmet instead, thus altering the course of human history because Emmet was just about to invent the flux capacitor, which would have made time travel a reality.)

When done well, a complete stranger should able to pick up the story map and follow your tale from beginning to end, without actually reading the story. This is particularly important if you anticipate working with someone else at some point; you don't want to make the map unreadable by bulleting little memory-joggers that mean something to you—and nothing to everyone else. The story map's usefulness is not limited to adaptations; I use it when helping clients with concept and story development, heavy revisions—and of course adaptations. The process is equally applicable to books, screenplays, comics, plays, short stories—virtually any medium in which a story can be told.

CREATING THE STORY MAP

I don't know the story you want to tell, so as an example, I'll use a tale that nearly everyone is familiar with: *Harry Potter and the Sorcerer's Stone*. What follows is a story map of the book's first chapter.

- MR., MRS., and baby DUDLEY DURSLEY in kitchen: Mrs. Dursley gossips, Dudley throws tantrum; owl flies past window, no one sees it.
- Mr. Dursley leaves for work, sees cat reading map; looks again, just sees cat, which seems to be reading street sign; Dursley nearing town, stuck in traffic, spots oddly dressed people, some wearing cloaks.
- Dursley at work, doesn't see owls flying past outside.
- Dursley goes out for a doughnut, overhears people whispering about Harry Potter.
- Back at work, he starts to call home, hangs up, thinking bit of conversation he heard about "Harry Potter" must be about some other Potter and not his nephew (he's never seen nephew, isn't sure of first name).
- Dursley leaves work, bumps into man in cloak, who hugs him saying "You-Know-Who has gone at last" and calls him a Muggle.
- Dursley goes home, spots same cat by his house, tries to shoo it then goes inside, watches news report on unusual daylight owl activity and shooting stars falling instead of rain; asks wife if she's heard from her sister lately; she gets upset and says no, why?; he says odd things are happening, thought it might have something to do with her sister's crowd; Dursley inquires about nephew's age (about same as Dudley's) and first name (Harry).
- Just before bed, Dursley looks out window, sees cat staring down street, expectant; wonders if it has anything do to with the Potters he and his wife are related to and avoid, tells himself nothing the Potters did could possibly affect his own family.
- Cat sits outside as owls fly over, watches as DUMBLEDORE appears on corner in long robe and purple cloak; he eyes the cat with amusement, pulls

device from his cloak, clicks it to kill streetlamps; he sits
beside cat, starts conversation.

- Cat turns into PROFESSOR McGONAGALL; they
  speak of celebration (owls and shooting stars a part of
  this) eleven years in the making, Muggles noticing
  odd things, and You-Know-Who's disappearance;
  Dumbledore refers to Y-K-W by name others fear to say:
  VOLDEMORT.
- McGonagall says Dumbledore the only one Voldemort
  was afraid of, Dumbledore calls this flattery: V had
  powers he never did; PMG says that's only because DD
  chose not to use dark powers, and says rumor is V went
  after the Potters last night, killed Lily and James, but
  when he tried to kill their son Harry, V's power
  somehow broke.
- DD says they may never know what happened or why V
  couldn't kill the boy, says Hagrid (who tipped PMG off to
  DD's pending arrival) is late; DD has come to bring
  Harry Potter to his aunt and uncle, along with a letter to
  help them explain things to Harry when he's older; PMG
  argues against leaving him with the Dursleys, says Harry
  will be world-famous among their own people; DD
  explains that's why he must be with the Dursleys—they
  know nothing of this, and Harry can grow up in peace
  until he's old enough to handle the truth.
- When DD says Hagrid's bringing Harry, PMG calls
  Hagrid careless, but DD would trust him with his life;
  the giant HAGRID arrives on huge motorcycle that falls
  from sky, a bundle of blankets in his arms, says he got
  Harry out of house ahead of swarming Muggles.
- DD takes HARRY POTTER—a baby with a lightning
  bolt-shaped scar on his forehead; HAG kisses Harry's
  forehead goodbye, starts bawling about Harry being left

with Muggles; DD quiets him and leaves Harry in
blankets on Dursley doorstep, with letter.

- DD, PMG and HAG say their goodbyes; Hagrid leaves on
the flying bike; PMG leaves as cat; DD turns streetlamps
back on as he leaves, wishing Harry good luck; Harry
sleeps on doorstep, unaware of fame or future.

That's the first seventeen pages of Harry Potter—all of chapter one—in 46 lines, or one single-spaced page. At this rate—compressing seventeen story pages into one bullet-point page—the entire story map for this 309-page novel will be a mere nineteen pages long. Nothing of real story significance has been left out, and anyone can follow the tale without having read the book.

Character names are capitalized the first time the character appears, which acts as a quick reference when you're wondering who's been introduced at any given point, and who has not. Abbreviations are used to shorten names and save space; Dumbledore's clothes are mentioned only to show his kinship with the oddly dressed folk Mr. Dursley noticed earlier. (To see a complete story map of the first Harry Potter novel *and* the first film, check out the Bonus Chapter, Story Map Workshop: *Harry Potter* (Book and Film).)

As you go through your story and (starting on a fresh page) create your map, keep the seven structural pillars (or plot points) from Chapter 18 in mind: inciting incident, first act turn, midpoint, low point, second act turn, climax and wrap-up. When you spot one of these (or spot a likely candidate for one), break the bullets and plug its name (and page number) into your story map, just before the bullet where the plot point begins—like this:

- Harry asks the plump woman how to find platform 9¾;
she tells him to wheel his luggage cart straight at the
barrier between platforms 9 and 10, and not to stop.

FIRST ACT TURN (p93)

- Harry pushes his luggage cart toward the barrier, first walking, then running; he closes his eyes, expecting to crash into it—but the crash never comes.
- Harry opens his eyes, finds himself at platform 9¾ of a different train station; a Hogwarts Express steam engine waits nearby, students lining up to board.

This acts as a quick visual reference to where you are in the story, and makes the map appear less dense. If you're not sure about a plot point, put a question mark in brackets after its name: "FIRST ACT TURN [?]." If you wrote the story without structure in mind, you may have more than one candidate—or none—for any given plot point. We'll come back and finalize structure later. For now, it's best to insert these points when you spot them. You might want to bold these as well, or set them off from the main text by giving them a different color than the bullet-points.

Go through the whole story this way, from first scene to last, bulleting important events (emotional as well as physical—and even spiritual, if that's relevant to your story) and ignoring everything else (the water in the bottom of the rowboat taken by Harry and Hagrid in the last beat above, for instance). When the plot point is not sharply defined (when an act break takes place over several pages, for example), insert the structure heading (Inciting Incident, First Act Turn, etc.) just before the first bullet in the sequence.

When you reach the story's end, take a break. Then go over the map alone, rooting out typos and clarifying anything that might be unclear or confusing to someone else. This time, refer to your structure sheet, and be on the lookout for (or double-check) those plot points: Are they all there? Are they in the right order, and in approximately the right places? Are there multiple candidates for single plot points? Refer to the previous chapter and try to clean things up.

If you still come up with missing plot points, plug in placeholders where they should be. Inciting incident and first act turn, for example, typically appear 10 percent and 25 percent of the way into the story—so place those headings (all caps, bolded or different color) 10 percent and 25 percent of the way into your story map, followed by the word "[NEEDED]" in brackets. (Using brackets allows you to quickly locate missing structure points with the search function.)

This placement is approximate, as it may turn out that the 10 percent mark in your story map doesn't quite line up with the 10 percent mark in your source material or (later) remapped story or screenplay. It doesn't have to be perfect at this point; we'll make any necessary adjustments and lock the structure in place as we go.

In the next step, we'll remap the story for the screen.

CHAPTER 20
REMAPPING FOR THE SCREEN

The story map we created in the last chapter is a starting point, representing the story as it is now (most likely in some other medium), or as you imagine it might be (if no fixed story currently exists). In this chapter, we'll begin the process of transforming that into an outline that can serve as the basis for a screenplay. (Options for the creation of the screenplay itself are the subject of Part IV (Chapters 22–24).)

This is where it helps to be (or to work with someone who is) intimately familiar not only with story in general, as realized in books, games, oral tradition and other nonfilm media—but also with the demands and expectations of Hollywood. Because I'm not working with you personally (in which case we'd brainstorm things together, and I'd make specific suggestions tailored to the needs of your particular story), I'm going to lay out a number of guidelines that will help you move this outline closer to what it needs to be.

How close you'll get, and how long that will take, depends on factors that—again, not knowing your story—I cannot fully take into account. If your tale is already fairly cinematic, or if you find it easy to slide into the "Hollywood mindset" and view your story with industry eyes, then this chapter may be enough to take you all the way, at least on the big points.

But even if not, it will get you a good deal closer to the finish line, and establish a foundation for similar work on future projects, which should go more smoothly. It also stands a good chance of speeding up the process should you decide to hire outside help down the road (see Chapters 23–24), because you've already done some of the groundwork.

So, grab your concept and structure sheets, along with your story map. Then sit down, strap in, and turn on all you've got. . . .

FIRST PASS

Reread your concept and structure sheets. Now breeze through your story map, paying particular attention to the structure headings. You want to make sure that they're in proper order, and that you have a scene or sequence that fulfills the requirements of each structural pillar. If any structural element is still missing, give some hard thought to what existing story event might fit the bill—or to coming up with new "beats" (events) to plug the gaps. Remember, nothing's set in stone, so your solutions don't have to be perfect. Yet.

There's a good chance that some of your structural beats are going to seem too far off the 10 percent, 25 percent, etc. marks— but don't worry about that either; they may or may not have to be moved. Because much of what currently surrounds them is going to change or disappear during the adaptation, it's too soon to tell.

Do your best to get those seven structural pillars in place, be- cause they're going to be holding up your story. When you're done, take another look at your concept sheet, and ask yourself: Does this concept match the story map I just read? If not, you have one of two problems: the story isn't measuring up to the concept, or the con- cept doesn't match the story you're telling. You can change story, concept, or both—but the two *must* match.

CONCEPT "REVEAL"

Even if concept and story are already in harmony, reevaluate the concept while reviewing the twelve points listed in Chapter 4 (and if you've read Chapter 4, you'll know that there are actually thirteen points): pitchable concept, relatable hero, emotionally compelling story, ticking clock, visual potential, classical structure, actor-friendly lead, average length, reasonable budget, low-fat story, franchise potential, four-quadrant appeal, and merchandising potential. (The last three points are often optional at lower budget levels.)

Is there anything inherent in your concept that conflicts with these points? If not, you're ready to move on. If there is something about the concept that flies in the face of one or more of these elements, "re-vision" the concept until it's movie-friendly—then move on.

And know that it's not at all uncommon to shift, tweak, or change the emphasis of a source material's concept to render the adaptation more cinematic. The important thing is to keep the story's "heart" alive and beating strongly in the new medium. Think of it as changing clothes for different weather, or different social occasions; though you may look different from a distance, it's still you—and your story—underneath.

SECOND PASS

On your second pass through the story map, you're going to do to the map—on a larger scale—what you just did to the concept. Read through the story map, again referring to the checklist in Chapter 4 (and Chapters 5–15 if you need more detail). Adjust the beats (bullet-points) as you go.

Don't rewrite the story itself, just the bullet-points. You can lighten the load of future passes by striking out or coloring text to be deleted, and choosing another color for new or altered text. In some cases, you may want to axe an entire beat and rewrite/revise it just below. The aim here is to create a single document that shows both original and revised beats, while also allowing you to review revised beats only—which will come in handy later. (This might seem like a perfect opportunity to make use of Word's "track changes" feature, but resist the temptation; that way—trust me— lies madness.)

Your basic concept should by now be fairly pitchable in terms of Who-Goal-Obstacle. If any of these points were left unclear, return to them now, because it's going to be hard to continue without having these pretty well solidified. (See Chapter 17 for more on this.)

If your hero is not relatable to a large number of people, make him so by adding relatable attributes, deleting unrelatable attributes, or both. The hero needn't be perfect—shouldn't be, in fact—but relatability is key. (Or at least, as detailed in Chapter 6, sympathy/ empathy or compelling presence. Still, if you're looking for a hit, relatability is the surest path in this regard.)

Make sure the story is in some way emotionally compelling. It's no coincidence that movie reviewers use phrases like "the ride of the summer"; the reading/viewing experience is driven by emotion, and should—like Christopher Lockhart's roller coaster—have its ups and downs. An overabundance of cool technology or clinical description at the expense of character depth is (if left unaddressed) a sure sign of troubles to come.

Look for that ticking clock that adds tension, suspense, urgency. Again, this doesn't mean that the whole story has to take place in a few hours or days. (Though it is worth noting that when Hollywood made a movie out of James Grady's novel *Six Days of the Condor,* it became *Three Days of the Condor.*) But you do need some kind of pressure driving your hero to act now rather than later or "someday." So if the clock's not there, add it. (For more on this, refer to Chapter 8.)

Unlike most other media, movies do not inspire images in people's minds. The movies are the images. Reevaluate your story map for visual potential, things the camera—and the audience—can see.

Keep an eye out for "internal" passages which would be difficult or impossible to show onscreen. These will have to be modified to make them more shootable, or cut entirely. Particularly important events that cannot be filmed might be referred to in dialogue, but care must be taken to avoid a story that's "too talky" or contains obvious exposition. Remember: if the camera can't see it in some way, it shouldn't be there. But also remember that good actors can be extremely effective at conveying (externalizing) emotions both subtle and grand. (For more on visual potential, see Chapter 9.)

Keep structure in mind, double-checking your seven plot points and their positions within the story map. If any are still missing, give some more thought to filling them in. By the time you're done, all seven will be in place. (If you have any doubts, reread Chapter 18.)

Whether your full story is 250 pages or 500, it needs to be shorter. If it's short-form (novella, comic, short story, magazine article, etc.) or nonexistent (real-life experience, board game, toy, theme park ride and so on) to begin with, it needs to be longer. In the end—assuming the beats are tightly written, and after trimming down (or building up) the story and cutting all the old beats—you will in most cases wind up with a story map of 20 to 30 pages or so.

Take off your writer's hat and view your story from an actor's perspective. Is the main role interesting, different, challenging—perhaps even unique? If you hope to see an established star in your movie, you need to know that they're flooded with offers. They're not going to choose yours because it's just another paycheck; they're past that (if they were ever there at all). They want something that lets them show their stuff and turn on all they've got, so to speak—especially when the qualities of the role demand skills most moviegoers and critics don't yet realize they possess. (See Chapter 11 for more on this.)

Remember that time is at a premium, and you have perhaps two hours in which to tell your story. Consider this your own, personal ticking clock. There is no truer incarnation of the adage "time is money" than Hollywood. (For a refresher on why this is so, review Chapter 8.)

If you come across anything that would be stupendously expensive to film, consider cutting it outright. Brainstorm other, less expensive ways to achieve whatever story purpose those costly beats accomplish. Remember that the best films—the best stories, period—are about people. Events large and small are important only because they affect characters we care about.

If your stupendously expensive scene seems crucial to the story (which most, despite their authors' protestations, are not), keep it—for now. And make damned sure you don't have a whole gaggle of them in the same story. If you do choose to keep such a scene, it should probably be in the climax—otherwise you're presented with the dilemma of topping it without equaling or surpassing its expense. The climactic sequence must be the biggest, most intense portion of your story. (See Chapter 13 for more on budgetary matters.)

Always, always look to cut the fat. Recall Vinge's Law from Chapter 14: every scene must accomplish two, and preferably three things: advance plot, reveal character, build backstory. If any scene fails to meet this standard, revise the beats until it does—or cut it.

One of the most common sources of story fat is repetition: do your characters repeat the same actions—visit the same place, go to see the same person, take the same drive—more than once? Look for ways to condense such repeats into fewer scenes. If more than one trip etc. is necessary, make them significantly different in some way. In the first Harry Potter book, Harry leaves with Hagrid, comes back, then leaves for Hogwarts. In the movie, he leaves once. There's a reason for that.

Also look to keep your focus on one or a few main characters, even if this means condensing multiple characters into a few, or one.

Do the same with minor players as well; an overabundance of characters diffuses focus, and often spawns confusion. (Chapter 14 goes into more detail on fat-free filmmaking.)

Are sequels, prequels, or spinoffs a possibility—and if not, could they be? Unless it's going to do your story irreparable harm, consider leaving this door open.

Will your story appeal to everyone—young and old, male and female? If not, that's okay, so long as the budget is reasonable. The higher the budget, the more people you need to pull into theaters for the film to turn a profit. Again, unless it's going to damage your story, consider what you might do to broaden your prospective audience. Male writers, for example, often neglect to create strong female characters; this, in turn, lessens a story's appeal to women.

Keep merchandising in the back of your mind as you read— does your tale lend itself to toys, T-shirts, Happy Meals? If not— could it? Again, this is far from mandatory at low or even mid-range budget levels. But if your story can only be produced as a "tentpole" (big-budget or "event" picture), the studio is going to want as many revenue streams as possible to lessen their risk and maximize their profit. (Chapter 15 covers franchise appeal, four-quadrant and merchandising potential.)

If all of that's too much to keep in mind while navigating your story map for the second time, do multiple passes, keeping just a few points in mind during each. The important thing is to strongly consider each of these points. Because whether you do or you don't— the people who ultimately decide whether to option or buy your project will be looking for precisely these things.

And if they're not there, your prospective buyer is likely to move on to someone else's project.

CONSULT PASS

You may be the best writer in the world, but there's one thing you cannot do—see your work for the first time, or through another's eyes. For that, you need to borrow someone else's eyes (and preferably the rest of them as well). Even those who are, in fact, the best writers in the world routinely have their work privately critiqued by others. When you're not only creating a story, but working out the blueprint for adapting that story into another medium, this becomes doubly important.

Your "consultant" may be a friend or family member, fellow writer, screenwriter or professional adaptation consultant (see Chapters 23–24 for more on finding and working with these). The greater their understanding of story, novels (or whatever it is you're adapting), screenplays and adaptations—and the film industry itself—the better. The more likely they are to soft-peddle or overlook problems for fear of hurting your feelings, the worse.

As mentioned, even the most accomplished writers in the business seek feedback from other professionals. Oscar-winner William Goldman has long been considered one of the best, if not *the* best, screenwriter of all time. He's also a novelist. Among his many credits: *Chaplin* (NFBs/TRU), *Misery* (NOV), *The Princess Bride* (based on his own book, NOV), *The General's Daughter* (NOV), *Absolute Power* (NOV), *The Chamber* (NOV), *Maverick* (TVS), *A Bridge Too Far* (NFB/HIS), *Marathon Man* (based on his own book, NOV), *All the President's Men* (NFB/TRU), *The Great Waldo Pepper, The Stepford Wives* (NOV), *The Hot Rock* (NOV), and *Butch Cassidy and the Sundance Kid.*

Interviewed by Moriarty for Ain't-It-Cool News, he spoke of showing his work to others before going out with it: "Thank God all those respected writers savaged it when they read it. I loved that . . . I'm thrilled because if they'd all said nice things, I'd be dead. The more savage they could be, the better it would be for anyone reading it. Anyone who wants to be a scriptwriter had better learn to have thick skin. You'd better learn it. Kill all your darlings when you write. So many young writers can't do that. They say, 'No, this is my favorite thing, I love this,' but you have to be able to kill anything if it's not working." F. Scott Fitzgerald said much the same thing.

A good consultant will help you figure out what's working,

what's not, and how best to address potential problem areas. Ideally, they can savage the work politely. The consult pass may be your first pass (if you go with a consultant right off the bat) or your twentieth (if you're really obsessive).

At this point—if you were the source material's creator (or rights-holder) and I were the consultant—we'd go through the story map beat by beat, several times. But because I'm writing a book and you're reading it, I'm unfamiliar with the specifics of your particular story. What I can do is summarize what should happen here. (For advice on finding and working with a pro, refer to Chapters 23–24.)

This is where the process becomes dynamic. While it can help considerably to have someone (or several someones) read through your story map and get back to you with notes or comments, the real magic takes place when you and another creative soul go through the whole map bullet by bullet, brainstorming all the way. Each of you will come up with things the other never would have thought of alone—and even when those suggestions don't work or don't seem quite right, they cause the conversation to spin off in still new directions, which often result in workable solutions.

This is story development at its best—alive and cooking, constantly evolving, electric. Written notes represent the thoughts of one mind—but get the right two people in a room or on the phone, and the result is somehow far greater than the combined thoughts of both minds working alone.

Anyone can have a great suggestion. What you're looking for is someone close to, at or (preferably) above your level of story, screenplay and adaptation understanding. This will ensure consistently useful suggestions over the course of your efforts. That's what you want.

Revise the story map after each pass—adding and changing, cleaning up typos and such, and deleting things you're sure you won't be using. *But . . .* be sure to save each version as you go. For example: you brainstorm through a pass with your consultant, making notes along the way (preferably in digital format, rather than writing in the margins of a hardcopy). Save that version—with notes—as (let's say) Your Title story map v02. Now go in, make your changes and do a cleanup. Save it again, this time as Your Title story map v03. And so on.

In this way, you never lose your notes, never lose old beats you might later decide to revive, and always have a recent draft saved if your computer has a meltdown while you're working on the next one. The most recently saved draft will always be the one with the highest number.

REPEAT

When you find the right person, go over the story map with them, start to finish (in several sessions), until your brains start steaming or you both pretty much agree that it's as good as the two of you can make it. Take a break—and then hit it again a few days later to be sure. You should be looking at the map at least twice as often as your consultant, because you'll be revising it (in accordance with the notes you've been taking) between development sessions.

Ideally, you and your consultant go over the whole map several times. This is useful for two reasons. One is that early passes can change the story significantly—meaning that, with subsequent passes, you'll be looking at (and working to improve) a somewhat different story. You can't improve things on the first pass that aren't even there until the second or third pass.

The second reason is that, once the major work of the big changes has been taken care of, you start to see smaller things that escaped your notice before, because your focus was elsewhere (on the big things). It's tough to spot that black widow by your big toe when an elephant is charging. This is where you catch inconsistencies (some caused by previous changes), connect errant dots, smooth out the rough edges and in general come up with some of the finer details that often "make" a story—little touches that add emotion, depth, realism, humor, etc.

Following each revision, you should scan the story map and review changed material only (which will be easy to spot if you've used a different color for altered text). Make sure the changes remain in line with the story you want to tell—for while brainstorming is an incredible story-booster, you may find there are times when you get carried away in the heat of the moment. In such instances, later reflection serves as a check on this, and prevents you from going off the rails by continuing blindly from the previous session.

AIM AND LIMITATIONS

The ultimate aim of all of this is to arrive at a story that has been mapped for the screen—a blueprint for a screenplay. To help ensure that you've achieved this, the next chapter provides several checklists to use during your final passes.

There's really only one limitation here, which is this: before there can be a movie, there must be an actual screenplay—which you may, or may not, be able to write yourself. (For more on this, see Part IV: Creating the Screenplay, Chapters 22–24.) And it's there, in the writing of that screenplay, that some of the things we've been working on here—the precise placement of the seven plot points, for example—will become finalized.

Some things may need to be moved, added, deleted or tweaked at that stage, simply because you can't know the final pace or page count until you actually have the pages to look at. If, for example, the story map has too much happening before the first act turn (which must come about 25 percent of the way into the script), something's going to be shortened, moved, or deleted in order to make that act turn come at precisely the right time. This is common, even with original (nonadapted) screenplays, so don't sweat the small stuff just yet.

And remember: the better the map, the easier the journey. Every hour spent in this process will save you and the screenwriter (if that's not you, too) many hours of frustration, dead ends, and regret—because it's a hell of a lot easier to change things on the story map than it is to write three dozen different versions of the script, hoping to get things right.

Think of it as an investment in your project's future.

CHAPTER 21
LAUNCH-CHECKING YOUR PROJECT

Just prior to every shuttle flight, NASA's Launch Control Center would run through a preflight checklist of 20,000 items. The list presented in this chapter is considerably shorter, but no less important. In a way, this list is more comprehensive because it allows you to identify and eliminate design flaws—structural weaknesses—that can wreck you with major malfunctions down the road.

If you answer no to any of these questions, or are unsure, scrub the launch and refer to the indicated chapters before moving forward with the adaptation. If, after that, you still find yourself at an impasse, refer to Chapters 24–25 (on finding and working with an adaptation specialist).

RIGHTS CHECKLIST
- Do you own or control the rights necessary to sell the project in Hollywood? (Chapters 3 and 31.)

CONCEPT CHECKLIST
Look over your three-sentence concept sheet, and ask yourself the following questions:

- Does your concept have a clear WHO, or protagonist/ hero? (Chapter 17.)
- Does the concept have a clear GOAL that your protagonist/hero must struggle to reach? (Chapter 17.)
- Is there a clearly-defined OBSTACLE which your protagonist/hero must overcome in order to reach the goal? (Chapter 17.)
- Can the basics of your WHO-GOAL-OBSTACLE be boiled down to a ten-second pitch? (Chapters 5, 17, and 25.) If not, you may be in indieland.

STRUCTURE CHECKLIST

Review your updated structure sheet (or refer to the structure headings on your story map), and look for the following:

- Is your story classically structured into three major acts? (Chapter 10.) If not—and you've no intention of structuring it this way—you're most likely in indieland, and much of the following may not apply.
- Do you have an inciting incident roughly 10 percent of the way into your story? This will be page 10–15 of the finished script of 120 pages. (Chapters 10 and 18.)
- Is there a clear first act turn about 25 percent of the way into the story? This should be very close to script page 30, in a 120-page script. (Chapters 10 and 18.)
- Do you have a definite midpoint at or very near the halfway point? This will be around script page 60. (Chapters 10 and 18.)
- Is there a clearly defined low point, somewhere between the midpoint and the second act turn—most likely very close to the latter? (Chapters 10 and 18.)
- Does the story have a clear second act turn, about 75 percent of the way in? This would be page 90 of a 120-page script. (Chapters 10 and 18.)

- Is there an unmistakable climax near the end of the third act? (Chapters 10 and 18.)
- Do you have a denouement or wrap-up just after the climax, to conclude the story and indicate what happens next for your hero/es? (Chapters 10 and 18.)

STORY CHECKLIST

Read through your new, screen-friendly story map, and immediately ask yourself the following questions:

- Is your hero in some way relatable/sympathetic/ empathetic/compelling to millions of people; will they *feel* for him/her/them? (Chapter 6.)
- Is the story emotionally compelling? (Chapter 7.)
- Does the story have a "ticking clock" of some kind? (Chapter 8.)
- Can the story built around your concept be told in a way that is largely visual? (Chapter 9.)
- Does the story have an actor-friendly lead? (Chapter 11.)
- Can this story be told within the confines of 105 to 120 script pages? (Chapter 12.)
- Do you tell this story in a way that is not prohibitively expensive to film? (Chapter 13.)
- Does your telling of this story conform to Vinge's Law? (*Every scene* must accomplish at least two—and preferably all three—of the following objectives: advance plot, reveal character, build backstory. But also note that this can be finalized in the screenplay itself.) (Chapter 14.)
- Does your story have sequel, prequel, or spinoff potential? This is often optional, but a big plus. (Chapter 15.)
- Does the story have "four-quadrant" appeal? Also optional—and the gold standard at higher budget levels. (Chapter 15.)

- Does the tale have merchandising potential? Again optional, but very nice to have—and often essential at higher budget levels. (Chapter 15.)

SUMMING UP

Only when you can answer yes to each of these questions (except perhaps the "optional" ones, listed just above), should you move forward with the adaptation. The only exceptions are these:

- The project is intended to be an independent film—in which case you *might* get away without the ten-second pitch and the structure checklist.
- You're planning to get help from someone else (an adaptation consultant or specialist, for example) to iron out the trouble spots before proceeding. (Chapters 23–24.)
- You're not planning to sell the project at all, but are doing it for personal and noncommercial reasons—that is, you don't expect to make money with it.

PART IV

CREATING THE SCREENPLAY

The next step in the adaptation process is, of course, the screenplay itself—without which there can be no movie. There are three options here: writing it yourself, writing it with professional guidance, and hiring a professional to write it for you. Which course you choose depends upon several factors, including desired quality and speed, personal finances, and whether or not you plan to become a professional screenwriter yourself.

The next three chapters will help you choose the path that's best for you.

CHAPTER 22
GOING IT ALONE

Writing Your Own Screenplay

Whether the source material is your own or someone else's, it's possible to write the screenplay yourself. It's even possible to sell the first script you write, the first time you go out with it. And while this last may not be the way to bet, it has, on occasion, been done. Be aware, though, that adaptations can be particularly challenging—and that neither path is a picnic.

"You have to be mindful," says screenwriter John August, "that knowing how to write a great book, and how to market a great book, has very little bearing on how to make a good movie, or how to deal with this completely separate system that is the film and television industry."

When it comes to adaptations, screenwriter Jonathan Hensleigh minces no words. "Writing any screenplay, adaptation or original, is murder," he says. "It's just a question of how painful being murdered is. You can be murdered with an injection that puts you to sleep, and you drift off and die in a narcotic-fueled haze or what-have-you. Or you can be bled out over the course of four days in the desert while scorpions eat your appendix. They're different. And I would say that the one is an adaptation and the other an original screenplay."

Still, there are those who've successfully adapted their own works. Hensleigh aims to be among them, and is currently working on a series of young adult novels which he then plans to adapt. (For details on how he intends to give the books built-in cinematic appeal while writing them, see Chapter 36.)

PROS AND CONS

The pros of the do-it-yourself approach are easy to see: cost and control. Writing the screenplay entirely on your own means you don't have to pay someone else to help, or to write it for you. It also puts you—like a book author (or film director)—in control of every nuance of plot and character, every line of dialogue, every period and comma. It's going to be exactly what you want it to be, and no one (not yet, anyway) can tell you any different.

The cons are closely related. The cost, in terms of time spent, will be high, perhaps enormous. If your learning curve is fairly typical, you'll be writing screenplays for three to ten years before your work is good enough to catch the eyes of agents, managers, and buyers. Which isn't to say it will be bought; rather, it will be considered.

The other major con is the same as the pro: you—and not someone more experienced, who's already put in their three to ten-plus years—are in charge of every smallest detail, and that's likely to show. One way to mitigate this would be to hire a screenwriter (preferably an adaptation specialist) to look over the finished product when you're done, and help smooth out the rough edges. How much time this is going to take, and how much it's going to cost, will of course depend on just how rough your screenplay turns out to be.

ON SCREENWRITING

If seeing this one story brought to life on the screen is what you really want to do, turning yourself into a screenwriter to get that done is a bit like building an airplane because you want to go to

Paris. There are easier and more sensible (if not cheaper) paths to pursue. "I think the author with one book," John August advises, "trying to write the screenplay to get the movie version of that one book made, is likely going to have a very frustrating time, and will probably be better off writing another book."

If, on the other hand, what you really want to do is write screenplays, and you see this as but the first of many—then taking an active hand in the writing is something you're going to have to do, and you might as well start now. "And if it feels like it's not going where you want it to go," counsels Oscar-nominated screenwriter Susannah Grant, "then maybe someone else can contribute."

Though this is not a book about the nitty-gritty details of how-to-write-a-screenplay, for those considering this path, a few general tips appear below.

The first of these is this: you can't write a screenplay the same way you'd write a book because a) it would be too long, and b) no one would read it. Books are about richness and depth of detail; scripts are about brevity and saying more with less. Remember the ten-second pitch or logline (see Chapters 5 and 25), the point of which is to condense the immensity of your story into a sentence or two? In many ways, screenwriting is like that, on a bigger scale.

FINDING SCREENPLAYS

There's a specific format to be adhered to, which is best learned by reading scripts that have already sold, and preferably sold very recently. Looking at recently sold scripts allows you to see what actually sold, as opposed to what was eventually filmed after ten revisions by five different writers and the director. The two can be, and very often are, radically different—and even if there was only one writer and one draft, the director adds things (shot numbers, numerous camera directions) that no selling script should contain.

The scripts you'll find published as books or offered for sale (or free) over the internet are, almost without exception, "shooting scripts" (the final versions that were actually filmed) which did not exist until years after the "selling script" was purchased. Worse, some of those free "scripts" found online are actually transcripts—which are the result of someone watching the movie, and typing out what they see and hear. Which is about as far removed from a professionally written screenplay as you can get. It may be an accurate description of events, as far as it goes, but it's not going to show you what actually sold.

You need to know what buyers consider to be good story, plot, character, dialogue, style, and so on—in today's world, not yesterday's or last year's or when the script for your favorite movie sold ten years back.

If you want to see the actual screenplay that caused some executive somewhere to say, "I, must have this, even if it costs $3 million"—you need to track down the selling script. Probably 95 percent of all spec screenplays from 2010 onward can be found online within a few weeks of the date of sale. The same is true of those specs that went out and didn't sell, but were nonetheless good enough to convince an agent and/or manager to take them out to the town. The catch is, you have to know where to look. The best sources are not accessible to the general public, and also tend to change from time to time. (Updated information on current sources can be found online at http://makeyourstoryamovie.com/bookbonus.html.)

LEARNING FROM THE PROS

Bonus features found on DVDs often provide a wealth of information as to exactly what the writer, director, or producer were thinking when they wrote, shot, and edited the movie. Many times, they'll also explain what attracted them to the project in the first place, and why specific changes were made along the way. Actor commentaries can also be useful. If you think those "special edition" DVDs are overpriced, think again: where else can you get inside info like this, directly from the people most closely involved with the project? Just make sure you review all available DVDs, and choose the edition that promises to be most helpful. In other words, make sure you're paying for useful information, and not a limited edition, gold-plated, miniature Batmobile.

Another thing you can do is sit down with the script (again, preferably the selling script) and watch the movie—following along one page at a time. Unless the writer also directed (and often even then), you'll see quite a few changes. Try to figure out why those changes were made. Sometimes this will be impossible, because the reasons have to do with shooting schedules or financing issues or clashing personalities. But much of the time, you'll be able to figure it out. And each time you do that, you learn something about story as it relates to filmmaking—about what works onscreen and what doesn't.

Perhaps the best thing you can do is also the most difficult: sit down with the writer of a successful film you admire and ask screenwriting- and adaptation-specific questions. If you're thinking that seems easier said than done, you're right. If you're reading this book, though, that task just got a whole lot easier; many of those people offer their advice in these pages—and you'll find extreme-depth interviews with most of these as well as other working writers, producers and directors online at http://makeyourstoryamovie.com/bookbonus.html.

THE ANYONE-CAN-DO-IT MYTH

We've all read stories about ordinary people selling their first screenplay. And while these stories are often inspiring (and rightly so), they're seldom exactly what they seem. In fact, let's examine that sentence: "We've all read stories about ordinary people selling their first screenplay." There are, basically, three probable inaccuracies here: the people aren't ordinary (they're writers), the first script they sold is almost never the first one they wrote (it's more likely the tenth or twentieth), and they didn't sell it (their agent did). Let's take a closer look at some of this.

Stories about waitresses (Diane Thomas, *Romancing the Stone*), truck drivers (James Cameron, whose films include *Avatar, Titanic,* and *The Terminator* franchise) and strippers (Diablo Cody, *Juno, Jennifer's Body, Young Adult, United States of Tara*) selling screenplays promulgate the unfortunate perception that anyone can write a commercial screenplay.

The truth of the matter is closer to this: writers of all kinds (screenwriters included) tend by their very nature to be unsuitable for (or unfulfilled by) pretty much any other job. And so they often drift into something—anything—that promises to pay the bills while they continue to write. The job may be high-powered (Ron Bass, who now has dozens of film credits, was an entertainment attorney) or menial; either way, it's not who they really are.

Eventually, they sell something. The headlines say "School Janitor Sells First Screenplay for $1.5 Million"—which, after all, makes for a better read than "Unemployed Writer Sells Screenplay After 5 Years Working as Janitor and Writing 20 Scripts that Didn't Sell." And the general perception becomes that, "Hey, if a janitor can do it, if a stripper can do it—so can I."

Some of those thinking this are right, because they—like *that* particular janitor, or *that* particular stripper—are really writers waiting (or, more correctly, working their *derrieres* off) to blossom. Some of them are even ready now. Most, though, are not. They may have a fabulous idea, or a brilliant concept and—who knows?—maybe three or five or ten years from now (if they keep at the craft and the premise remains marketable and no one else sells a similar project first) they'll be good enough to pull it off, to make it work.

But if they really want to go the distance with it, now, they're going to need help. That could mean hiring someone to consult and help flesh things out, or finding someone to write the whole thing for them. The next two chapters will explore both options.

CHAPTER 23
GETTING HELP

Consulting with a Pro

Nothing cuts the learning curve like consulting with someone who's been there before you, and few things—maybe no things—can teach you more about screenwriting, faster, than having someone like that working with you, applying the principles of screenwriting to your particular story. And you really do need to come up to speed because, make no mistake—you're competing with some of the best writers in the world.

Great concepts may not be common, but there are a lot of them out there. What's really rare is the ability to develop or flesh those out into full-blown stories that completely realize their inherent potential—and then sustain that greatness over the course of the entire story.

On the upside for you, most of the writers who can do that are, at any given time, busy with studio and production company assignments. So for the most part, your script won't be competing with theirs. But make no mistake: you'll be in the game with some very, very good writers. None of them have your particular story to tell (usually), so you may not be competing directly—but if your script doesn't measure up, this will not be your year.

What you want is your unique story, told in the best way possible. You may be capable of doing that yourself, with no help from anyone—but for every writer who thinks that and is right, a thousand (conservatively) are wrong. And so, personal budget allowing, you might want to enlist the services of a coach, so to speak.

"If you aspire to be a screenwriter yourself," advises Oscar-nominated producer Michael Nozik, "find someone knowledgeable who will be editorially tough with you, to get you to adapt your own material in a critical way. Someone who'll be honest and say: you've got to cut these characters and cut that storyline; here's the essence of the story; this is the movie, and this is how you should write it."

Whether you plan to enlist professional help with your own writing or oversee the project as it's written by someone else (the subject of the next chapter), you need to sort out some basic story issues up front. "For the rights-holder," Susannah Grant advises, "you want to talk to the screenwriter and really hear why the person is drawn to the material. Make sure the qualities that attract them are the things you value as well.

"If you've got a story about a woman who breeds dogs and what you really care about is the woman, and what the screenwriter really cares about is this one dog who ends up in the wrong house, that's a different movie. And that's a conversation you need to have before you join in with someone."

PROS AND CONS

The pros of this approach are getting a professional eye on your story and format, a brainstorming partner for creative input, total control of every aspect of the project (because you'll still be the one writing it), an experienced guide to keep you out of trouble from start to finish, and speed (because the story map or adaptation is going to come together faster with professional help).

The only real con here is money, as consultants don't work for free. On the other hand, a good one will save you gobs of time, so you have to balance the time-vs.-money equation in a way that fits your schedule and your budget.

FIRST STEPS

Once you've found the right consultant, who is preferably someone with adaptation experience (for more on finding the best writer/consultant, see Chapter 24), have them read whatever source material you may have, and get their feedback. You might also show them your logline (Chapter 25), pitch sheet (Chapter 26), and structure sheet (Chapter 18); these will help fill out the big picture and convey some idea of where you intended to go (which sometimes differs from where you actually wind up).

At this point, you're looking for a frank evaluation of the material's strengths and weaknesses, as well as suggestions (both general and specific) as to how the story might be rendered more cinematic for the screen. It's important to keep an open mind and maintain some story flexibility, as it's pretty much impossible to adapt anything from any other medium without significant alterations.

You may not like all of your consultant's suggestions. You may actively dislike some of them. That doesn't matter. What matters is that he consistently comes up with good, usable ideas that make sense; that he can explain the reasoning behind his suggestions (including the ones you don't like); and that he "gets" what you're trying to do in telling this story.

It's particularly important that your consultant be able to explain *why* certain things should be done, because your objective here is not only to create a good screenplay, but to learn how that's done. What you're really looking for is a consultant-slash-mentor—and not everyone who's good at something is also good at teaching it to others. Some are unable to verbalize what they somehow grasp intuitively; others simply don't have the patience.

If all of that lines up, and you're convinced you've found the right adaptation consultant, it's time to get cooking.

MAPPING IT

If you have a logline, pitch sheet and structure sheet for your source material (which you should), review them with your consultant, making whatever alterations seem appropriate given your story's onscreen destination. It's possible that you'll make no alterations at this point, but instead wait until you're into the next step—but you should review nonetheless.

Next, get on the phone, or in a room together, and roll through that story map. This is where the real work takes place. (For more on this process, see Chapter 20.) Using Skype can save you quite a bit on phone bills.

Think of your story as a base-model car which can be heavily modified, depending on where you want to go with it. If you want to take it over asphalt at 200 miles an hour, that's one thing; taking the scenic route at a stately pace is another; fording rivers and climbing mountains yet another. If you try to do all of these things with one vehicle, you are doomed—at best—to mediocrity. At worst, you'll crash and burn, or break down and get stranded.

If, on the other hand, you want to do just one of these superbly, you're going to need some pretty substantial modifications made by someone who knows exactly what they're doing. One day, that will be you. Right now, you need help. You're ready to drive the thing, but someone more experienced needs to do some serious work to support you—because you don't want to break something your first time out.

Together with your consultant, hit that story map again, and again, and again—as many times as it takes to get it right. When working with reasonable clients and source material of reasonable length that's in reasonably good shape, I find that this can almost always be accomplished in twenty hours or less. Particularly stubborn clients, and those with unusually long source material or with material that still needs major work in its native medium, occasionally require more time.

At the end of this step, you should have a new, completed story map for a properly structured, well-paced tale with a relatable lead and good character arcs, etc. It should also be something that both you and your consultant are happy with. This will serve as the jumping-off point for the first draft of your screenplay. Before we go there, though, you want to take another look at your logline, pitch sheet and structure sheet—and bring them into line with your newly-remapped story. *Then* it's time to be . . .

JUMPING IN

Writers write, and it's time to buckle down and get to it. Consultants consult—so don't be shy about checking in with yours as you go, particularly if you get stuck somewhere, or come up with something new and want a second opinion as to how it might (or might not) fit in with what you have now. That's what they're there for: to bounce ideas off of and evaluate your progress.

Speaking of this last, be sure to check in every thirty pages or so to see how you're doing, as it's perfectly possible to follow the story map precisely, but err in matters of style, formatting and so forth—things you might not necessarily notice on your own. It's best to catch bad habits early, rather than backtrack later and fix a larger number of errors.

Remember to check in with your logline as well. The logline should trump everything else, because that's the story you set out to write. And while it need not be strictly accurate in every respect, it should be impossible for anyone who's read the logline to then read your script and think, "This is not the same story." Any time your story diverges from your logline, pull it back into line—or, if you consciously decide on a new direction for your story, revise the logline instead.

The same goes for your pitch sheet (Chapter 26). And of course any significant changes should be reflected in your story map (which includes the structure points) as well. In fact, you need to check your story map before executing that brilliant new idea, to see what additional changes might be required. Ripple effects are the norm; changing one thing means other things must change as well, and it's a lot easier to pick these out by reviewing the story map than by plowing through, say, a 500-page novel every time you want to change something.

FINISHING UP

Once you're done, run the whole thing by your consultant again and discuss. You'll likely catch some errors or inconsistencies you missed before (or that weren't there before), and maybe think up some significant improvements, now that you have the whole, finished story in front of you—which is something you've never had before.

You might also bring your story map up to date, and roll through that again as well, as it's often easier to spot glitches this way, without the constant distraction of wow-is-this-the-coolest-scene-ever-or-what? Also, because you get through the story map much faster, everything you've read is fresh in your mind, because you just saw it a few minutes ago—which makes those inconsistencies pop out at you like they're written in 3D.

Then it's time to do your polish, smoothing out the rough edges, tightening up and clarifying the writing. (Be particularly wary of phrases that can be read in more than one way, or have more than one meaning; if off-duty cop Dick and imperiled damsel Gwendolyn are hiding from a gang of bad guys in a warehouse, do not write "Dick shoots Gwendolyn a glance.") If you give this a shot before showing the finished draft to your consultant, then you can get feedback on a more refined draft.

Lastly, remember that what you have now is a draft. You may choose to have your consultant work it over and do an edit or polish, or not. Either way, you will later think of ways to make it better, and if it winds up bought and made it will change yet again.

Because unlike books, scripts are never finished until the movie has been shot and edited—and released.

CHAPTER 24
HIRING A PRO

Taking the Express Lane

The final option is to turn the actual writing over to someone who's done this kind of thing before, and done it well. Why might you do that? Well, think about something you're good at, perhaps even what you're best at. Then ask yourself: how good were you at that thing, whatever it is, the first time you tried it? The first ten times you tried it? The first hundred? Do you look back now and cringe at the quality of your early efforts?

Put another way: if you looked in your garage one day and found a formula race car preapproved for the Indy 500—would you race it yourself, or hire a pro? Fantasies aside, the truth is that without a top-notch driver behind the wheel, you'll never know what that vehicle can really do. And you have to figure the odds, in each case, of crashing and burning.

"Writing," cautions producer Gale Anne Hurd, "is the most difficult aspect of filmmaking. Staring at a blank page and having to fill it with meaningful stories and well-rounded characters is the most daunting challenge in the business. And while there are exceptions, I would generally recommend approaching professional screenwriters or producers to undertake adaptations—because it's a rare author who has sufficient objectivity to make the best choices when adapting their own material."

For Oscar-winning writer Paul Haggis, it's about different skill sets—and pain-avoidance. "I've seen very few authors who are good screenwriters. I think they're two different beasts. I wouldn't dare to write a novel. I would be no good at it because I don't have a novelist's skills, just as most novelists don't have the skills to write a good screenplay.

"Also, it's very hard to kill the things you love. You know a story so well, all the intricacies and all the little things you've fallen in love with. And in the process of adapting it you may just have to jettison major parts of the story, things that you don't want to part with. I think that would be too painful. Get someone else to break your heart for you."

Haggis' producing partner Michael Nozik sums up his own views: "Authors," he observes, "tend to write screenplays that more closely reflect their book than what the movie should be. At the end of the day, if your goal is simply to get your book made into a movie, you probably want to get the best screenwriter possible to come on and do the writing for you."

PROS AND CONS

The pros here include quality and speed; instead of having a draft of uncertain quality at the end of anything from six months to several years, you should (if you've chosen your writer well) have a polished and professional screenplay in the space of a few months.

The potential cons are lack of absolute, sentence-level control—and cost. If you follow the steps suggested in this book and agree on a detailed story map (see Chapters 19 and 20 for more on this) before the writing begins, the finished script should be the story you wanted to tell, though it might not be told with exactly the same words you'd have used yourself. For most people, this is a relatively minor quibble.

The other con—cost—can (depending on your budget) be a

serious consideration. Good help doesn't come cheap, and a screaming bargain by Hollywood standards is still a significant amount to
most. Making it all that much more important, should you choose
this route, to find the best writer for your project.

FINDING A GOOD (AND AFFORDABLE) WRITER

Good and *affordable* are often mutually exclusive. But not always, so
read on. The Writers Guild "scale" or minimum wage is $50,000
to $90,000, depending on the projected budget for the movie,
with the $50k figure applying to a "low budget" film costing $5
million or less. No WGA member is permitted to accept a smaller
amount.

Which presents something of a dilemma, as most writers with
produced credits are Guild members—meaning, basically, that if
you saw their name on a movie that didn't go straight-to-DVD, you're
looking at paying, best-case, $50,000 to $90,000 for a script. (And
if all of their movies did go straight-to-DVD, you probably don't
want them writing your script.)

The situation isn't actually that rosy, though, because most
working screenwriters whose movies you've seen are doing a lot
better than minimum wage. Some of the best ask—and receive—a
million or more per script. So, you can probably scratch them all off
your list on that basis alone.

Which leaves you in a sort of Wild West populated by a few
good screenwriters, fewer still with adaptation experience—and a
great many who either aren't yet good enough to do what you need,
or never will be. So how do you, as someone with little or no Hollywood experience, tell the difference—how do you pick out a
budding Wyatt Earp or Doc Holliday, before the script shootout
that skyrockets their reputation and price? The answer is easier
than you might expect: you simply rely on the opinions of those
who do have Hollywood experience. No industry connections
needed.

One thing you can do is look for writers who've placed highly in major, legitimate screenwriting competitions. I use the word *legitimate* because many contests are designed more to fatten the wallets of their promoters than anything else, and placing highly or even winning one of these may mean little. "Some of these contests," says WME story editor Christopher Lockhart, "are like beauty pageants in Uglyville. *Some*body's gotta win.")

The most prestigious and respected competition is The Nicholl Fellowships in Screenwriting Program, which is put on by the Academy of Motion Picture Arts and Sciences—the same organization that awards the Oscars. Of the 5,000+ screenplays entered each year, ten are selected as finalists. The writers of those ten scripts, therefore, represent (as judged by the Academy) the top 0.2 percent of all entries. Previous finalists have gone on to write films like *Air Force One, Arlington Road, Armored, Erin Brockovich, Finding Forrester, Pocahontas,* the *Transformers* movies, *28 Days,* and the *Castle* TV series. Finalist Jay Simpson's script *Armored* actually sold during the competition—for $400,000. "As far as I'm concerned," says Lockhart, "if you want to talk about screenwriting contests, the Nicholl is the only contest to win."

Oscar-nominated producer Michael Nozik is among the many industry players who read the top ten Nicholl scripts every year. The committee that judges the top ten scripts has included people like producer Gale Anne Hurd, screenwriter Susannah Grant (who began her career by winning the Nicholl competition), former Fox Chairman and CEO Bill Mechanic and others.

The Disney Fellowship is also highly respected, but a condition of winning is that any script written during the fellowship year will be owned by Disney. The studio then pays the writer, who becomes a WGA member—so by the time you find out someone's won, it's too late to hire them unless you want to wait a year and pay "scale" (WGA minimum) or better. The Chesterfield was another top-notch competition, but is no longer active. (For more on screenwriting contests, visit http://makeyourstoryamovie.com/bookbonus.html.)

Useful as the contest method can be, it does have limitations.

Some high-ranking scripts are obviously commercial. But because commerciality is often not a factor in the judging—scripts are evaluated on other criteria—a substantial number of the highest-ranking scripts are, though well-written, unlikely to sell for reasons of subject matter, dark tone, etc.

"Even in one of the better contests," Lockhart confirms, "the scripts that win wouldn't necessarily translate into successful films. There are scripts I read and I think, 'Wow, this guy's a good writer—but Hollywood's never going to make this movie.' So then I ask myself: 'Is this *really* a good writer?' Because if you're writing scripts that will never be movies, you're in the wrong business."

There are writers who place consistently well in contests—and that's all. Ultimately, you want more than just a great screenplay—you want one that will *sell*.

Ironically, some competitions exclude writers who've managed to get paid for their writing. Obviously, this is done with the best of intentions, and is meant to keep the contest restricted to newer and unproven writers, who would in most cases not fare well if they had to compete against seasoned pros. Still, the earnings threshold can be fairly low; in the case of the Nicholl Fellowships, for example, writers who've earned a cumulative total of $5,000 or more by screenwriting are declared ineligible. Which is just about everyone who's ever earned anything—so many good writers who haven't yet made it big do not enter these contests.

Another approach is to look for a screenwriter who's already been optioned or put into development by a real company or producer with solid credits. If industry professionals at that level feel a particular writer is worth their time, it's a good indication he or she is close to "breaking" (selling outright and/or getting produced—at which point they'll likely become WGA members and, so, unaffordable). The ideal "find" is someone who's begun to attract this kind of attention, but isn't yet making the big bucks. Perhaps someone who placed highly in a prestigious competition, and has since been optioned or in development.

Someone like this is also more likely to be well connected (or, at least, better connected than you). And while it is definitely *not* true that Hollywood is more about who you know than how good you are, it *is* true that who you know can speed things up. So a writer who is both good and at least somewhat connected may be able to help get the script seen by the right people after it's written. This doesn't guarantee a sale, nothing can do that—but it may up your chances.

THE ADAPTATION SPECIALIST

Another thing to look for is adaptation experience—because while writing an adapted screenplay and writing an original are similar, they're not quite the same. With the original, anything goes; with the adaptation, there's an existing story whose soul must be preserved and nurtured, and some story paths simply cannot be taken because to do so would betray the spirit of the source material. There are writers who are fabulous at originals *or* adaptations, and merely competent at the other. And there are some who do both well.

There are even a few who also write novels, nonfiction books, comics, etc., though this is rare. It's possible someone like this will have a deeper understanding of where you're coming from, particularly if they've adapted their own works into screenplays—which, despite what most might think, is considerably more difficult than adapting someone else's work.

Regardless, someone who's already done several adaptations— someone who has come, basically, to specialize in adaptations—is likely to do a better and faster job with yours than someone with no such experience. Which isn't to say an accomplished screenwriter's first adaptation won't be a good one; it's just playing the odds.

THE PERFECT WRITER

On top of all that, there's one more quality you're looking for. Because it's not enough to find a good writer; you need to find the *right* writer for *your* project. There will be those who have all the write stuff—but just don't "get" what you're trying to do, and bringing someone like that on board is going to make every step a battle, and the end result something no one's really happy with. As Leslie Dixon says of on-set situations with clashing visions: "It's like a bunch of lions fighting for scraps of meat and in the end you just get kind of a bloody pulp."

On the other hand, you don't want someone who just agrees with everything you say, no questions asked and no suggestions made. That indicates someone who really has no interest in telling the best story, but is just looking for a fast paycheck.

What you really need is something in between: a collaborator who sees your project for what it is and understands what you're trying to do, but at the same time brings a fresh perspective both creatively and businesswise. They'll suggest new things, always backing up those suggestions with creative or industry-specific reasons. They will occasionally disagree with you and say as much, because they want the story to be the best it can be and also something with a realistic shot at selling. At the same time, they understand and acknowledge that it is, in the end, your story—and the final decisions are yours.

You, in turn, have to realize that the end product—the completed script—is likely to differ in many respects from the idea, book, true-life experience or other source of adaptation or inspiration. Sometimes this will be because you or the writer (or the two of you together) come up with something better, other times it will be due to commercial considerations. So it's important—as always—to keep an open mind.

The only real exception to this would be a situation in which you want what you want, and you really don't care whether it's commercial or not—in which case, you need to let the writer know this up-front. I once spent several months working with a writer whose story—a trilogy of unpublished novels—was (in my opinion) in need of substantial revision before presentation to book agents or publishers. I made all sorts of suggestions, most of which were dismissed without any real explanation. It seemed to me that just about every decision this guy made, every instinct he had, was wrong. I'd never seen anything like it.

Finally, I learned that he really, literally couldn't care less about the work's commercial potential; all he wanted was a good story to be shown to family and friends. Rooted as I am in a world of people who have sold or hope to sell their stories, this had never occurred to me. If I'd known his goal from the start, our relationship would have been totally different, and radically more productive. We were working at cross purposes the whole time, and never knew it.

I now ask every client right up front: what are you looking to do here, what is it you hope to accomplish? Be sure you're clear on this with your writer, as well as yourself. You can't reach the destination if you don't know where you're headed. (Which, incidentally, is the single strongest argument for mapping any story before the writing begins.)

Lastly, you want someone who is able to see the story as you do, who understands what it is at its core—its "heart"—and will keep that heart alive and beating strongly in the new medium, regardless of whatever other changes might be made along the way.

THE PROCESS

The process here begins, as before, with the story map, which the two of you should work through and agree on before the writing starts. Once underway, make sure your writer checks in with you every thirty pages or thereabouts, so you can review the work's quality and make sure everything's going according to plan (the story map)—and that your sweet ballerina hasn't morphed into a murderous cannibal transvestite amputee werewolf hooker with a coke habit.

And if you think that's far-fetched (well, okay, it's a little far-fetched—but less so than you might imagine), consider the experience of comic writer and screenwriter Steve Niles, who ran a comic book imprint some years back. "There were times when I'd hire someone to adapt a story into comic form, and they'd hand in a [comic] script that had nothing to do with the original. And I'd say, 'What are you doing?' People get confused about adaptations, they think it means 'I make it about me, right?' No, to me the job has always been preserving the original material and the author's voice. It's the same with movies."

But we digress. Point being, you do want to keep tabs on the writing as it progresses, and this is the time to do it. If your writer somehow strays from what the two of you agreed on, better to catch it early than find out on page 120 that things went wrong on page 2. All the same, you don't want to micromanage, and the writer should be free to make whatever minor adjustments might seem necessary along the way. Significant deviations from the story map, however, should be okayed by you before going forward. This is one area where the best surprise, is no surprise.

PAYMENT ARRANGEMENTS

Writers may write, but—like everyone else—they also need to eat, pay rent and keep the power turned on. Be aware that asking someone to write an entire script for a percentage of what the screenplay might sell for—and nothing else—is a classic amateur move that will quickly eliminate pretty much every writer with any talent right off the bat. You wouldn't expect someone to build a house to your specifications for no money up front and a percentage of the home's eventual sale price. Same thing here.

It's not that they don't believe in your project; it's that, much like publishing, the fate of any given property is uncertain, and there are far too many variables involved to be able to say that *this* script, if executed in *this* way, is absolutely going to sell. (Whereas it is quite possible to say, with a reasonable degree of certainty, that *that* script, executed by a guy who has so few other prospects that he's working for free on someone else's project, will *not* sell, *ever,* under any circumstances.) The only certainty is this: the better the script, the better its chances—and the better the writer, the better the script.

I mention this whole thing only because such no-pay offers are extremely common, and extremely commonly ignored by those capable of making a living by writing. Which leaves—people who aren't. Not your best option. Look at it from the writer's perspective: why should they set aside their own brilliant ideas (and their 100 percent profit share) to work on someone else's (for a smaller percentage)? Take on a few of those, and pretty soon there's no time for your own projects, and no money either; it's a lose-lose proposition.

Moving on. . . .

You're not looking for cheapest guy around, because there's a reason he's the cheapest guy around. So the overall cost is going to be (for most) significant. You can reduce the bite by paying in several installments—for example: 50 percent at the start, 50 percent on completion; or 33⅓ percent up front, 33⅓ percent at page 60, 33⅓ percent on completion. If the project takes several months, you've got several months to pay.

Someone who's also looking for a percentage (in addition to the initial payments) can be a good thing, because that's a motivation to help move your project along after it's been written—whereas someone who takes a flat fee and nothing else has less incentive to do their best, and none at all to push the project afterward.

OWNERSHIP

In all cases, it must be crystal clear that—once all payments have been made (except, of course, any percentage-of-sale)—you own the script, just as you'd own a house you paid someone else to build. The difference here being that you don't need a construction worker to help sell your house—whereas a connected screenwriter could come in handy. Your agreement may guarantee the writer proper credit (subject to WGA jurisdiction)—but when you hire someone else to write something for you, the final product (and its copyright) should belong to you. Technically, it's a "work-for-hire," and you are—for copyright purposes—the legal owner.

PART V

SUBMISSION AND DEAL MAKING: HOW STORIES ARE SOLD

Tales of high-selling scripts abound but, for the most part, lack any specific information as to just exactly how the selling process works. Sure, Agent A or Manager B or, occasionally, Producer C sold the script—but how does that work? For all the detail such reports provide (or don't provide), one might conclude the scripts are displayed in a shop window on Rodeo Drive for the perusal of passing studio execs and other interested parties. When in fact, the selling process starts with a sentence or two, and those in the business of selling scripts rarely send them directly to studio execs.

The following eleven chapters will shed considerable light on this process, from the construction of the initial pitch or logline, through sale, contract, and credits.

CHAPTER 25
THE LOGLINE

Loglines and pitch sheets are tools of the trade. The logline should come first, followed by the pitch sheet—which is, when you get right down to it, an expanded version of the logline.

Before moving forward, reread Chapter 5 (which explains why you need a logline in the first place, and why you're most likely dead in the water without one). Then reread Chapter 17 (on creating a rough, working logline).

Now, let's workshop the loglines for two stories you already know. First up . . .

LOGLINE WORKSHOP: *HARRY POTTER*

Harry Potter and the Sorcerer's Stone (aka *Harry Potter and the Philosopher's Stone*) was a massively successful novel that went on to become one of the biggest movies of all time. I've never had occasion to logline this before, so I'll do it now, in the same way I'd logline a client's story or one of my own—except I'll write out the thoughts I have along the way, to illustrate the process. Remembering the WHO-GOAL-OBSTACLE format that all good loglines share— how do we build one for this?

First up: WHO (or maybe What) is this story about? Those inexperienced with loglines might be tempted to say "magic," or "a school for wizards." They might even take a hint from the title and say "a sorcerer's stone." Let's follow those paths and see where they take us.

Magic. Okay—what is magic's goal? Whoops, we're stalled already; magic has no will of its own and, therefore, cannot formulate a goal. No goal means no logline, which means we've reached a dead end. In fact, the same is true of both the wizard's school and the sorcerer's stone, so all three are out the window right there.

The story is, of course, about Harry Potter—but for logline purposes, that's not our WHO. There are several reasons for this. The first is that "Harry Potter" tells us nothing. Think about it: you're an editor or producer, and someone tells you (back in the mid-1990s) that they have a great story about Harry Potter. So what? Who the hell is Harry Potter?

That's the question we must answer: WHO, exactly, *is* Harry Potter? A boy destined to follow in the footsteps of his magic-using parents and . . . ? That's already too complicated; we do not have time, within the confines of a ten-second pitch, to wander off into explanations about who his parents were or what his destiny is. (Knowing his destiny also kills any possible suspense; if we know he succeeds, what's the point?)

We need to get more basic than that. Harry is *a boy*. But not just any boy; that's too general. We need to add some sort of brief descriptor to help set him up. So—what kind of boy is he? One with latent powers, sure, but we need to keep our WHO simple and (just as importantly) relatable/sympathetic/empathetic. We know his parents are dead, so what does that make him? An orphan. So:

An orphaned boy.

Now we're getting somewhere. You don't know a thing about this kid, and already your heart goes out to him. In three words, we have an instantly sympathetic WHO.

All right—what's his GOAL? To have a good time? Not much

of a goal. To escape the wicked aunt and uncle (or step-uncle)? Let's try that on for size: *An orphaned boy must escape his unloving aunt and uncle* . . . Meh. Doesn't exactly grab you by the throat, does it? Besides, he's away from them a mere eighteen minutes into the movie (and headed back to them at the end), so this isn't exactly a story-spanning goal, either.

There is that sorcerer's stone; maybe he's after that. *An orphaned boy must find a magical gemstone* . . . Could be interesting. It's a start—but in the wrong direction, because Harry's not really after the stone at all (Voldemort is), and doesn't even know it exists until an hour and forty-eight minutes into the film. So, again, hardly an overarching objective.

There is that school he goes to when he leaves, and pretty much the whole story takes place in and around the school. Nonetheless, *An orphaned boy must attend school* sounds like a surefire snoozer, or perhaps a slow-paced indie drama. Again the reaction is: *So what?* Nothing special about that, because all boys go to school—and if there's nothing special about it, why should someone spend a million dollars (or a hundred million) to make a movie about it?

Still, if so much of the story revolves around the school, there must be something to that. Is there some reason he must attend *this* school and not some other? Because he happens to live nearby? No. Oh, right—it's a school for *wizards*. And he's going there because he wants to become one. Which gives us this: *An orphaned boy attends a school for wizards* . . . (Actually it's a school for witches *and* wizards, but we won't mention this here because a) Harry's not going there to become a witch and, b) it would clunk up the logline.)

Wow, that's different. Suddenly going to school has become a whole lot more exciting. Even so, it's not a GOAL. Who goes to wizard school? Someone who wants to be a wizard, that's who. And that is, in fact, Harry's goal: to become a wizard. The school for wizards thing is too good to drop, though, so let's keep that:

An orphaned boy attends a school for wizards, where he . . .

What does Harry do? Learn what's being taught, of course; that is why people go to school—those who go voluntarily, at any rate. So: *An orphaned boy attends a school for wizards, where he has fun learning the ways of magic and . . .* Ehhh what's wrong with that? No urgency. Why do we care what he has *fun* doing? We don't. So let's tweak that a bit and see what we get:

An orphaned boy attends a school for wizards, where he must learn the ways of magic . . .

Okay, *must* sounds urgent. But why is it urgent? What happens if he doesn't? And what's in his way—what's the OBSTACLE? Voldemort, of course. But again, names mean nothing at this point, and so serve no function in a logline. So let's do the same thing with Voldemort that we did with Harry: say what he is and add a descriptor. Voldemort is a *wizard*. What kind of wizard? Powerful, to be sure, but that's not quite what we're looking for; it is not Voldemort's defining quality, and it doesn't really set the stage, because for all anyone else knows at this point, the kid and his parents are evildoers who have it coming.

Wait, there's something: evil. Voldemort is an *evil wizard*. Now the stage is set, we know who's who—meaning who the good guy is, and who the bad guy is. And there's our OBSTACLE: the evil wizard Voldemort. How hard was that? Right away we see this kid is up against it, facing long and perhaps impossible odds. Here he is, facing a full-blown evil wizard, and he has to go to school to learn magic? That's like pitting a West Point cadet against Caesar. The only quibble I have with this is that the word *wizard* repeats, but in this particular case substituting something else dilutes the impact, and in fact the first use sets up the second, reinforcing the fact that the villain is already far more accomplished (and therefore more formidable) than our boy Harry.

Now, why is Voldemort an OBSTACLE? Because he wants to kill our hero, of course. Harry is actually Voldemort's obstacle as well, but we want to keep the logline focused on the hero whose story it is and not the villain whose story it's not. Let's try this: *An orphaned boy attends a school for wizards, where he must learn the ways of magic to defend himself against the evil wizard who killed his parents . . .*

Not bad, but *defend* seems a bit passive for a rousing logline, and we're veering longish if there's going to be much more to this. At the same time, *to attack the evil wizard who killed his parents* sounds a bit aggressive, particularly for a young adult audience. So what else can we say here? How about *to defeat the evil wizard who killed his parents*? The word *defeat* leaves room for interpretation, and also leaves open the possibility that the evil wizard survives to fight again another day.

Which gives us *An orphaned boy attends a school for wizards, where he must learn the ways of magic to defeat the evil wizard who killed his parents.* Getting better; now we have a sort of quest-for-vengeance thing implied but not actually stated. It's important to avoid setting up false expectations, and we certainly don't want to mislead the reader. So this strikes a nice balance.

We might be tempted to add more—something about thwarting the evil wizard's quest for immortality, perhaps, or preventing him from getting a body, or even mentioning that the evil wizard tried to kill Harry when he was still an infant. But to do so would render the logline bloated and overly complex. Sure, there's a lot of good stuff we'd like to cram in here—but when it comes to loglines, less can indeed be more.

And, less being more, we might also be tempted to shorten it to something like, say, *An orphaned boy must learn the ways of magic to defeat the evil wizard who killed his parents.* But this would be incomplete because . . . how is he supposed to do that? The school-for-wizards bit is crucial, because the concept doesn't quite make sense without it.

What we have now is pretty good: *An orphaned boy attends a school for wizards, where he must learn the ways of magic to defeat the evil wizard who killed his parents.* But as important as it is to avoid going overboard and saying too much, it's equally important to know when saying just a little more can make a big difference. And the one thing this logline still lacks is a solid sense of urgency, a ticking clock of some sort. After all, if going to school to become a wizard is like going to school to become a doctor or lawyer, our protagonist could be middle-aged by the time he graduates. It just won't do. Also, for all we know the evil wizard is living as a recluse in Botswana, making a confrontation somewhat unlikely and, again, somewhat less than urgent.

So let's add this, and—to avoid messing up the smooth-flowing text we already have—let's tack it on the end:—*and now comes for him*. Giving us this: *An orphaned boy attends a school for wizards, where he must learn the ways of magic to defeat the evil wizard who killed his parents—and now comes for him.*

Okay, plenty of urgency now; our hero has to learn this stuff or die, and he's being hunted right now. With this addition, we're almost there. It says what we want it to say, but could nonetheless use a bit of refinement. We could try upping the emotional content by replacing *killed* with *murdered*. But for something aimed largely at kids, that might be just a little too heavy, so let's not.

And now comes for him could perhaps be clarified, in the interests of making absolutely everything absolutely crystal clear. We could, for example, say—*and who now comes for him*. Still, that wording is a tad . . . highbrow, proper, formal, whatever-you-want-to-call-it. So let's simplify by saying:—*and is now after him*. Like defeat, *after* is open to interpretation, and the clear implication is that he means to kill our hero.

Now, most of the times when Voldemort is after Harry it's because Harry is in his way, acting as an obstacle to his pursuit of the stone (which, as mentioned, requires too much explaining to be part of the logline). But even so, he still tried to kill Harry before the story began, and tried again in the forest (before Harry knew about the stone). All in all, then, this is perfectly accurate.

And so we arrive at this:

An orphaned boy attends a school for wizards, where he must
learn the ways of magic to defeat the evil wizard who killed his
parents—and is now after him.

Is that a story you'd want to read, or see on the screen? If so, you've got plenty of company. WHO: *an orphaned boy* . . . GOAL: *learn the ways of magic to defeat* . . . OBSTACLE (with urgency): *the evil wizard who killed his parents—and is now after him.* And notice what we didn't need: the sorcerer's stone. The mere fact that it's part of the title suggests that it's an object of contention—in fact *the* object of contention—between hero and villain. And, obviously, a sorcerer's stone sounds like something any wizard might want.

Because the logline is so indescribably crucial, let's run through that process again, with a different adaptation. . . .

LOGLINE WORKSHOP: *JURASSIC PARK*

Jurassic Park was a hugely successful novel that went on to become one of Hollywood's biggest hits. Keeping that logline mantra in mind—WHO, GOAL, OBSTACLE—how do we build a logline for this story?

WHO (or perhaps What) is this story about?

Most of those new to loglines begin by saying something about dinosaurs. Many of those who don't, start with the park itself. Still others kick things off with "An experiment" or "A scientist." Let's take those roads and see where they lead . . .

Dinosaurs. Okay, what do they do—what's their goal? Run rampant, search for food, that kind of thing. What's their obstacle? An absence of food-bearing park personnel caused, basically, by a hurricane coupled with a power failure. So:

Dinosaurs run rampant on an island resort, trying to feed
themselves during a power outage caused by a hurricane.

What's wrong with this? It is, after all, an accurate description of what happens. But replace "dinosaurs" with "tigers" and you've got a documentary. Besides, running rampant and eating each other is what dinosaurs do. There are no real stakes involved here, unless you're a dinosaur. What's their obstacle—high winds and rain? That doesn't quite cut it. And what the hell are dinosaurs doing on an island resort?

Lastly, for all the hype, *Jurassic Park* is not, at its core, a story about dinosaurs. And even if it were, they are (in this tale) more than a little hard to relate to. So let's try . . .

A park. There's no denying that the park is a central element of this story. So we might be tempted to try something like this: *A park featuring dinosaurs descends into chaos when the power fails.*

Also accurate, as far as it goes—which isn't very. First problem: a "park" cannot have a goal. Which means it can't be our protagonist or hero. Second problem: we can't have an obstacle in the way of a nonexistent protagonist with no definable goal. There are three basic elements to a proper logline, and we've just struck out on all of them.

Even setting that aside, there are other issues here. A park descends into chaos. So what? Again, where are the stakes? Why do we care? "Park" is not something an audience can relate to, identify with, or root for. Why? Because there is no emotion associated with "park." It's a thing, not a character; a what and not a who. Building your logline around a park isn't much better than casting a brick as your lead. If we replace "dinosaurs" with "moose" in this park-centric logline, we've got another documentary. And, again—what's with the dinosaurs? So let's try . . .

A scientist. Which scientist? There are four: John, Alan, Ellie, and Ian. Immediate confusion. But let's go with John, who set the whole thing in motion by creating the park. What does he do? Well, he tries to restore order, mostly. Get things back the way they were before everything went to hell. What's in his way? Dinosaurs, basically. Thus: *A kindly scientist tries to restore order when a park full of dinosaurs descends into chaos during a power outage.*

Also accurate. But again: so what? Who cares? What are the stakes? Replace "dinosaurs" with "otters" and it's a National Geographic Special. And then there's that brachiosaur in the room: the dinosaurs themselves. What about . . .

An experiment. The whole thing is sort of an experiment, in terms of both science and profitable entertainment. Which might lead us to something like: *An experimental park featuring dinosaurs descends into chaos during a power outage.*

Already the old problems crop up: our protagonist cannot be "an experiment." "Experiment" has no will, and therefore no Goal. No Goal means no Obstacle—and again our logline winds up in loserville. Along with those unexplained dinosaurs.

Let's start over by stripping this story down to the bone. At its marrow—or, more to the point, at its heart—who (or what) is this story about? Dinosaurs? No. A park? No again. An experiment? Not at all. A scientist? Closer, but not really—making this, at best, a partial yes.

Following up on that—why is "scientist" closer than "dinosaurs," "park," or "experiment"? Well, "scientist" is a Who, not a What. People exercise will, pursue goals, tackle obstacles. Sounds familiar, doesn't it? Who-Goal-Obstacle. Still, "scientist" is not our protagonist.

Here's a shortcut to figuring out who is. Ask yourself this question: Who are we rooting for? In this case, just about everyone but Nedry, making this a rather broad answer. So let's narrow it down: who are we *most* rooting for? Who have we bonded with, emotionally? If we were to play god (which, let's face it, we do)—who is *not* expendable?

Let's run down the list. No one's going to miss the "bloodsucking attorney" (who is, in fact, the first to go) or the lazy, thieving Nedry. Ray is cool and has his uses, but he's not essential. Same goes for Muldoon.

John is likable but, all things considered, he's lived a long, full life and this whole mess is more or less his fault. Ian Malcolm is

both likable and entertaining—but when you come right down to
it, he's comic relief, hovering just outside the core group of characters. To be brutally honest, we can still have a relatively happy ending if all of these folks die (which, in the novel, they do).

But what about that core group? Who are they? Alan and Ellie
(two romantically involved scientists who are considering children;
in this respect, also, Ian is an outsider), Tim and Lex (John's young
grandchildren). This, really, is who our story is about.

Unfortunately, this also makes for an awkward logline: "Two
scientists and the two grandchildren of another scientist . . ." is already a mess. How can we smooth that out and make it flow, while
at the same time conveying the essence of Who the story revolves
around? We need a single word that summarizes what is actually a
multiple or ensemble protagonist. (Which, it should be noted, is an
unusual complication; most commercially successful fiction revolves
around one or two main characters.)

So what do these people have in common? Not much. In fact,
they meet for the first time during the course of our story. But is
there some brief term we might apply to them as a group—preferably
one that will strike an emotional chord with readers?

Two adults, two children. More specifically: a man, a woman,
and two young children (brother and sister). If we didn't know any
better (which the readers of our logline will not), we'd probably
call this *a family.* They may not qualify genetically, but they do fit
the archetype: man and woman, protecting children. Technically
incorrect or not—this is (for our purposes) a family.

How many members of this family can we afford to lose to hungry dinosaurs? Zero. We want them all to come out okay. Making
them—together—our main character. And so our logline begins:
A family . . .

Short, reasonably accurate, rich in emotional content. In a
word: perfect. That's our Who. Now, what is our Who's GOAL?

Well—what is our family doing? *Struggling* to stay alive,
obviously—but also something more. Because they're not looking

to find a nice cave, build fires and whittle spears for the next forty years. That would be "staying alive." There's a larger Goal here: they're looking to get the hell out of Dodge. In short (which loglines must be), their goal is *to escape*. So:

A family struggles to escape . . .

"Struggles," by the way, is a great word because it implies conflict, which all great tales must have. Still, *struggling to escape* is only half of the Goal. To get the other half, we need to figure out what it is they're struggling to escape from. Dinosaurs? Well, yes—but also no. We wouldn't say "A family struggles to escape dinosaurs." That's confusing. What are these, cave-people? Even that doesn't hold up, really, because dinosaurs were long gone when the first cave folk came down the pike.

Remember the basics: Who-Goal-Obstacle. Who's your protagonist, what does he want, and what's in his way? If we say *A family struggles to escape dinosaurs*—there's nowhere left to go, because . . . what's in their way?

We could try the hurricane: *A family struggles to escape dinosaurs while battered by a hurricane.* But this is also confusing, and raises difficult questions: Where the hell did the dinosaurs come from? What are people and dinosaurs doing together? Is this a comedy? A time-travel tale? Is the setting prehistoric, or modern-day?

That's way too much to think about at this stage, where clarity is vital. Back to the goal: what is the family struggling to escape from? Well, where are they trapped? In the *park,* of course. They're struggling to escape from the park.

Still, it's not that simple. Why don't they just walk (or drive) out the front gate? Call the cops, the army, order an airstrike? Because . . . what? Because the park is located on an *island*. And not Manhattan, but a *remote island*. This is where things start coming together:

A family struggles to escape a remote island park . . .

So far, so good. Now for the final element: What is our Who's OBSTACLE?

What's in the way of the family as it struggles to escape the re-mote island park? *Dinosaurs!* But we can't just drop "dinosaurs" into a logline and expect it to work. Plague, pirates, armed revolution-aries, sure. But—dinosaurs? That is, to say the least, a stretch.

True, it makes perfect sense when you're reading the story. But no one's going to get that far if they don't buy the premise. Our challenge is to get that premise across; to make "dinosaurs" work—quickly, efficiently, believably—within the confines of a logline. (This explanation or *setup* is a second unusual complication, which most loglines do not require because we're already familiar with the everyday world in which their stories take place. Note that the *Minority Report* logline cited in Chapter 5 also requires a setup line, because—as with *Jurassic Park*—the story makes no sense without it.)

So what do we have in the story itself? A program to recreate dinosaurs using genetic engineering and the DNA of—well, that's too long already. While we do need explanation, it must be concise. So how about this: a remote island park *whose main attractions—genetically restored dinosaurs—*?

Quick, reasonably accurate, explanatory without being kludgy. How can there be dinosaurs and people? The dinosaurs were re-created through genetic engineering. Okay; possible, maybe. There's the science. But why would anyone do that? To make money. That's why the park: charges admission, makes a mint.

This tells the reader we're talking present-day, rules out time travel (or there'd be no need to recreate the dinosaurs), and gives us motive—which adds believability to the mix. Now we're cooking:

> *A family struggles to escape a remote island park whose main attractions—genetically restored dinosaurs—*

The rest almost writes itself. Naturally, the critters must be confined within the park. And so something must have gone wrong, or we'd have no story. The main attractions *have been set loose.* All right—but how? *A power failure.* No need to mention Nedry or the hurricane; they're the warm-up; the power failure is the main event triggering the chaos.

And so we arrive at this:

A family struggles to escape a remote island park whose main attractions—genetically restored dinosaurs—have been set loose by a power failure.

Even with the added complexity of an ensemble protagonist and the necessary "dinosaur" explanation, this comes to twenty-three words. Read aloud, it's a mere ten seconds of someone's time. More than that—it's something they'll want to read.

A FEW MORE POINTS

Those (above) are loglines: WHO the story's about; what their GOAL is; and the OBSTACLE that stands in their way. No subplots, names, deep characterization or cast of thousands. Instead: bare-bones concept. Complete, concise, intriguing. Certainly enough to keep you focused while writing the story—or keep the attention of someone reading or listening to your ten-second pitch. If the bones are good enough—and you've managed to convey them effectively—your audience will want to see how you've fleshed them out with your story.

And that's what the logline is all about: getting someone to want more. Of course, you must also target your audience: a company that adapts romance novels for the direct-to-DVD market is unlikely to bite on *Jurassic Park,* no matter how intriguing the logline.

If all goes well, you'll be asked to submit your pitch sheet (see next chapter) or complete story for consideration. And your story had better live up to the promise of your logline. Remember (from Chapter 5) that the WHO, the GOAL, and the OBSTACLE needn't necessarily be presented in that order, and that sometimes (as with *Minority Report* and *Jurassic Park*) a setup line may be needed. Most of the time, however, WHO-GOAL-OBSTACLE will be the order that reads most smoothly, and no setup line is necessary. Start there, and be willing to change your approach if you get stuck. When you think you're there, go over it again and see if it can be shortened or refined. Don't be satisfied with it until you're convinced it's as good as it can possibly be.

BUT I CAN'T LOGLINE THIS STORY!

If you find yourself utterly unable to come up with a good logline, this could mean one of several things. Your story may be non-classically structured, meaning it does not fall into the expected three-act structure (which drastically reduces the pool of potential buyers, and probably means you're looking at pursuing the independent film route with a lower budget). Such tales, even when well-executed, do not generally make for good loglines. (Recall Christopher Lockhart's comments (Chapter 5) on *Juno* versus *Liar Liar*.)

It may also be that the story can't be loglined because it has serious problems: the hero is never clearly defined, or has no clearly defined goal that spans most of the story, or there's no consistent obstacle, no urgency, etc. It's hard to put these things in the logline if they're simply not there.

Or you could just suck at loglines. Really. Some people are good at it, some aren't. And just as most novelists couldn't write a good screenplay to save their lives, and vice versa—some folks just can't cut things to the bone and turn a whole story into a ten-second concept. It's not a skill that comes easily (when it comes at all), and—like adapting a story for the screen—it's actually harder to logline your own work than someone else's, because you lack the perspective of an objective observer.

One trick you can try is this: ask yourself what you'd have to change to make whatever logline you've come up with fit the WHO-GOAL-OBSTACLE format (and don't forget the urgency). Then tweak the logline until it's there. Now ask yourself if you'd be willing to alter your story to match. Sure, this entails a good deal of work—but better that than trying to pitch something that is, basically, unpitchable. On future projects, come up with the logline first—before you write the story—and you'll never have this problem again.

CONCLUSION

Ultimately (as mentioned in Chapter 5), you're going to need a logline, or 99 percent of the people in town will never read or hear your pitch. Now, getting them to read or listen doesn't guarantee they'll take the next step (your particular project may not be right for their particular needs at this particular moment, regardless of quality)—but a substandard logline guarantees they won't. Because the logline is where it all begins—and if you can't hold their interest for ten seconds, that's also where it ends.

To be sure that no one can possibly misread your logline the first time around, see that it's always accompanied by the genre of your tale—for example HARRY POTTER (YA adventure)—followed by the logline. This puts the reader or listener in the proper frame of mind before the all-important pitch.

For more on logline-building (including additional examples and workshopped loglines), visit http://makeyourstoryamovie.com/bookbonus.html.

CHAPTER 26
THE PITCH SHEET

Okay, so you have a great logline. That's your calling card, and its purpose is to get people to want more. If it works, they may dive right in and ask to see the script. Or they may prefer to get their feet wet first—in which case they'll say (or write) something like, "Tell me more." Now you (or your agent, manager, etc.) need something bigger than a logline.

THE BASICS

With a pitch sheet you are, in essence, courting the other party. So if a logline is that first intriguing glance, the pitch sheet would be your first conversation. You want to be flirtatious and intriguing, but at the same time, not give too much away. Enter the pitch sheet. If this were a movie, the pitch sheet would be the trailer. If a book, the flap copy or back-cover blurb. (In fact, the pitch sheet I wrote to sell my first novel *Nano* was actually used verbatim by the publisher, on the back cover. The same may happen with this book.)

Accordingly, the pitch sheet, while longer than a logline, is still fairly brief—one page at most, and likely just a few short paragraphs. It's not meant to be a synopsis; more like a teaser. As literary agent Andrea Brown once said of queries: "It should be like a skirt. Long enough to cover everything, but short enough to be exciting."

As with a trailer or blurb (or first conversation), the goal here is simple: to persuade the other party that you're interesting enough to warrant a few hours of their time. The successful trailer leads to a movie ticket or rental; the blurb to a book purchase; the conversation to a first date—and the pitch sheet to a script request.

THE LEAD-IN

Taking things from the top, the pitch sheet starts with your script or project title. Below that is the genre (action, thriller, comedy, drama, whatever). Then the writer's name (perhaps preceded by "screenplay by"), then (if the script or project is an adaptation) the title and author of the original work ("based on the novel *Terribly Intriguing* by Hungry Author"). If the title of the source material is the same as the script or project title, just say "based on the novel by Hungry Author." If the author is also the same, say "based on his [or her] novel."

Drop down a few lines and insert your logline. This serves as a quick introduction to those who may not be familiar with the concept, and a reminder to those who've already heard or read it. ("Oh yeah, I remember liking this/asking to see this/speaking with the charming writer/etc.") Below this, some sort of separator—a line, a few dashes, etc.

THE ONE-MINUTE PITCH

A few lines farther down, the pitch begins. If the logline is your-concept-in-ten-seconds, this is your-story-in-one-minute. The pitch itself should be an expansion of the logline, which will include both the logline's three essential elements (WHO, GOAL, OBSTACLE) and some (but likely not all) of the seven structural elements or plot points you've already worked out (in Chapter 18): inciting incident, first act turn, midpoint, low point, second act turn, climax, and wrap-up.

Typically, the pitch will cover the inciting incident and the first act turn, which will of necessity include the WHO and the GOAL as well. The climax will be implied by the nature of the OBSTA-CLE, which will also be here. Low point and second act turn are usually (but not always) absent, as these generally take too long to explain and distract from a fast, smooth-flowing read.

The midpoint may or may not be present; when it is, it's nearly always of the point-of-no-return rather than the something-unsuspected-is-going-on variety (because the former is usually more easily and quickly explained).

The wrap-up or denouement is optional; I prefer to leave it out, because revealing this gives away the outcome of the climax—and I like to retain an element of mystery/suspense for the reader. (If they want to know what happens, they can ask or—better yet—read.)

CHARACTER AND STORY SETUP

The first paragraph should introduce both your hero and his (or her) day-to-day life or "ordinary world." As with the logline, you want your hero to be relatable/sympathetic/empathetic/compelling. The whole first paragraph (each of the paragraphs, in fact) should be no more than a few lines long.

CENTRAL DILEMMA

The next paragraph should introduce you're hero's dilemma, which—again like the logline—should be compelling. The inciting incident goes here, as this is the source of the dilemma. The goal and first act turn will be here, or just after.

STORY BUILDUP

The next paragraph should focus on building up the story—adding a few essential details to deepen/broaden the reader's grasp of where things are going. This proves that you have more than a bare-bones concept. If the hero's goal was not revealed (or at least implied) in the first paragraph, it should be here. (Generally speaking, the same goes for your villain or other obstacle.)

Remember, the point at which your protagonist knows what he must do and sets out to do it (decision coupled with action)—your first act turn—should come about 25 percent of the way into the story itself. So it's going to look odd if it appears much later than that in the pitch.

COMPLICATIONS, STAKES, AND CLIMAX

The next paragraph (or several, depending on story and format), should delve into or strongly imply how the hero's challenge becomes greater or harder (complications), how the stakes go up (stakes) for the hero and perhaps others, and the nature of the final confrontation (the climax). Occasionally, this section will reveal the midpoint and/or (less frequently) the low point. The second act turn may also appear here, particularly if it serves to up the stakes and directly triggers the climax. The climax itself should appear in the final paragraph, and is sometimes coupled with the severest expression of the stakes. The resolution or outcome should (in my opinion) be absent.

CONTACT INFO

It doesn't do much good to get someone hot for a read, only to leave them wondering who to contact. So be sure to put your contact info (name, e-mail, and perhaps phone number) at the bottom of the page. Once that's done, your pitch sheet is complete.

SAMPLE PITCH SHEET

Here's an example of a completed pitch sheet I worked up for *Harry Potter and the Sorcerer's Stone*. (For a detailed explanation of exactly how the logline at the top of the pitch sheet was constructed, see the preceding chapter.) I chose to do this as an example because it's something just about everyone has seen—and something that, if you haven't seen it, is easy to find. Using an example with which you're already familiar allows you to see just exactly what was deemed important enough to include, and what was left out—something that would be impossible were I to use, say, the pitch sheet for an unproduced script. Keep in mind that the sheet below is about as long as a pitch sheet can reasonably be—so if yours runs longer than this, look for ways to trim or condense.

HARRY POTTER AND THE SORCERER'S STONE
(YA/adventure)

a screenplay by Steve Kloves
based on the novel by J. K. Rowling

An orphaned boy attends a school for wizards, where he must learn the ways of magic to defeat the evil wizard who killed his parents—and is now after him.

As a baby, Harry Potter was left on the doorstep of an aunt and uncle who never wanted him. Treated like a slave and forced to live in the cupboard under the stairs, he longs for a better life.

When Harry is ten, he starts getting letters, which his foster parents keep from him. That is, until a giant kicks down their door and delivers one in person—an invitation to the Hogwarts School of Witchcraft and Wizardry. Harry learns that his real parents were killed by an evil wizard, who also tried to kill him—and that his foster parents knew, but never told him. To protect himself and honor his parents, he must learn the ways of magic.

But Hogwarts has its own challenges: rival students, miscast spells, haunted passages, a homicidal instructor, a newborn dragon and a marauding troll among them. And there's something hidden on the grounds. Something Voldemort—the wizard who murdered Harry's parents—is desperate to find. The sorcerer's stone that will restore Voldemort's shattered strength, and render him immortal.

Together with newfound friends Ron and Hermione, Harry must find a way to keep the stone from Voldemort—and keep himself alive while hunted by a wizard no man has ever defeated.

[contact info here]

(For more examples of completed pitch sheets, visit http://makeyourstoryamovie.com/bookbonus.html.)

THINGS TO AVOID

Don't go over one page, and don't make that one page too dense. It should not be covered with text; rather, it should consist of a few light paragraphs and lots of white space. You want only the most essential, most important details here; crowding the page with secondary characters or plot twists will make your story seem overly complex, or your pitch unfocused. Either can be lethal.

Do not festoon the page with nonstandard fonts, which can be difficult to read and are almost certain to annoy those readers who bother to squint through it. Very few things scream *"AMATEUR!"* before the pitch is even read. This is one of them. You're here to sell the story, not the typeface.

Outside the curious world of pitch fests (where such things have come to be accepted), do not include graphics of any kind whatsoever. No images of what you think the movie poster should look like, no photos of yourself, your pets, car, house, pretty butterflies, etc.—all of which also scream *"AMATEUR!"* from a distance.

The one general exception to this last caveat would be a situation where the property being pitched is for some reason graphics-dependent or -based (illustrated children's book, graphic novel, and so on), or is based upon an already widely recognized property or brand (in which case it might get the reader excited even before he starts reading). And of course if the person you're submitting to actually asks for graphics, then by all means provide them. Also, if your agent or manager wants to add something, you might want to go along with that, as he or she presumably knows the tastes of the people being pitched.

PITCH SHEET AS WRITING GUIDE

The pitch sheet is more than just a selling tool; it can also be used as a guide while writing. Let's say you do your logline first, followed by your seven-point structure sheet. If you then move to the pitch sheet, you can refer to that while writing the story, to help keep things on track. You can also use a pitch sheet to help determine the overall direction of the story—the broad strokes—before filling in the nitty-gritty details with the story map itself.

CHAPTER 27
HOW SCRIPTS GET SOLD

A Peek Behind the Curtain

Most people want money now and to a large extent, a few hundred grand to a million in the hand is worth the more than the uncertain prospect of a greater amount later. This is particularly true of your first deal, where the goal is often to amass enough cash to quit the day job and write (or whatever it is you want to do) full-time with no one switching off the lights or repossessing the car. There are no guarantees of any kind in Hollywood. Still, if you want cash now, nothing beats . . .

GOING FOR THE SALE

So. Your rep (agent or manager) goes out the door looking for a sale. That means approaching the studios. But—as mentioned elsewhere—you don't approach the studios directly. In order to give your project the best possible chance of acceptance there, what you do instead is send the script out to a number of different production companies you feel might be right for the project. When choosing these companies, you (or, more likely, your rep, whose job it is to keep track of all this) also take into account which studios they're tight with. This is important because, if all goes well,

you're going to wind up with several different production companies wanting to make your movie, and (for reasons explained below) if they're all working with the same studio, that's a problem.

In almost all cases, making your movie is going to take a lot
more money than the production company can get its hands on—
and so they'll want to take your script in to whatever studio they're
cozy with and ask the studio to buy it for them (in which case the
production company will be involved in, and profit from, any
movie that eventually gets made).

Because your goal is to get paid the highest amount possible,
your aim is to incite a bidding war among the studios. For this to
become a possibility, you need to have several different prodcos
(production companies) taking the script in to several different studios, all at the same time. You don't want to piss anyone off, so you
generally approach your first-choice production companies first
(meaning the ones you want to take the script into each of the studios), and work your way down the list if any of those aren't interested. Ideally, you wind up with one prodco willing to take your
project into each of the different studios. If Prodco A has a great
relationship with Studio B, then they're the ones who take it in.
And so on. In some cases, you might authorize a single company to
take the script in to several studios, either because they have several
great relationships—or because you're running short on interested
prodcos.

Once you have these companies lined up, you give them permission to go to the studios, where they say, basically, "We think
this is a movie, we want it to be our movie, and we'd like you to
buy it for us because we'll both make tons of money." The theory
being that the studio is more likely to say yes to the prodco (which
has probably enriched the studio with a tidy sum of money on past
projects) than it is to say yes to some random agent or manager who
wants to sell a script to enrich himself and his client with a tidy sum
of money. Which may not make a lot of sense, but does go a long
way toward explaining why you can't just drive into Hollywood,

bang on the studio head's door, and expect to sell a script all by yourself.

When everything goes astonishingly well, two or more studios get interested and bid against each other for the script—or one studio becomes so convinced of this possibility that it makes a large, million-dollar-plus "preemptive" offer to induce you to sell the script to them before any other offers come in. Such offers sometimes come at close of business on Friday, with a one-hour deadline, because the studio knows you are unlikely to be able to get hold of anyone at another studio who is authorized to top their offer until Monday. (You might want to keep your cell phone handy.)

When things go reasonably well, you get one offer—usually for several hundred thousand dollars, against several hundred thousand more. "I've sold six scripts that I've written on spec," says *Transformers* (GAM) screenwriter Ehren Kruger, "and not once did I have multiple financiers wanting to buy the script. It was always one place making an offer, and fourteen other places saying, 'No, it's not good enough,' or 'It's not right for us,' 'Not interested,' or what-have-you.

"You can look at that and say, 'Wow, one out of fifteen places thought my script was worth investing in; that's pretty bad.' Or you can be realistic about the business and say, 'One is all I need.'"

The above explanation of the selling process is (believe it or not) somewhat simplified, and there are nuances of timing and "early looks" not covered here—but you get the idea. Given a great script and a good team, you can go from first approach to done deal in a week or two, sometimes faster (and sometimes slower).

SCREENPLAY RELOADED: THE PACKAGE DEAL

If Fate rings up "No Sale," all is not lost. You might be offered an option—which is, in some cases, decent money (and in some cases not); either way, it has the potential to pay off big later. Simply put, an option allows someone (usually a producer or production company) to tie up the rights to your property while they try to put a deal together and find a buyer. (For more on options, see Chapter 31.) If, for example, a production company wants to make your project, but can't get their favorite studio to bite, they might option it and then seek to "package" it or secure independent financing (covered below).

Another thing you can do is retreat, regroup—and look to "package" the script yourself with one or more "elements" (stars, directors, powerful producers) to make it more attractive to prospective buyers. The logic here being that, while your script may not land a buyer, your script starring George Clooney directed by Ridley Scott most likely will. Hell, either one alone would probably do the trick. And so you set about trying to "attach" (meaning secure a commitment from) a "bankable" element (or several). Technically, you don't do this yourself; your agent or manager or producer (or some combination thereof) does it for you.

Packaging is where the larger agencies really shine, in large part because they have such massive collections of talented clients—and attaching some big names to your script means big commissions for them if the project gets made. Suddenly this screenplay that might have brought them 10 percent of a million dollars might now bring them a percentage of 10, 20, 30 million or more.

Of course, your project has to be something that stands a good chance of interesting these people in the first place—but if it is, and the big agency packaging apparatus swings into motion, the sale of your script (which, ironically, quickly becomes the least significant part of the financial equation) can turn into a foregone conclusion. Now, that doesn't always happen—but it does happen, and each new year brings with it several sales of packaged scripts that failed to sell the year (or two) before.

It may seem more than a little strange that a process which skyrockets the price of acquiring the project makes it more likely to sell, particularly when it was already turned down at a lower price—but look at it from the buyer's perspective: instead of a script that may or may not interest bankable elements (who will need to be talked into doing the project) at some point down the line (which could be years), you're now looking at a project where someone else has done the legwork for you, you know exactly who's going to be involved, you know (or hope) that their involvement comes closer to guaranteeing a profitable venture, you know for a fact the financing will be easier, the film already looks marketable because of the "names" involved, and you won't look stupid for recommending it to your boss.

Basically, the project appears to have momentum before the race has even started; this thing is going to hit the ground running. Which means it stands a better chance of getting "greenlighted" (authorized for production). Which, in turn, means your status as an executive is going to go up because you're the genius who said, "Gee, if Huge Star A and Giant Director B really want to do this, maybe that's not such a bad idea."

And so, although this increases the financial risk to the buyer (probably more money paid for your script, and definitely gobs more money paid to the other elements once things get rolling), they actually perceive the overall risk as having been lowered because they now think the project will get made and be successful. And if everything goes wrong (the script is rewritten into mediocrity, the star bails, the director's over budget, the film is worse than *Plan 9 from Outer Space,* and even the DVD sales are flatlined), the guys who recommended and bought it are less likely to be fired—because how could they have known, when everything looked so right? Whereas buying an original script from a total unknown is (or appears to be) a more uncertain venture.

Buyers—studios in particular—are all about risk avoidance. The lower their perceived risk, the higher your chances of a sale. Sometimes a great script alone is enough—and sometimes it isn't.

For obvious reasons, packaging is a longer process than going for the sale right out of the gate. Just as there's no guarantee that any given script will sell on its own merits, there's also no guarantee that bankable elements will attach themselves to any given script. And so most folks tend to go for the sale first, and then try to package if that doesn't work. Sometimes, though, the stars align and an agency moves to package something right out of the box. When successful, the results can be impressive.

Evan Daugherty's script *Snow White and the Huntsman* was packaged the first time it went out. Evan's agent and manager showed the script to powerhouse producer Joe Roth, because Roth had produced the recent megahit *Alice in Wonderland* (NOVs), one of very few films to have grossed over $1 billion at the box office. Roth liked the script and attached Rupert Sanders, a director of commercials who'd thus far turned down every script he'd been offered to direct, which of course only made the studios more eager to work with him. As it turned out, he liked the *Snow White* script, and provided a number of notes which Daugherty then implemented.

"There was a huge team of reps working together on this," says Daugherty. "My agent and manager, Joe Roth's agents, Rupert Sanders's agents. And then all the execs at the studios. Everybody negotiating. All of these elements coming together help to explain the way the script sold, and how much it sold for [$3.2 million]. And of course I like to think it being a pretty good script had something to do with it."

CHAPTER 28
THE SELLERS

Agents, Managers, and (Sometimes) Producers

So, you have something you want to sell, and you need someone to help you sell it. Congratulations! Now take a number. Really. Hollywood "reps" (meaning agents and managers) are notoriously hard to land. In fact, if getting a good book agent is the equivalent of scaling Mount Everest, then finding a good manager is something akin to, say, a journey to the moon—and landing an agent more like a mission to Mars.*

Before we even get into the nitty-gritty of finding a rep, though, you may be wondering about a more fundamental question. . . .

WHO NEEDS A REP?
No one—and everyone. Here's the thing: it *is* possible to sell something without a rep. It has been done. But here's the other thing: unless you turn out to be the occasional freakish exception you've probably read about (the fact that it's freakishly rare is, in fact, why

---

*Then again, there are exceptions. See the Bonus Chapter, How I Got an Agent in 48 Hours, Over the Christmas Holiday, Without Asking to Be Represented.

you've read about it), choosing to rep yourself will make every step of the journey harder, longer—and less likely to succeed.

Christopher Lockhart is executive story editor at WME. Before that, he ran the story department and oversaw the agent trainee program at ICM, another superagency. When asked about the chances of making it in Hollywood without a good rep, his answer is direct: "I don't think there's any possibility at all—not in the world of studio films."

You've probably asked yourself, as everyone does when they first get into this, why you should pay an agent or manager (or both) 10 percent. What you should be asking, instead, is why everyone else who's succeeded in the business is willing to pay that 10 percent. And why even those aforementioned freakish exceptions who sold their first project alone, now have reps. There must be a reason. Actually, there are several. Most of this goes for book agents as well.

First off, unless you or your work are in some way famous already, the people you're trying to reach have never heard of you. To them, you're just another one of the tens of thousands of unknown writers whose mostly terrible scripts barrage Hollywood on a daily basis. Many, perhaps even most companies won't even look at material from people they don't already know or haven't already heard of (in a good way), unless the material has been personally referred by someone they do know. So, right there, you've cut your chances of finding a buyer in half at best.

Secondly, those who are willing to look at such material are not in any hurry to do so. There are plenty of projects from more important people to look at, and those get first priority. Your script may be read a week, a month, or six months from now; in short, whenever they get around to it.

Third, when it does get read, it's going to be read by the newest assistant or the greenest reader, because there's no particular importance attached to it. Also because, frankly, the chances of finding a real gem among the mountains of turds that people send in are, to say the least, remote. After all (the thinking goes), if you were any good, you'd have a rep.

Finally, if all goes fabulously well and an offer is made, it's likely to be a lowball offer and a less-than-ideal contract because you might be so thrilled by any offer at all that you'll quickly accept, well . . . any offer at all.

"Contracts give me a headache, even to look at," says *Dark Fields/Limitless* author Alan Glynn. "I was so happy to get that first deal with a publisher that I would have accepted any terms at all. I did read it and understood what I was signing, but I didn't have anything to compare it with and was in no real position to question any of the details. I suppose I have been very lucky. My agent, Antony Harwood, who now runs his own agency, negotiated the contract with the publisher. They went back and forth on the details, and then when he was satisfied he presented it to me as a good contract. So technically, I guess it wasn't the first contract they sent out, but it was the first one I saw."

Others have been less fortunate. *Q&A/Slumdog Millionaire* author Vikas Swarup cautions those new to the industry. "In some cases, writers have signed away everything, you know? Once they sign a film contract or a book contract. And in fact, there is a case I know of where the writer had signed away everything to the film people, in return for a one-time, lump sum fee. And later on, that movie became a mega, megahit and the writer said, 'But, you know, you're not giving me due credit.' And the filmmaker said, 'Get lost. We told you we would give you some money, we gave you some money, now you have no business even questioning us.' They did put his name on it, but he was more or less sandwiched in between the makeup man and the transport coordinator, that kind of thing." And while this is an extreme example that took place outside the United States, the lesson is clear. (To find out how to keep this sort of thing from happening to you, see Chapters 31 and 32.)

If things go poorly and everyone passes (not getting back to you is also a pass), your name and your project's name get entered in the company computer as a pass, along with whatever uncomplimentary comments the reader who passed might have made. Should you approach that company again at some point in the future, perhaps with a revised version of the same project—they'll find you right there in the computer, see that they've already passed on this, and more than likely refuse to read it again. Placing you in an even worse position than you were the first time around (if you can imagine that). This also creates a hurdle for any future rep going out with a revision, because now the work is "tainted." (Should you find yourself in such a situation, be sure to inform your rep, so he can adjust his approach accordingly.)

Contrast all of this with what happens when a rep approaches the same companies with the same script. First off, the rep is someone known to the buyers. If he's a good rep, he's known for bringing in good material. He's a filter, sifting out all the garbage and bringing them only the best. Furthermore, he knows what they're looking for, so the material is likely to be genre-appropriate for the company's needs. So right off the bat, more companies are going to look at it, and the interest level is higher going in. The rep is going to pitch your project like it's the Next Big Thing. That's his job, and practice makes perfect.

Secondly, everyone knows that this rep is or soon will be showing the same property to half a dozen or more other companies. That creates urgency. If this script turns out to be hot—and the chances of this are far greater if it's already convinced the rep to go out with it in the first place—no one can afford to let it sit around unread, because everyone knows the competition will be reading it quickly. Which means they have to read it quickly, too, or lose their spot at the table if the game heats up.

Third, it's not going to get read by the new kid in the office; rather, it's going to get read by the story editor, director of development, etc., or by their most trusted assistant (and then the exec, if it gets a good report).

Finally, if an offer is made, the company isn't going to lowball the rep or send out a contract they know he won't accept. They will, for the most part, dispense with the bullshit. They also know that the second they make an offer, the rep is going to tell the competition about it, in hopes of creating even more urgency and drawing even higher offers. If successful, this can lead to a bidding war. Knowing this, the first company might well make a high "preemptive" offer to take the property off the table at the start and avoid the potentially higher cost of a bidding situation. (These two scenarios—bidding wars and preemptive offers—are responsible for the staggering, multimillion-dollar sums paid for scripts like *Déjà Vu* ($5 million) and *Snow White and the Huntsman* ($3.2 million, MLF).)

The rep and/or an entertainment attorney (who may be suggested by the rep) can then negotiate the deal with an experienced eye and make sure it's a good one.

If by any chance you've now concluded you may want a rep, read on. . . .

GETTING NOTICED

There are three bazillion other people vying for the same reps you are, which is bad. On the other hand, well over 99 percent of them are peddling properties that (in their current form) have zero chance of drawing a rep's interest or of selling. Which is not so bad—for you, anyway. Still, these people can clog up the works in much the same way that looky-loos stop traffic for miles as they slow down to gawk out the window at an accident on the freeway.

You need a way to bypass the mess and get noticed—like a monster truck rolling over the top of all those stopped cars on the freeway. The only guaranteed way to do that is to have a great— and I mean great—property to sell, preferably a screenplay. Greatness is so indescribably rare that it commands attention. Selling something on your own, if you can manage it, also draws attention (but see above for the pitfalls of this approach).

Still, someone has to look at the thing to realize it's great. Which means arming yourself with an awesome logline and pitch sheet, as well as a fabulous (and fabulously-told) story. This works for nonfiction as well as fiction. (For a detailed account of how I landed the agent who sold this book, see the Bonus Chapter, How I Got an Agent in 48 Hours, Over the Christmas Holiday, Without Asking to Be Represented.)

AGENTS VS. MANAGERS

The typical wisdom holds that managers are more interested in the long-haul and the overall career-spanning potential of any given client, while agents are there for the quick kill: if you have something they think they can sell, right now, today—then they're interested. Managers may (and may not) be interested in signing someone whose work is almost but not quite all-the-way there; agents generally are not.

A good blind query *might* wind up getting you a manager, whereas many agents require a referral from a current client or someone else whose opinion they trust to even read your material. (A referral never hurts with a manager, either.) Often, that "someone else" is a producer who's optioned something he's trying to sell.

Just the same, the best referral in the world does no good at all if the material itself doesn't deliver, and those who spend all their time trying to make connections, trying to get closer in some way to the people they want to know, have got things exactly backward. Rather, the focus should be on creating great material—which will cause those people to want to know *you*.

"Agents do not come in six packs," notes screenwriter Terry Rossio. "A good manager is better than a bad agent. What matters is building a team, finding that person who is competent and is truly on your side. That can be an agent, manager, or producer; that can be a studio executive, that can turn out to be a production assistant who eventually goes on to run a studio. Individuals matter, not titles."

AGENTS

If you've ever watched the *Entourage* TV series (and if you haven't, you should), keep in mind that Ari Gold's character is based on a real-life agent—perhaps the most successful in the business. And while not all agents are like this, Ari Gold's character embodies most if not all of the qualities generally associated with agents, and one that isn't—a soft side. (For a quick dose of Ari, search "Ari Gold's Best" on YouTube.)

Most agents work for agencies, which may employ several (or several hundred) agents. The internal workings of agencies are far too complex to detail here, but there are some important things you should know. First off: the bigger the agency, the greater their clout. Giants like WME and CAA have so many clients that they can provide what is essentially one-stop shopping when packaging projects: writer, director, major actors, and so on. Unfortunately, these same factors mean that a new or smaller client is more likely to get lost at a big agency, because there are so many other, more established clients to serve. It can also mean the agency prefers to attach their own clients to your project (because their fees are commissionable), rather than other people who might be better for the project (but whose commissions go to other agencies).

A smaller agency may well give you a higher priority, because you're more important to their bottom line. On the other hand, they may not be able to do as much for you, or do it as quickly, as a big agency. On the third hand, you could be their big break, or (potentially) biggest moneymaker—so they may work much harder to push you than a bigger agency will, which may increase the likelihood that your work will sell, or that (if you're a writer) you will be hired to write other projects.

Either way, big or small, the first step is up to you because, as Terry Rossio notes, "Really it's only after you get something to happen, that's when the agents start to circle."

Says Christopher Lockart: "I think that you have to look at where you are in the world, and find a place that is commensurate with that. If you win the Nicholl competition, that may not necessarily mean you belong at WME or CAA—but maybe you don't have to go to the ABC Talent Agency either. Perhaps you can go into a place like Gersh, or Innovative, or UTA. Be realistic.

"Some say it's more about the agent than the agency, and I don't disagree with that—but the big agencies can package projects. Agencies like WME, CAA, ICM. They have the talent that can attach to a project and get it financed and greenlit. That's an important qualification. They also have access to all of the information—the available jobs in town—and they have a team of people who pursue those jobs for them. That's why the big agencies' writers land the most work."

Another difference between big and small agencies is this: at the smaller agency, one agent may be able to sign you because he believes in you, regardless of whether others agree or disagree. At the larger agencies, it doesn't work that way.

"New writers don't understand why agents don't want to represent them," explains Lockhart. "They question why an agent won't take a chance on a new writer. They think, 'What's the big deal?' The big deal is that agents have very high overhead. They also have bosses. And the boss looks at the client list and says, 'How many of these clients are making money? Because for every client you have, we spend x amount of dollars trying to promote that client—and if the client isn't making any money, then we're wasting our investment.'

"Again, it's a business. Most agents can't just sign anyone they want. Agencies have signing meetings, where agents have to get into a room with all of their colleagues and say, 'I want to sign Joe Screenwriter.' And the colleagues in that room are going to ask that agent, 'Who the hell is Joe Screenwriter?' And the agent had better have a good answer. So agents look for writers with some sort of heat. They won the Nicholl competition, they wrote a script for a hot movie at a film festival—whatever it is, there's some heat. Now the agent can justify adding that writer to his client list.

"Because you know what happens? When it comes time for the agent's contract to be renewed, the agency says. 'Okay, you cost us $250,000 last year, and your client list brought in $85,000.' Then, when they renegotiate the contract, the agent is making half what he did before—or they don't renew the contract at all; they let him go. And so that's why agents aren't so quick to sign people. An agent has to be really passionate about a script and a writer to sell. And that's not easy to get. Most scripts simply don't inspire that sort of passion in others."

MANAGERS

Unlike agents, who are licensed by the state, limited to commissions of no more than 10 percent, and legally prohibited from being producers on client projects—managers require no state license, are not limited to 10 percent, and may produce. And while there are many excellent managers and manager/producers, there are also a lot of bozos, simply because any idiot can call himself a manager, and many do. (Which is not to say that agents can't be bozos as well.)

THE GOOD, THE BAD, AND THE UGLY

"For new writers," says Lockhart, "I think that finding a manager is a great way to go. They're a different breed, and they tend to be hungrier. They're more open to new talent, and there are more benefits for managers because they can attach as producers. So from the manager's perspective, there's the possibility of making more than a straight 10 percent. Agents can't do that because they can't attach as producers."

The amount of the commission isn't usually a problem; with perhaps a handful of exceptions by very specialized managers, anyone who charges more than 10 percent is likely to price himself out of the market in short order. The manager/producer, on the other hand, can be a good thing—or a bad one. A lot depends on whether the guy knows what he's doing.

Most if not all of the best managers in the business are now manager/producers, for the quite simple reason that it's more profitable to produce than to manage. Why manage at all, then? Because if they didn't represent the client and the project from the start, they couldn't attach themselves as producers. From the manager/producer's perspective, this can (given the right clients and properties) be a very sweet deal.

For the writer, it means a manager who's likely working even harder to get projects made (because there's more in it for him), and—sometimes—a kickback on the management fee: because the rep is making so much as a producer, he'll sometimes decline to accept (or later refund) the 10 percent management fee. Leaving the writer 10 percent richer on any given deal.

The downside is that a manager/producer who doesn't know what he's doing, or doesn't have the client's best interests in mind, can scare off buyers by demanding a fee that's too high or a credit the buyer will not agree to (because, for example, other, bigger producers don't want to share their credits with a manager)—or by just being an asshole no one wants to deal with. (The latter tend to get fired from companies owned by others, but when they're the ones running the company, it's a different story.)

The other danger is the clueless manager, who means well but either doesn't quite know what he's doing, or lacks the connections to get your material seriously considered. You want someone professional and well connected (first choice)—or professional and able to forge the connections needed to get your project seen by the right people (second choice).

Making the wrong choice can have consequences even after the relationship has ended. I once found myself in a situation where, years after having parted ways with a particular manager/producer, I went out through another manager with a revised version of a script the former manager had at one time represented. Much to my surprise, I received an e-mail from him saying that as far as he was concerned, he was attached to that script and, furthermore, he'd make the town aware of that fact at the appropriate time. Meaning, essentially, that (in his mind, at least) any prospective buyer was going to have to bring him on as a producer, and pay him a producer fee.

The effect of such a stunt, were he to go through with it, would be to render the project both problematical (if the buyer doesn't want him involved) and potentially more expensive (because of his fee) to purchase. And while the first issue can often be dealt with by paying a fee to make an unwanted producer go away, the second would remain—and possibly reduce any purchase price as well, in order to pay the unwanted producer. Worst case, the buyer might simply lose interest.

Fortunately, we had a written management agreement into which I had inserted a clause explicitly stating that he would have no involvement with or claim on any property sold after the management agreement terminated, unless it was a deal he had initiated during the term of the agreement. Apparently, he'd forgotten about that.

Looking into these kinds of situations at the time, I learned that the Writers Guild will sometimes represent nonmembers seeking to fend off clingy managers, because the practice is something the Guild wishes to discourage. At the time, no manager had ever prevailed against the Guild in such a case, and frankly, no manager is likely to. Still, it's a hassle you don't want to go through, and a complication you don't want impairing your ability to close a deal.

And speaking of closing deals, managers cannot (technically speaking) do this for you. As Lockhart notes, "Managers cannot negotiate; it's forbidden by law. So you could have a manager and a lawyer, and have both angles covered because lawyers can negotiate. You can have an agent and a manager—or all three." (For more on lawyers, see Chapters 31 and 32.)

A FINAL NOTE ON AGENTS AND MANAGERS

Neither is a substitute for a good entertainment attorney, and even those who are also attorneys have a split focus. When it comes down to negotiating the actual terms of the contract, you want and need a full-time entertainment attorney. Not only do they know the territory better than any agent or manager, they're also there to see that you get what you want (within reason). An agent, or a manager who is also an attorney (and can therefore negotiate), may have little or no interest in securing terms that do not affect their commission—but that may nonetheless be important to you.

Attorney Cathleen Blackburn encounters issues like this in her work for the estate of *Lord of the Rings* author J. R. R. Tolkien. "The Estate," she notes, "is a complicated business to administer as there is widespread commercial interest in its rights and an ever greater need to protect those rights from forms of exploitation which do not accord Tolkien's works appropriate respect. A literary estate will usually put respect before commercial concerns, but would-be exploiters of rights often do not understand this and believe that all one has to do is offer the right price."

(For more on contracts and attorneys, see Chapters 31 and 32.)

PRODUCERS

Producers and production companies can also put a deal together, by developing and/or taking a project to people and companies they know who might be interested in making the movie. (For more on this, see Chapter 31.) Occasionally, they'll even buy the project themselves, but this is rare—as even those few who can afford this, generally prefer to have someone else foot the bill. As with agents and managers, there are Big Producers, small producers, and everything in between.

Producer Marc Turtletaub (who himself received the script from two other producers, Ron Yerxa and Albert Berger) paid first-time screenwriter Michael Arndt $250,000 for the decidedly independent-minded *Little Miss Sunshine,* got it into development with Focus Features (which fired Arndt as writer, then rehired him after the head of the company was himself replaced), paid $400,000 to buy it back from Focus when they dropped it two years later, then came up with the $8 million budget needed to shoot the film. That's a full-service producer.

The movie was shot in thirty days, and post-production was completed just four days before the Sundance Film Festival, where the film triggered a bidding war and sold to Fox Searchlight for $10.5 million plus 10 percent of the gross—a Sundance record. Reviled by many critics (whose opinions, in the end, cannot make or break a movie), it went on to top $100 million at the box office, and won two of the four Academy Awards for which it was nominated. (Best Original Screenplay and Best Supporting Actor; it was also up for Best Picture and Best Supporting Actress.)

Producer Julie Richardson found *Collateral* writer Stuart Beattie while he was waiting tables, worked with him to develop the story, and brought the script to writer-producer Frank Darabont, who (with his producing partners Rob Fried and Chuck Russell) was looking for low-budget projects he could pitch to HBO. The network passed, but when Beattie mentioned the script in a meeting at DreamWorks, studio exec Marc Haimes read the script overnight and made an offer the following day. The film, starring Tom Cruise and Jamie Foxx, grossed over $200 million worldwide. It was Julie's first producing credit—and Stuart's first sale.

When you can't get an agency or a manager behind you, it may still be possible to ally yourself with an independent producer who believes in your project. He (or she) is most likely to option your project for little or nothing, perhaps do some development (probably with the original writer), and then try to interest others (actors, directors, other producers, financiers, execs—even agents and managers) in climbing on board.

There are scads of small producers and wannabe-producers out there, often with no company behind them. And while it's true that many of them will never amount to much in a professional sense, it's also true that some of them will—and that just about every household-name producer started out this way. Back in the 1990s, for example, there was a small production company whose head would ask people not to fax him after a certain hour, because the fax machine was in his mother's room, and she went to bed early. That company is now a mini-major studio whose films rake in hundreds of millions. In Hollywood, all things are possible.

Hungry producers are looking to make a name for themselves, and can be willing to take chances on things that larger, more established producers (or agents or managers) consider too risky or too small to warrant their attention. The little guy doesn't have everyone on the planet bringing projects to him and, indeed, may become more invested in yours because he doesn't have a zillion other things from which to choose. Your project, which more established pros might pass up, could be his best shot.

And so, in the absence of other options, the producer could be your best shot. And though it may take him longer to put a deal together (if it can be done at all), the right producer, with the right project, at the right time—can be solid gold. In fact, when it comes to the particular project they're interested in, a persistent and talented producer can be better than an agent or manager (or both) who gives up after the first round if no prospective buyer shows up.

A good producer is like a pit bull on a raw steak; once they get their teeth into something they like, it takes a crowbar to pry them loose.

CONNECTING

When trying to reach these people, remember to explore any existing connection you may have, however tenuous it may be. Michael Douglas bought *Romancing the Stone* from his waitress, Diane Thomas. *Erin Brockovich* became a movie because chiropractor and bodywork (on people, not cars) specialist Pamela DuMond (more recently author of the novel *Cupcakes, Lies, and Dead Guys*) heard the story from one client (Erin Brockovich) and told it to another (producer Carla Shamberg). A different screenwriter of my acquaintance landed the manager who sold his first script (and several more soon after) when a friend whose mother lived next to the manager asked his mother to show the script to her neighbor.

I once found myself pitching a studio head because the born-again client I was working with on a true story/nonfiction book adaptation had changed the life of a hard-core biker related to the exec. Such stories are legion, and every one is different.

There are also a great many failures, which no one reads about. You can't make a pest of yourself, and you can't expect someone to pass along something that isn't very good or simply isn't appropriate for the intended recipient—because by doing that, they burn their own connection. People who find good material are valued; those who find bad material—or who don't know the difference—are not. Referrals from the former, and even from friends (and sometimes acquaintances) whose acumen is not yet known, do get attention.

Finally, "the most idiotic approach will work if the writing is genius," counsels screenwriter Terry Rossio, whose films have earned billions. "The best approach in the world won't work if the writing is mediocre. The biggest mistake a writer can make regarding their approach is to worry about their approach. Win the game by having better content than anyone else, and the whole approach issue goes away."

CHAPTER 29
THE BUYERS

Studios and Production Companies

Two types of purchasers account for the vast majority of screenplay purchases: studios and production companies. The reason is simple: this is, for the most part, where the money is. And so, it's also where your (or your rep's) selling efforts will be concentrated. Let's take a closer look. . . .

THE STUDIOS

These are the Big Guys with familiar names. When you read about a jaw-dropping seven-figure spec sale, chances are, the buyer was a studio. The six "major" studios are Warner Brothers Pictures, Paramount Pictures, 20th Century Fox, Walt Disney Pictures/Touchstone Pictures, Columbia Pictures/TriStar Pictures, and Universal Pictures. They've been around since the dawn of time, and occupy Los Angeles—area properties of staggering size.

Each studio has multiple divisions, defined by the kinds of pictures they make or, in some cases, distribute (when the films were made by others). Castle Rock Entertainment, HBO Films, New Line Cinema, Turner Entertainment and Warner Brothers Animation, for example, are all owned by Warner Brothers.

Each studio itself is ultimately owned by an even larger company: Warner by Time Warner; Paramount by Viacom; Fox by News Corporation; Disney/Touchstone by The Walt Disney Company; Columbia/TriStar by Sony Corporation of America; Universal by Comcast/General Electric.

Next come the so-called "mini-majors" which are (with the exception of MGM, once an old-school major) relative newcomers founded between 1991 and 2007. These include Summit Entertainment, Lionsgate (which bought Summit in early 2012), The Weinstein Company, MGM, DreamWorks, and CBS Films. (For an updated list of studios, their divisions and corporate ownership, visit http://makeyourstoryamovie.com/bookbonus.html.)

The landscape is shifting, with companies merging, buying each other, cutting distribution deals with other companies, and so on. It's your agent's/manager's/attorney's job to keep track of all this, but the distinctions are important to you for several reasons. One of these is that you don't (generally speaking) just take a project into "Warner Brothers" because (for the most part) they wouldn't know what to do with it. Instead, you must first figure out which subdivision of the studio is most likely to be interested in whatever it is you have to offer—and then you don't approach them. (That's not a typo; you have someone else approach them, as explained in Chapter 27.)

Another reason these distinctions are important is because, when you option something, the amount of the bonuses you receive is often dependent upon the "major" or "mini-major" status of the studio you're dealing with, on the theory that the minis can't afford to pay what the majors can. The contract will actually spell out the differing amounts, because at the time of the option, it's not yet known who the eventual buyer may be.

A third reason is this: the majors are publicly held companies, beholden to their stockholders. If what you have to sell looks like a surefire moneymaker, your project may well find a home there. If it's more a labor of love that you want to see made simply because it *should* be made (as, indeed, some pictures should) regardless of whether or not it hauls in a pile of cash—or if you're looking for an Oscar—you're more likely to find a home at one of the mini-majors or at an independent production company (though an "indie" division of a major is still a possibility). Make no mistake: these companies are also looking for surefire moneymakers. But they're also more willing to take a chance on something unconventional.

In Hollywoodspeak, studios are sometimes referred to as "territories." Be warned: these are not territories you want to enter alone and unarmed. As a seller, you do not (in most cases) approach the studios directly, even when you know which division—and executive—you're aiming for. This is because when a studio turns down or "passes" on a project, that decision is usually final and unappealable. And so, what you do instead is approach . . .

PRODUCTION COMPANIES

Production companies do what studios do, on a (mostly) smaller scale: acquire properties, assemble creative teams, secure financing and get movies made, marketed, and distributed. Sometimes, they rely on studios or agencies to fulfill some of these functions. Production companies may be owned by producers, actors, directors, financiers, even studios.

The films they make or distribute reflect the sometimes very particular tastes of their owners. James Cameron's Lightstorm Entertainment (*Avatar*, *Titanic*, HIS; *True Lies*, MOV; *Terminator 2: Judgment Day*) is not going to be interested in the same kind of material that might attract, say, Focus Features (*Traffic*, TVS; *Lost in Translation, Eternal Sunshine of the Spotless Mind, Brokeback Mountain*, STO).

Producer-run production companies are looking for films to produce. Actor- and director-run companies may be looking to produce only projects that their principals (owners) can act in or direct—or they may cast a broader net and look for things where they might produce alone, without acting or directing.

Once again, it's your rep's job to know who's-looking-for-what—though it never hurts to keep yourself informed by, for example, taking note of the opening credits on films that seem to be in the same ballpark as the project or projects you'd like to see on the screen.

Some production companies have "first look" deals with studios, in which the studio provides office space and pays the company's overhead (or some of it) in exchange for getting a first look at any project the company wants to pursue. A small subset of these prodcos-with-studio-deals are also provided with "discretionary funds" they can use to option or (in some cases) buy material. But even companies without studio deals of any kind often maintain close relationships with studios and the executives who work there.

Production companies also cultivate relationships with financiers, which allows them to raise part or all of a project's financing outside the studio system. Raising part of the amount makes a studio more likely to come up with the rest (because the risk is lower), while coming up with all of it frees the company to make the movie they want to make, with the people they want to work with, free of studio influence, demands, and ultimatums.

It also means keeping a bigger piece of the pie should the film prove successful, because now the studio will be acting as a distributor only (where the opportunities for creative accounting are fewer), or buying the completed film outright (and perhaps agreeing to split a percentage of the gross, which is impossible to conceal). Larger films with substantial budgets are less likely to be sold than offered for distribution, while smaller films can go either way.

That bigger piece of the pie may or may not translate to you. Generally speaking, prodcos that team with studios from the start pay studio-level prices up front or on commencement—meaning you get a pile of money on signing the deal, and/or another pile on the commencement of principal photography. This happens because the studio (and not the prodco) is footing your bill.

Production companies that fly solo may offer a sweeter deal on the back end, after the film is released (studios typically offer you "net points" on the back end, which translates to "zero")—but far less on the front. Thus, if the film is successful and the accounting honest (or the contract good), your payday could be quite a bit bigger overall. On the other hand, if the film flops, you could do quite a bit worse—and if it's never made at all, you could wind up with nothing.

Which is one reason it's good to have the people on your team working for a percentage: if you lose, they lose—so they're usually very motivated to seek out the best possible deal. Call it enlightened self-interest.

A NOTE ON SELLING

Keep in mind that most of the above describes the process of selling to studios. As mentioned, production companies can also be buyers, and for them, everything revolves around the financing. For more on this, see the "Financing" section of Chapter 30.

CHAPTER 30
TIMING, BUDGETS, FINANCING, AND MARKETS

Most writers give little thought to any of this, but a basic understanding of how these things can work for—and against—you, is essential. What follows is a quick guide to the essentials.

TIMING

As mentioned earlier, success in Hollywood is a combination of three things: talent, access, and timing—which most often translate as writing ability, reps (agent, manager, sometimes producer) and, well, timing. Of the three, you have the least control over the last. If there is indeed an element of chance, of blind luck (good or bad) or a Hand of Fate involved in the whole process, this would be it. Let's take a look. . . .

At the most basic level, you have to approach people at a time that's right for them. If Peter Jackson is shooting a *Hobbit* movie in New Zealand, he's not going to be reading your script at the same time, though it's possible someone else at his company might. If Jerry Bruckheimer has already done two time-travel movies, he might not (as I recently found out when shopping mine) want to do a third, no matter how good the script is—whereas several years back (when *Déjà Vu* sold), they were actively looking.

Fortunes can turn on a dime. Perhaps you want to do a biopic about a deceased first lady, but a hot director had his favorite studio buy a similar script about the same first lady for him, because he's married to an actress who wants to play the lead. This seems likely to doom your script—until the divorce, after which the director loses interest in the project, but doesn't want his now ex-wife to have it. The studio doesn't want to piss him off, so they hang on to it, but don't make it. The whole thing is stalled, and possibly dead— which is bad news for others but good news for you, because your similar project may now get a second chance, assuming you or "your people" are informed enough to know what's going on and make your move. (And, no, I didn't make that up.)

Sometimes, world events can derail your project; immediately after 9/11, interest in screenplays featuring terrorists flatlined for quite a while, and even completed movies had key scenes reworked or release dates delayed, or both. Book authors, too, took a hit from this. As Walter Kirn recalls: "*Up in the Air* was published in July of 2001, had a front-page review in *The New York Times* Sunday Book Review, was as they say climbing the lists, and was poised to be my first bestseller. And then 9/11 happened. Unfortunately, the book's cover art showed businessmen flying around with briefcases, and one of them crashing into the ground in flames.

"The whole country suddenly became preoccupied with completely different things and totally averse to the setting of the book. The novel's tone of dark precise irony and rueful alienation didn't seem possible to stage in airports anymore. Even for people who were reading it in the comfort of their own homes, images of airplanes and airports being infernos and places of incredible mortal vulnerability wouldn't shake.

"Fox had just bought the rights, maybe a week before, and I was working on the screenplay. Within a few weeks after, I got the very strong impression from the studio that this was a movie that couldn't and wouldn't be made." The project drifted in limbo for years—which, ironically, led to completely different people becoming involved, and the making of a fabulous movie.

Current events can also make your project suddenly hot; something happens on the world stage, it's on everyone's mind, and you already have a script about just that kind of thing—making you the only game in town, because no one else has had time to write a script yet, or even get a decent pitch together.

Something like this happened to screenwriter and former war correspondent Mark Boal in 2011. Though his *Kill Bin Laden* (TRU) script about the global manhunt for Osama bin Laden had found a home with *Hurt Locker* director Kathryn Bigelow, the general impression around town was that movies based on the recent war had run their course. Consequently, financing was a problem.

Then came reports of bin Laden's assassination. Suddenly, the project was fully funded, with buyers lining up as Boal busied himself with revisions and a new ending. Not long after, political backlash over the film's scheduled release date (one month before the presidential election) caused the release to be pushed beyond November.

Or maybe you have a script sitting in a pile on the desk at the production company of the biggest star in the world, who's gearing up to shoot his next film—when the big project falls apart. Suddenly, he's got this big empty hole in his schedule that he's not getting paid for (or at least, not getting paid as much as he would have had the project gone forward). After getting the bad news, one of the producers at his company picks up the top script on his to-read stack—and it's just what he's looking for, right then, gets bought and fast-tracked and becomes Tom Cruise's next movie. Some years ago, this precise scenario took place.

Timing was also instrumental in the biggest spec script sale to date: *Déjà Vu*. "There is something to be said for good fortune," screenwriter Bill Marsilii relates. "Though I believe that Terry and I wrote the best script we could write out of that story at the time, the factors that went into the sale were a celestial alignment that

I'm just kind of a witness to. About a month before we finished the screenplay, Mike Stenson from Jerry Bruckheimer's office asked Terry—completely out of the blue—do you know anybody who's got a good time-travel script, because we've been thinking we'd like to do that. And Terry laughed and said, oh boy, do I. Bruckheimer's company had money and a hole in their schedule. We showed them the script exclusively the Tuesday after Memorial Day, forty-eight hours before the rest of the town would get it, and they took it to Disney immediately. I heard later that when they took it to Disney, the business affairs person who would usually approve such an offer was on vacation. We closed the sale Friday for $3 million against $5 million, and for all I know the regular guy came back from vacation and said, 'You paid *what?*'

"So luck is a factor, but to believe that it's all luck, or a crapshoot or a lottery, is I think the wrong attitude. There were a number of very well-considered factors that led to Bruckheimer and Disney taking that script off the market with the offer they did. It was a business decision. And the only reason, I think, that someone would offer $5 million preemptively, is because they were convinced that if anyone else were allowed to see the script, it would have cost them $6 million." Bill and Terry recently sold a second project called *Lightspeed*—for $3.5 million.

Time is funny stuff, as Einstein pointed out, and what's good for one project may be bad for another. One timing gremlin which eventually happens to everyone who's been in the business for a while is this: you're working on a fabulous project that no one else (or almost no one else) knows about. And then, before you can get it out there—someone else sells another project just like it. In most cases, this spells certain death, as the first script to sell generally kills the market for all similar scripts—to the point where those with similar scripts in the works often just give up and move on to something else. Down the line, if the other script gets made and the other movie succeeds—or if the other project is indefinitely sidelined for some reason—there might be another chance. (If the other movie does stupendously badly, it can kill the market for similar projects for years to come.)

Occasionally, though, two similar projects have gained such momentum—or have such powerful people pushing them—that both projects move forward. Sometimes the projects wind up merged (as with *Gorillas in the Mist*, TRU); other times both films go head-to-head, or nearly so (as happened with *Armageddon* and *Deep Impact*). In the latter case, one of the films might slaughter the other at the box office, or the audience might be split, pulling both films down—for which reason, studios are loathe to compete with big, similarly themed pictures. (Even though both *Armageddon* and *Deep Impact*—released two months apart—did extremely well.)

In yet other instances, similar projects may be pursued through different channels. In late 2011, for instance, I was revising an adapted screenplay of mine—based on a comic script I'd written—called *War Gods* (logline: *Rome's most powerful emperor faces his most lethal enemy: a time-traveling general with warplanes and attack choppers, bent on looting the Roman treasury of $2 trillion in gold*). I'd already arranged to take it out through my former manager, now acting as producer.

While I was doing this, a friend at a major agency sent me a link to an article in *Variety,* about a pitch sold by a game show contestant to a major studio. The concept: a U.S. military unit travels back in time and faces off against a Roman emperor and his legions. I couldn't believe it. What are the chances? Everyone I consulted on this offered condolences, including my ex-manager.

After a few hours of black depression, I took a hard look at the facts, uncovered some interesting details online, and realized that my particular situation differed from the usual lethal dilemma in several respects. For one thing, I had a script, the other guy did not; for another, my completed first draft predated his pitch by several years, so I could hardly be accused of copycatting. Thirdly, the other project had a potentially messy rights situation because portions of it first appeared in an online forum. Lastly, the other project cast the Romans as the bad guys—which, to me at least, seemed much less interesting. I then explained my take on things to my former manager—and we went out with the script.

And while this other project was cited by several prodcos and a studio exec as the reason for passing, *War Gods* (talent) found a home with Informant Media, whose CEO my ex-manager has known for decades (access). He also knew that Informant—whose credits at the time included *Crazy Heart, Hysteria,* and *The Expatriate* (the last still unreleased at that point)—was now looking to do something orders of magnitude bigger than their previous projects (timing). To cap it off, I'll be executive producing.

And so the situation as I write is this: I have a completed script with crystal-clear rights and several years' worth of development behind it at a lean and mean company with independent financing, which (if the cards fall right) may be able to move into production very quickly. The other guy—a game show contestant who's never written a script before—has a brand-new pitch with possible rights issues in studio development (which often takes years, and sometimes takes forever), competing with who-knows-how-many other projects at the same studio.

How things play out from here remains to be seen—but as it turns out, failing to sell my project to a studio may just be the best thing that could possibly have happened. Or not. Only time will tell. (For updates on this, visit http://makeyourstoryamovie.com/book bonus.html.)

Point being, once you're in the game, you do everything you can to stay in the game. Timing can be good or bad. Some timing glitches are obviously and immediately fatal. Others, not so much. And sometimes, you have to go with your gut to find out which is which.

In the end, such matters of timing, fortunate or unfortunate, are things over which you have absolutely no control and which— short of being psychic—you have no ability to predict. And so, for the most part, you simply deal with them if and when they crop up.

As Seneca the Younger said over 2,000 years ago, "Luck is what happens when preparation meets opportunity."

BUDGET LEVELS

This is perhaps the best place to say something about budget as it relates to your particular project (or projects). That something is this: if what you want to do is going to cost less than $10 million or so, you will in almost all cases seek out independent production companies or financing, for the very simple reason that studios have near-zero interest in making films at this level. They may be happy to buy or distribute the film once it's done (as happened with *Little Miss Sunshine*), but they're not likely to become involved at any point prior to that that because the production and marketing costs associated with studio films render studios, for the most part, incapable of operating at such a small scale.

"It's harder to make cheaper movies at the studios," notes producer Gail Lyon, whose credits include *Erin Brockovich* (TRU), *Gattaca, Edge of Darkness* (TVS) and *Stuart Little 2* (NOV), "because you're paying for their infrastructure. It's not that that isn't fair, it's just expensive."

There are other reasons as well. "What they don't want," says screenwriter/producer Jonathan Hensleigh, "is a film that costs $10 million, $15 million and it's just sort of a programmer; they're not quite sure how it's going to perform, so piling on another $20 million to $40 million to market it doesn't make sense. Because the cost of marketing is so exorbitant, to get a film launched at all and do any kind of media buy the conversation begins at $20 million. Spending say $11 million or $12 million marketing a film, you may as well just not. I'm not kidding, it's like flushing the money down the toilet. You're throwing the punch but pulling it before it lands, so it has no impact.

"All marketing executives know that if you're going to go for it, you've got to throw the punch and make it land. And that's a certain high figure. And so because of that, because of the huge cost of marketing for a theatrical release, they don't want to pull the trigger on a lot of these films. That middle ground of over $10 million, they've just gotten out of that business.

"The smaller films and art house films, the ones that cost a couple of million bucks, those are still going in the small, studio 'independent' arms, and that's still a profitable business for them. Other than that, studio interest in these projects has plummeted."

At the other end of the equation, if the budget for your project is going to run north of about $80 million, you must find a studio buyer because independent financiers are (so far) unable or unwilling to pony up such a scary amount of cash. (The sole exception being billionaire George Lucas, who sometimes funds his own $100M epics and, as a result, is able to pay the studio a distribution fee and retain all other profits.) This is, no doubt, one of the reasons for the studios' focus on blockbusterland, where the sheer magnitude of potential profit is unrivaled—and where there is no competition. (Contrast this with each year's crop of Academy Award–winning films which—in the major categories—are overwhelmingly independent productions.)

And while this may seem contradictory for companies whose mantra is risk avoidance, look at the projects that get produced at this level. In fact, the vast bulk of studio projects are franchises, remakes, sequels, prequels, spinoffs and adaptations of existing works in other media (which are often already successful and so have existing fan bases).

As screenwriter and director Jonathan Hensleigh points out, "Anyone working in Hollywood who would disagree with that statement is in a coma, or blind, deaf, and dumb." In short and relatively speaking: the studios are primarily interested in things that have worked before and are thus perceived (rightly or wrongly) as low-risk projects—though they will sometimes foot the bill for what they feel to be a promising comedy or thriller with a midrange budget, or something with major star power.

"By all means," says Hensleigh, "vehemently, italicized and underscored, the independent world is a much more receptive place to original material than the studios." Also lower-budget projects. Again, your agent or manager should know best who to target for any given project.

Screenwriter Terry Rossio suggests a dual approach. "The industry is moving toward the big and the small," he notes, "I think studios will always want a few of the high-budget, high-profile projects. And there will be more and more of the microbudget stuff. Everything in between is getting cut back, the marketing costs and production costs are too high, they don't make sense in a world of YouTube, video games, cable programming, etc.

"By all means, try to make your way to one of those big-budget projects. But also take time to write and produce on the microbudget scale, because that's where we're all going to live in a few years."

FINANCING

Generally speaking, when a studio buys something, the studio finances production and claims most of the profit. In extraordinary cases (James Cameron's *Titanic* and *Avatar,* for example), two studios may split the cost and the profits.

Independent production companies (or "indieprods") operate on a different model. Higher-level indieprods typically option something first (though they will in some cases buy up front), figure out what the budget is likely to be, and then find a "foreign sales agent" whose job it is to sell the project to financiers outside of North America.

Consulting with the sales agent (who knows what he can sell and where), they'll figure out which director and/or star(s) they want to attach to the project, and an order of preference. (They actually have a formula for determining the box office potential of any given project, with any given star/director combination—assuming, of course, the film turns out well.) These people will then be approached through their companies or reps. If they commit to the project, an announcement is made (often at a major film festival or market).

The global film market is divided into territories, some of which encompass more than one country. The sales agent's task is to "presell" enough specific territories to fund the film. In other words, based on the project, the people involved and the production company's and sales agent's reputation and track record, financiers will (hopefully) agree to advance enough money (collectively) to produce the film. In return for this, they get the right to distribute the film in the presold territories, and retain a sizable share of the profits from those territories.

By projecting the finished film's likely revenue in all territories (based in part on the past performance of similar films with similar elements attached), and factoring in the return the investors want to see, the production company figures out exactly how much it can spend to make the movie. And then—when the financing has closed and the money is in the bank—the script is bought and the movie made.

Afterward, the prodco (again acting through the sales agent) shows the completed film to distributors in the unsold territories, who pay for the right to distribute the film and retain a portion of the profits (which is much smaller than the portion retained by the presold territory investors, because the risk is now much smaller; the film has been successfully completed, and they can see what they're getting before buying). The prodco typically deals with domestic distributors itself, making a U.S. distribution deal with a studio.

Finally, the film is released.

The practical effect of all of this is that when a studio buys something, it pays the up-front portion (generally one-third to one-half the overall purchase price) pretty quickly—whereas when a production company buys something, it usually happens months, even a year or more after the (usually fairly low) option. On the other hand, most of the scripts that get bought by studios never get made, so you wind up with maybe half of the total purchase price you would have gotten had the film actually gone into production. Still, that's a lot more than you're likely to get from a prodco that doesn't make your movie and only paid you for an option.

If a large independent production company actually buys your script, the amount can be comparable to what a studio would pay you—and chances are your movie's getting made, quickly.

If the prodco option expires and they haven't made your movie, you're free to try again elsewhere. When a studio buys your script, it's often gone forever, whether they make the film or not.

Yet another thing to ponder is financing security. As producer Gail Lyon points out, "Independently financed films can fall apart on a dime, literally. They're much more fragile, for a number of reasons." Whereas studio financing is pretty much guaranteed once the project is greenlit. Except . . . studio projects can also crash. When, for example, a regime change takes place—and the new regime does its best to kill the old regime's projects in favor of its own, because the success of the former will do nothing for them, but will make the old regime look good. Regime change is often unpredictable; it was for many years an industry cliché that ousted studio heads first learn of their status by reading the trades.

And, as Lyon also points out, "Times are changing a little bit and studios are much more willing to pull the plug on a ridiculously expensive movie, because at the end of the day they realize that unless it's the size of a hit that you can't program for, a phenomenon that you'd be stupid to think you could program for, there's no chance to make any money on it.

"Would studios like to make their movies more cheaply?" asks Lyon. "Of course. Would they prefer a lower cost? Well, yes. . . . But then are they going to get the actors they think they need to market the film? It's a whole cyclical argument that could go on until hell freezes over."

In the words of *Terminator*'s Sarah Connor, "A person could go crazy thinking about this." So, don't. Just do your best to get your project to the right people—and let them deal with it.

DOMESTIC VS. INTERNATIONAL MARKETS

Time was, 60 percent to 80 percent of all box office receipts were domestic, and 20 percent to 30 percent foreign. Today, the situation has reversed—with 60 percent to 80 percent of total box office coming from foreign sources. There are a number of reasons for this, perhaps the most prominent being that the U.S. is a "mature" market. Just about everyone in the country lives close to one or more theaters (which are often multiplexes).

Consequently, just about everyone who wants to see a movie in the theater, can. Population growth is small, meaning there's no huge influx of new moviegoers. And the vast number of alternative entertainment sources available to the average American means that some of those who might have gone to see a movie will choose to do something else instead. After all, they can always catch the flick on DVD.

Europe—particularly the fairly recently liberated eastern Europe—is not quite in that position, and countries like India and China are very far from it. New theaters are being built, people who had no easy access to theaters now do or soon will, growing populations ensure a steady supply of new moviegoers, and the relative scarcity of alternative forms of entertainment tends to funnel people into theaters.

So while it might take a $250 million "event film" to get huge numbers of Americans into theaters, this is not generally true overseas. Event films are huge there, too—in most instances bigger than they are here—but to audiences in some emerging markets, every film is (more or less) an event, and catching it later on DVD is not an option.

What this means for you and your project is that (oddly enough) the greater its potential appeal outside the U.S., the better its prospects in Hollywood. Action films do incredibly well overseas not because they're simpleminded; in fact, many are now quite sophisticated—but because you don't have to be immersed in American culture to understand them. Even movies based on such

American cultural icons as *Batman, Iron Man, Spider-Man,* and *Thor* (all COM) are thematically universal. Everyone "gets" them, because "kicking ass" is something everyone understands. Some things—oppressed indigenous populations at the mercy of ravenous corporations, for example—are even better understood in foreign markets than here at home (though we're learning quickly). It's also one of the major themes of *Avatar,* which made nearly 75 percent of its total box office in foreign markets.

Comedies sometimes work internationally, and sometimes not, because humor can be culture-specific, and some things just don't translate. Even the biggest comedies seldom do as well internationally as they do at home, and the difference is often striking. Which is not to say that comedies can't be raging successes; they can (particularly when their lower budgets are taken into account)—but they have yet to approach the staggering box office numbers of the action/adventure genre.

When you start delving into things that are so culture-specific that you have to be American to really grasp what's going on, it becomes like an "in joke" that's not funny—or even comprehensible—to those outside your social circle. And when it comes to global movie markets, there are far more people outside our culture than in. (In 2012, for the first time, the total number of movie screens in China exceeded the U.S. total—and that's just one country.)

One obvious way of upping the foreign-market appeal (and, often, lowering the budget) is to set the story itself outside the United States. *The Hangover,* set in Las Vegas, was wildly successful. Still, 60 percent of the film's total box office revenue came from the United States.

The Hangover Part II was set in Thailand—and reversed the box office split, which became 60 percent foreign, 40 percent domestic. The U.S. figure actually dropped from $277 million (*The Hangover*) to $254 million (*The Hangover Part II*). Foreign, however, jumped from $190 million to $327 million—taking the total worldwide box office from $467 million to $581 million, more than making up for the second film's bigger budget ($80 million vs. $35 million). The decision to set the film outside the U.S. was likely made quite consciously, with an eye toward upping foreign box office and DVD sales.

If your project seems to lack foreign appeal, it can't be a budget-buster. Conversely, the more universal or global your theme, the bigger your budget can be. The ultimate personification of this principle is of course filmmaker James Cameron, whose *Avatar* and *Titanic* (HIS) films have redefined the limits of the possible in both areas—budget and box office.

The takeaway? Think locally; write globally.

THE HOLLYWOOD SOB STORY

Finally, you will at some point see dire headlines bemoaning the decline of box office income over the past quarter, past year, whatever. Invariably, when you get right down to it, the numbers they cite refer to domestic box office only.

So they'll whine about the numbers being down in, say, 2011, despite the fact that the numbers for 2009/2010 were skewed upward to begin with by *Avatar*, the biggest hit of all time. And they'll talk about how last year's box office take is down 6 or 7 percent from the previous year, while completely ignoring that fact that foreign box office is up by something like 17 percent over the same period.

Which means the overall is up quite a bit, because (as we've seen) foreign comprises 60 percent to 80 percent of the total and, thus, a 17 percent foreign gain completely wipes out a 7 percent domestic loss and results in an overall revenue increase. So while these scary headlines are busy shouting doom and gloom from the rooftops (presumably because gloomy headlines pull more readers than happy ones, and the perception thus conveyed neatly dovetails with the popular studio narrative about piracy), don't let them fool you. Hollywood's coffers are filling faster than ever.

CHAPTER 31
OPTIONS AND SALES

The entertainment industry is, in almost all respects, unlike any other. Nowhere is this more evident—and nowhere are the consequences of failing to understand this more severe—than in the area of . . .

ENTERTAINMENT LAW

I'm not an attorney, nor do I play one on TV. Bonnie Eskenazi, on the other hand, is a partner at Greenberg Glusker, which is perhaps the most feared entertainment law firm in Hollywood. In addition to handling transactional (contract) work, Greenberg Glusker—unlike most firms—specializes in litigation, often against major studios, which they refuse to represent. The firm's clients, past and present, include such luminaries as James Cameron, Steven Spielberg, Jerry Bruckheimer, Tom Clancy, the estate of J. R. R. Tolkien, and The Beatles.

"Entertainment law," says Eskenazi, who teaches a course on the subject at Stanford, "is not a legal discipline in and of itself, like copyright or trademark law. Instead, it stands at the crossroads of a number of different legal disciplines like contracts and torts and copyright and securities and waiver and trademark and many others, all laid over a really unusual and unique industry that attorneys from other fields know little or nothing about. You do not want to go up against lawyers who have been practicing in this area for twenty or thirty years and are exceptionally good at it.

"A neophyte probably will not be able to afford having an entertainment attorney negotiate his or her first book contract. But if Hollywood wants to make that book a movie, and you don't have an entertainment attorney to negotiate your deal, you will be badly hurt in the process.

The worst that can happen is that whatever you've worked on, for however many years, can be deemed to be owned by the other side—typically a studio or producer—and maybe you didn't get paid what you thought you should get paid for it. Maybe there's some clause in the contract that basically allows the studio to pay you less, or even nothing."

Sound impossible? One studio admitted to making $6 billion off *The Lord of the Rings* trilogy (based on J. R. R. Tolkien's books), then claimed to owe the Tolkien estate nothing, despite a contract that required them to pay 7.5 percent of the adjusted gross.

Cathleen Blackburn of UK firm Maier Blackburn is the principal lawyer for the estate of J. R. R. Tolkien, advising on matters of copyright, publishing, and contracts. Her explanation is politely British. "Movie contracts," she notes, "often have in them a provision which ensures that the studio fully recovers its production costs before paying profit participants. The operation of this calculation by the studio repeatedly showed zero due to the Estate. It was necessary to commence legal proceedings in California in order that a court should decide whether the calculation was being made correctly."

Bonnie Eskenazi led the lawsuit, and the studio promptly backed down. The same studio also paid trilogy director Peter Jackson $100 million less than he said he was owed. When he sued, the studio publicly stated that it would never work with him again. They settled quickly, and Jackson was soon directing two more

Tolkien-based movies—for the same studio. Welcome to Hollywood. In both cases, says Eskenazi, "the contracts were very solid and negotiated by good attorneys up front, which forced the studio into a position where they had to settle."

Indeed, issues that could have been dealt with up front by a good entertainment attorney can later cost millions to fix—if they can be fixed at all. Still, first-timers are often so excited at the prospect of a genuine Hollywood contract that they can be inclined to sign the first deal put in front of them, no questions asked.

"What's typically put in front of them," Eskenazi warns, "is a draft which is completely one-sided, and that side is not in their favor. There will be issues about the definition of what they're going to be paid, when they're going to be paid, how they're going to be paid. There will be rights issues that won't necessarily be apparent to the average lay person on the face of the agreement, to the point where they can actually be signing away rights without even knowing it."

Though many first-timers rely on an agent for everything, there is no substitute for a good entertainment attorney. "Agents first of all are typically not attorneys," says Eskenazi. "They don't focus so much on the rights issues as they focus on the money and the credits, and in many cases, the part that they don't carefully go over concerns the rights you're retaining. If you're an actor or director, you're still safer with an attorney, but it probably doesn't matter all that much. "But if you're a writer, the bundle of rights that you own in the copyright of your work is absolutely critical."

One quite successful rights-owner I spoke with (who prefers to remain anonymous) recalls getting a ridiculously one-sided agreement a number of years back, when their work was lesser-known, and their credits smaller in number. "We all signed off on it," he said, "because of course we wanted the movie to be made, and were just so excited about the idea that [Huge Director] would be directing. And if we saw that same document today of course, we'd say, 'What the hell, why should we sign this? You want us to just screw ourselves and save you the trouble?' We now have someone different handling our deals."

Obviously, this is an area where the well-meaning advice of Cousin-Elmer-the-lawyer is not sufficient. Using an attorney who doesn't specialize in entertainment law is like asking the local Best Buy associate to help defuse a nuclear bomb; your chances of survival are, shall we say, less than optimal.

Still, there are some basics you need to understand, which we can—in general terms—cover here. Things like . . .

OPTIONS

Options and sales (covered below) are different, but can be the same—so if you're interested in either, read about both. That's because an option is actually more technically an "option/purchase agreement"—so if all goes well, the option becomes a sale.

An option is just that—an option to purchase specific rights at a later time for an agreed-upon price. It's not an obligation: the option-holder can buy the rights later, transfer the option to someone else, or stick it in a shoebox and never look at it again. (Which is why you want a time limit on your option.)

An option is, at its best and when everything goes right, a slow-motion sale. Sort of like a date that might lead to marriage. The difference is that the option-holder, unlike a buyer (or spouse), can bail on the project without investing a significant amount of money. More properties are optioned than sold, for that very simple reason: it's cheaper to option something than it is to buy it. That's good for the option-holder, not so good for the rights-owner. Make no mistake, things can and often do work out wonderfully—but your first choice is almost always a sale.

"The option process," attorney Bonnie Eskenazi explains, "gives the studio or production company the ability to pay as little as possible for the exclusive right to make an underlying work into a movie. They'll typically pay a very small amount of money to tie up the rights for six months to a year and sometimes longer, while they determine whether they can make the project work.

"If they want to extend the option, then they have to pay more money to do that. And if they decide to go ahead and make the film, they have to make a substantial payment to 'exercise' the option and purchase the rights."

If you have a screenplay, go for the sale. If that doesn't work, try to package the script, or consider an option. Or, if you're not in a position to try to sell the script, perhaps option it to someone—like a producer—who is. If you don't have a screenplay, and the story you want to adapt isn't already well known or hugely successful, chances are that any interested party is going to offer an option and not a purchase.

WHY OPTION?

For the rights-holder, there's usually only one reason to option the rights: no one wants to buy them outright. There are exceptions. Stephen King optioned the rights to his short story "Rita Hayworth and the Shawshank Redemption" to writer/director Frank Darabont for one dollar. Then again, King didn't need the money, and Darabont was a writer/producer/director who convinced him he'd write, direct and produce a fabulous and Oscar-worthy movie—which he did.

For a producer (most options are acquired by producers), the option buys time. That time might be spent developing or adapting the property with the original owner (or with someone else); polishing an optioned script with the original writer (or with someone else); finding and paying someone else to adapt the property or rewrite the script; trying to interest actors, directors, or other producers in the project; looking for investors to help finance it; packaging the project alone or with the help of a manager or agent or another producer; trying to find a buyer—or some combination of the above.

All of these steps take time, and some of them cost money. Before investing that time or money on an uncertain venture (and all Hollywood projects are uncertain ventures), the producer needs to be sure that he or she can benefit if those efforts are successful. As long as the producer holds the option, he "controls" the rights, because he is (by the option's terms) the only one who can buy them—and, therefore, the only one who can sell them.

Look at it from the producer's perspective: Are you going to spend months, perhaps even years of your life trying to put a project together—when the rights-owner can sell it out from under you at any moment, leaving you with nothing? An option prevents that by locking up the rights.

Most options do not lead to sales. When they do, the buyer is almost never the option-holder. What happens is, the producer becomes a middleman and enters into an agreement with the buyer—usually a studio or (with increasing frequency) a production company with independent financing.

In exchange for a producer fee and credit on the movie (if it winds up being produced), the optioning producer transfers the agreement to the buyer, which then "exercises" the option by purchasing the rights for the price specified in the option. This is why options are transferable.

In relative terms, options are cheap; outright purchases are not—so even a producer who has the money to buy the rights up front will seldom choose to do so. Why spend a large amount of money on one project, when he can—for far less money—option multiple projects and pursue them simultaneously? Knowing that if any of those projects finds a buyer, someone else will pick up the tab?

It helps to look at things from a producer's viewpoint. "You work years and years and years to get a producer fee," says Oscar-nominated producer Michael Nozik. "And it seems like a big fee, but when you amortize it over the three or four years it took you to get it, it's not so much money unless you have multiple projects going, which is hard. It sounds glamorous, but you're still a working stiff like everybody else.

"The studio will try to grind you down on credits, on money, on everything, until you've established yourself as worthy in their eyes. And that's a sliding scale throughout time. Even though you put it together, and you signed the material—it's the nature of this business. It's all based on precedent: what did you get paid on the last one? If there was no last one, and you have no precedent, you're not in a good place.

"At the same time, we're in a world where, as hard as it is to break in and get recognized, everybody is looking for the next great thing. It's a little bit psychotic that way: it's a closed door, and it's a door that's open to anybody at the same moment.

"If you control the underlying rights with an option, then you can say, 'I want x, y, and z, or else you don't get the project.' And if the person replies, 'Well, then we don't want the project,' you walk away and you find out if someone else wants it.

"You have to be willing to play the nuclear card in any negotiation. Because it's all about strength. If they really want it, and you know they want it, and you don't care if they walk away because you know that what you have is so good that there will be another buyer, then you play that game—and eventually you'll get what you want, if it's reasonable, including a good price for the material."

This is exactly what screenwriter/producer Leslie Dixon did with *Limitless* (NOV), after securing film rights to the book and writing the screenplay herself. "I was willing to walk away and see it not get made," she says, "if it wasn't going to be a good picture."

Says Nozik: "If you can't do that, maybe this is your first project as a producer, then sometimes it's worth it, particularly if you're getting involved with people who can get the movie made, to do the deal knowing you're going to take a hit on it. As long as you're not completely closed out, and you get that credit, then you've got some added credibility going into the next deal."

Either way, if the rights are purchased, the rights-owner gets the full amount specified in the option agreement.

TIME LIMIT

Options have a built-in time limit. Think of it as a sort of progress-to-purchase clause: if the option-holder doesn't pay you (or cause you to be paid) by a certain date, he loses the option, and you are then free to sell or option the rights to someone else.

The option to renew or extend the option (once) may belong to either the option-holder or the rights-owner. The higher the cost of the option, the more likely it is that the option-holder will want to be able to renew the option for an additional payment. The lower the option price (or the more powerful the rights-holder), the more likely the rights-holder is to reserve that decision.

Options may be renewed a second time, or indefinitely, if both parties agree. Sometimes the option price is applied against (deducted from) the eventual purchase price, sometimes not. Again, consider the other guy's perspective.

"As a producer," says Jonathan Hensleigh, who produced *Armageddon, Con Air,* and *Gone in 60 Seconds* (MOV), "the first thing you want to know is, how long is the option and when is it going to expire? Because you do all this work on the screenplay and then you're shopping the thing, and maybe you can't get an actor involved, you can't get a director, and the clock is ticking, right? And it's terrifying, because at the expiration of the option, it could be game over. You can run into a brick wall very quickly, and you need time to get over it. You don't want to find out you were at a cocktail party and insulted the rights-holder's wife or what-have-you, so now you don't have the rights anymore. All kinds of crazy shit can happen."

OPTION DOWNSIDES

First and foremost, of course, options put less money in your pocket than sales. (For producers, this is an upside because it takes less money out of theirs.) Secondly, options tie up the rights for what can be long periods of time; if someone else becomes interested in your story while it's still under option, they can't have it unless the guy you optioned it to allows them to buy it—which, for various business or personal reasons, he may not. Progress-to-production clauses (see below) are less likely in option situations, particularly so when there is no finished script to base a movie on. (It's hard to produce what doesn't exist, much less do it in a hurry.)

There's also the possibility that, for whatever reason—higher priorities, the sale of a similar project by someone else, illness, laziness, emotional instability, incarceration, death, alien abduction—the project will just sit around collecting dust until the option runs out. During which time, of course, your hands are tied because someone else controls the rights.

Options that lead to sales also lead to step deals (see below), with the final payment coming due on or before the first day of principal photography. When the work being optioned is something other than a screenplay, though, it's going to take longer to start shooting the film because the screenplay has yet to be written. It will also likely be written by someone other than you, who will likely be paid more to write the script than you were paid for the rights.

Another potential option problem is seldom encountered, but does happen occasionally. Let's say you have a story that's similar to another story being pursued by someone else. You may not even know their story exists—but if they find out about yours, they may decide to option it, simply to stick it on a shelf and let it rot until their project moves so far forward that your potentially competing project will never be purchased or produced. Some would consider that cheap insurance—sort of like poking holes in the other guy's tires before the big race.

This can happen with screenplay purchases, too, but is less likely because of the higher cost—and leaves more money in your pocket if it does occur.

BONUS UPSIDE

But, again—options *can* work out quite nicely, and many successful films have resulted from them. Options also have one unique advantage that sales generally do not: you can option something two, twelve, or fifty different times, get paid to do it and—if the option is never exercised—still wind up owning the property.

OPTION TYPES

There are short-form options and long-form options. Short-form options cover the basic "material terms"—such as rights granted, price, time period, credits. Anything less than this is not a contract. "The courts will not enforce an agreement to agree," says attorney Eskenazi. "The material terms must all be there."

Long-form options include mandatory studio language, and cover all conceivable details—the idea here being to work out every aspect of the deal in advance, so there are no delays or misunderstandings later. "It takes longer to work out all the deal terms up front," says Eskenazi, "but it's safer for both sides. If you're a rights-holder, you don't want to find yourself in a position where the production company has the right to exercise the option but you're not happy with the deal terms they're giving you down the line."

Hammering out the details in advance also makes it easier—and faster—for the producer to transfer the option to the buyer, because there's nothing left to haggle over; it's a done deal. Long-form options run to dozens of pages, and include both studio boilerplate terms (without which no studio will purchase the rights), and those provisions which are negotiable.

To know which is which, and just how negotiable the latter are in your particular case, you will need an entertainment attorney. (For more on this, refer to Chapter 32.)

SALES

A sale is just what it sounds like: someone buys specific rights to your property—typically motion picture/TV, soundtrack, merchandising, and a laundry list of other "allied" and "ancillary" and "customarily or traditionally associated" rights. This is the ideal situation, and the one that brings the most money.

Because of the amount of money involved, the buyer is usually a studio or studio-affiliated company—though again, purchases by production companies with independent financing are becoming increasingly common.

Because of the risk involved, the property being bought is almost always a completed screenplay, or something that's already proven itself commercially successful in another medium (book, comic, game, well-known true story, etc.). "If you're selling a screenplay that the buyer already likes," Eskenazi confirms, "you've eliminated a big risk, because with anything else, the studio or production company doesn't know whether they'll be able to turn it into a workable script that people like, even if the underlying property is something they like very much."

In short, a finished screenplay offers some assurance that the story can be rendered in cinematic form—while success in some other medium guarantees an existing fan base already predisposed to buy tickets to (and hopefully say good things about) the movie.

Occasionally—and far less frequently these days (see Chapter 34)—a buyer may pay for something less substantial than a screenplay or adaptable work: a pitch, premise, or concept. Being less substantial and less proven by nature, and requiring serious time, effort and money to adapt, develop and expand, these typically fetch far smaller prices. You're more likely to pay the rent with such a sale than buy a house. Unless, say, you're selling the rights to something already extraordinarily successful—like, for example, A. L. James's novel *50 Shades of Grey,* the film rights to which were bought for $9 million in March 2012. (For updated information on record-setting deals, visit http://makeyourstoryamovie.com/bookbonus.html.)

THE HOLLYWOOD TWO-STEP

There may be many fools in Hollywood, but few of them work in studio legal departments. Just because something is bought doesn't mean it will be made. Like most folks, studios have their share of unfinished projects gathering dust in the garage. In order to avoid paying full price for all of these, studios arrange their purchases as step deals—so called because payment is spread out over several installments or "steps."

For example, let's say that you—like Evan Daugherty—sell an adapted screenplay for $3.2 million. You don't get all of that up front. Instead, you might get half on signing, or $1.6 million—enough to buy a decent house or a top-end supercar outright, but probably not both. The up-front payment is the first step. When you read that someone just sold a script for $1.5 million *against* $3 million, that's what it means.

The second step—the other $1.6 million, in this case—is due no later than the first day of principal photography on the movie. If that never happens—if there is no movie and so no first day of principal photography—there is no next step or second payment either, and you may find that camping out in your Bugatti Veyron is not as much fun as it used to be.

There may be additional steps based on various contingencies—sequels, prequels, remakes, TV spin-off (or movie spin-off, if sold for TV), back-end participation, and so on—but these are termed *bonuses,* and the up-front (on signing) and commencement (on filming) payments nearly always account for the bulk of the money. (A notable recent exception being the *50 Shades of Grey* deal, which was $4 million against another $5 million from the box office gross—allowing the studio to cover its bets if the film is not made, or is not successful.)

If you're a screenwriter with a rewrite provision, that may add another primary step, in which case you're looking at three payments: on signing, rewrite completion, and commencement.

DOWNSIDE

The only real downside to a sale is that there's no turning back: once it's sold, it's sold. Absent some kind of progress-to-production clause (explained in Chapter 32), you are unlikely to regain the rights at a later time. You may be able to *transfer* the rights from one studio to another in a process called "turnaround" (in which the first studio drops the project and then grossly inflates its development costs— and the second agrees to pay said grossly inflated costs in order to acquire the property), but that's not always possible either, as studios often prefer to bury their mistakes rather than risk the embarrassment of seeing someone else succeed where they failed.

A NOTE ON PACKAGING

As mentioned earlier, "packaging" is the act of attaching or committing one or more desirable "elements" (actors, directors, writers, producers) to your property on the theory that, if the property doesn't generate enough interest on its own, maybe the property-plus-Bruce-Willis (or whomever) will tip the balance in your favor.

A significant number of spec screenplays that did not sell when first offered to the town have gone on to sell (usually the following year) when packaged and offered again. It's the same script—with one or more bankable elements attached to up the buyer's confidence level. (For more on packaging, see Chapter 27.)

OWN IT

Because everything revolves around the property, it's vital to ensure that you retain ownership until someone pays you a good deal of money to sell your rights to them. So if you approach someone with a property you own, and they're not *buying* it from you, you should retain ownership, and this should be explicitly stated in any agreement you sign.

What you want to avoid is a situation where, say, a producer options your book or script and works with you to develop it—and then claims some kind of ownership or coauthorship of whatever changes/rewrites you personally made during the development process. (Beware of the phrase "work-for-hire.")

Should the option then lapse, you would retain full ownership of the original property only, and not the changes. Which, in turn, means that you can't sell the new-and-improved version to someone else without cutting that producer in on the deal. And if that producer's demands are excessive, or personality caustic, their attachment to your project can kill its chances in the market.

Do not assume that because ownership is not mentioned, or because there is no written contract (which there should be), that this issue will not come up. You want a clear statement of ownership in a written contract: your property, as well as any changes you yourself make to it, is yours, and all rights to the property and all of those changes revert to you if the option expires. Do not proceed without a written statement to this effect; just insert it into the option.

If and when someone actually purchases your property, on the other hand, your further contributions (if any) to that property will likely be considered as "work-for-hire" and owned by the purchaser.

Also keep in mind that any changes the producer might make—or hire someone else to make—will belong to the producer and not to you. If, for example, a producer options your book and then writes (or hires someone else to write) an adapted screenplay, that screenplay does not belong to you, even if the option expires. (On the other hand, it's not much use to the producer, either, unless it's radically different from your original property—because the producer needs your permission to sell anything that incorporates a legally substantial portion of your protected work.)

CHAPTER 32
CONTRACTS

If, as we've seen, industry contracts are so incredibly complex and deal-dependent—is there any general advice that applies to everyone? (Aside, that is, from the typical law school advice that "he who represents himself has a fool for a client?")

"As a rights-holder," counsels entertainment attorney Bonnie Eskenazi, "I would want a very clear, precise definition of the work that I'm selling. I would also want a very clear delineation of the rights that are being granted in that underlying work.

"Also, you need to have a really good reservation of rights clause. What you can hold on to varies tremendously depending on where you are in your career, who you're dealing with, and the kind of property being negotiated. But you want to make sure that you give away as few rights as possible, because that allows you to hedge your bets.

"If the film goes through the roof and becomes a major hit, then the more rights you have—and I don't care what those rights are— the better off you'll be. Because regardless of whether the motion picture company is being totally honest with you in terms of their back-end payments, you now have something they don't have, that you can go out and monetize if you want to do that.

"You have to give up some things—motion picture, television, home video rights at an absolute minimum. But you want a clause saying that any rights not specifically granted to the buyer remain with you. That, I would say, is the most important thing."

Naturally, the first-draft contract the buyer sends you will say just the opposite: anything not specifically reserved by you— including rights which do not yet exist or have not yet been devised— belongs to them.

"With *30 Days of Night*," says comic writer Steve Niles, "I sold the farm. They got everything. So I'm a little more careful now, and understand things I didn't before. I don't kid myself, I was well compensated for the movie, which I think is a good one, and I've gotten a lot more work because of it. But I wish I would have kept interactive and digital rights for certain aspects. They never did a video game, for example, when it's such a natural premise for a video game. Of course now nobody cares, it's over and done. But at the time we had game companies coming to us and we could not get the studio even vaguely interested. We really retain only publishing; we can do anything we want in print. I *think* we can do digital comics, but even that's up for debate."

Tolkien Estate attorney Cathleen Blackburn says "the simplest and best advice is always to grant only the rights that are needed for a particular form of exploitation and to grant them directly to the company doing the exploiting, as one is likely to lose an element of revenue when rights are sublicensed. Depending on the nature of the property, a film company may want to exercise merchandising rights alongside film rights, in order to maximize the revenue from both and cross-promote. However, it may seek to acquire other rights not to exploit them but to eliminate the competition which might arise if they are exploited by someone else. It is usually better to retain these rights, even if subject to a hold-back [delayed exploitation] period, than to give them away to a company which may not actively exploit them."

Isa Dick Hackett administers the rights of the late Philip K. Dick's dozens of novels and 120-plus short stories—which have been adapted into movies like *Blade Runner* (NOV), *Minority Report* (STO), *The Adjustment Bureau* (STO), and *Total Recall* (STO). She advises others to think ahead. "What I've learned over all of these years, having all these projects done, is that anything can happen in terms of how that particular title is ultimately adapted. Make sure you're thinking about—and the contract covers—every conceivable possibility, in terms of what it could become. Because something could start off really small, they're thinking to do an indie film, and then it ends up being this huge-budget thing like *Minority Report* (STO).

"Or the film could get made and nobody cares about it—and then suddenly it's *Blade Runner,* where all of a sudden it gets recognition and it becomes this whole other thing. And you're wishing that you had certain things built in so that you could enjoy certain creative controls, or participation or whatever it is. You want to hold on to any rights you can, because they can end up being a huge thing down the line.

"Novels now can potentially become interactive—but who has the rights, if the novel's optioned for a film? Because when you embed all this other stuff in an interactive novel, the literary work becomes almost filmlike, but in a different way. There's this whole other thing you can create—but what is it? It's not a game, it's not an ebook. Suddenly you're scratching you head thinking wait a minute, this didn't exist, we didn't contemplate this, what is this new animal? Our old contracts, from the early years when my dad was alive, didn't contemplate all of these different mediums. No one thought about digital; the internet didn't exist. And who knows what's next?

"You want to hold on to everything you can. I'm sure it's a terrible feeling that your baby, your creation can be exploited and used in many sorts of ways that you won't necessarily approve of or want out there. So you need good legal representation to hammer out all of those details. Because it's you against the studio, and you really need someone who's used to doing these contracts and has experience with studios. And if you don't have that, forget it."

Cathleen Blackburn, lead attorney for the Tolkien Estate, agrees. "Often, technology develops in a way that the original contract draftsmen could not foresee; television is a much more sophisticated medium today than in the 1960s, for example—and computers did not exist at all in the sense that we know them today.

"Also, deals involving adaptations are likely to be more complicated than those for original screenplays, as an existing work will probably have been exploited already and so there will be more existing interests to take into account—for example, the rights of book publishers, computer game developers, manufacturers of merchandise, and so on. So one needs lawyers who are well versed in the ways of the studios, supported by specialist auditors in the case of accounting disputes."

While it's clearly impossible to cover every possible contractual contingency here (that's your entertainment attorney's job), we can hit a few of the high points—important things you should be aware (or beware) of. If you've not yet read the "Entertainment Law" section of the previous chapter, be sure to check that out before diving in here.

MONKEY POINTS

Don't be taken in by the promise of sharing in the movie's profits or (worse) net profits. The most creative people in Hollywood work in studio accounting, and by the time they get done cooking the books, your project will have officially lost money on paper—even if they have to offset your film's staggering profits against the losses of three dozen other films (a practice called "cross-collateralization") to make it happen.

They will also pay various hefty fees for various things to various companies—many of which will turn out to be, in effect, nothing more than subdivisions of the studio itself. So while the money disappears on paper (and from your profit participation calculation), it never really leaves the studio's coffers. In some cases, it seems the more money a movie makes, the faster its paper losses accrue, making any possible net profit mathematically unattainable.

The Holy Grail of profit participation is "gross points," meaning a percentage of the film's actual earnings, which are much more difficult to conceal. People like James Cameron and Steven Spielberg and a very short list of actors get gross points—and even then, they sometimes (like Peter Jackson) have to sue to collect.

Everyone else gets what Eddie Murphy first termed "monkey points," or a percentage of the film's nonexistent "net profits." So while you do want to make sure your contract provides for some kind of back-end payment, on the wildly improbable chance there will be one—don't expect to actually collect on that, unless you're dealing with a nonstudio buyer. (And even there, your chances are not good.)

The upshot of all this being, you want as much of your money as possible up-front, on signing and commencement (plus the usual bonuses for sequels, spinoffs and so on). You do *not,* in *most* cases, want to accept a lower "front end" on the promise a "back-end" profit participation that will in all likelihood never happen.

There are very notable exceptions to this, but for those who fall outside the Cameron-Spielberg-Bruckheimer-Johnny Depp level, these exceptions are the exclusive province of independently financed, nonstudio projects. Writer/actor/producer Nia Vardalos, for example, made at least eight figures from the big screen adaptation of her one-woman stage show *My Big Fat Greek Wedding.* Made for $5 million, the film drew an Academy Award nomination for best screenplay, and grossed more than $350 million at the box office alone—with Vardalos, in a truly exceptional deal, getting a piece of the gross (rather than the net).

But remember: the only money you're guaranteed to receive is what you get on signing—and if *Big Fat* had failed (or the deal had been for net points rather than gross), Vardalos would have been left with the $500 she was paid for the script. So if someone offers you monkey points, ask for a banana instead. It's worth more, and will keep you from starving. (Even so, make sure your definition of net is no less favorable than the best definition accorded anyone else on the same project.)

For more on Nia Vardalos and other independent film success stories, visit http://makeyourstoryamovie.com/bookbonus.html.

BUMPS

One way to dispense with the monkey point dilemma is to ask for a performance bonus or "bump clause." In the book world, these are referred to as "escalator clauses," and are usually tied to bestseller status on specific lists (*The New York Times Best Seller List* being one of these), or number of books sold. Basically, every time you hit one of these predefined milestones (bestseller list status, number of weeks on list, specific number of books sold), you get a bump in your pay.

In Hollywood, such bonuses are tied to box office grosses as reported by third parties (*Variety, The Hollywood Reporter,* etc.). The third-party requirement is there to prevent the studios from working their usual magic with the numbers. If you think the purchase price should be higher, and the buyer doesn't, bumps can be a way to bridge the gap.

A buyer who is unwilling (or unable) to pay a higher up-front price may be willing to grant bumps because they add nothing to the project's up-front costs—and if the milestones are never hit, the money is never paid out. Bumps are often reserved for more established writers and you may not get this, but be sure to ask for it—and to tie the bumps to worldwide (and not domestic) box office.

PROGRESS-TO-PRODUCTION

It's sometimes possible to insert a "progress-to-production" clause in a purchase agreement. What this does, basically, is motivate the buyer to make your movie by requiring additional payments or rights reversion if production doesn't commence in a timely manner (the definition of which is negotiable, as it obviously takes more time to ramp up a $200 million movie than one that costs $2 million). It's also nice if you get to keep whatever money has been paid to you thus far. You can't always get this clause, but you'll never get it if you don't know to ask. The more eager the buyer is to acquire your project (bidding situations and preemptive offers are ideal), the more likely they are to agree to this.

Snow White and the Huntsman (MLF) is a recent and classic example of this. "It was one of those really fortunate situations that a writer hopes for," recalls screenwriter Evan Daugherty, "where several studios wanted to buy it. Which means you have a bidding war. Because of that, and because I had a hugely powerful producer in Joe Roth, he was able to incentivize the ultimate buyer to make the movie. He's been around a long time, he's run several studios, and he doesn't want to wait years to see a movie get made, if it ever gets made. So he said we want to be shooting this movie in *x* number of months, or we're taking it back and going to another studio. That was part of the agreement."

The film was released in June of 2012—less than two years after the script was purchased.

COVERING YOUR DERRIERE

Make sure you're covered under an "errors and omissions" insurance policy carried by the purchaser; this protects you in a number of unlikely-but-possible scenarios in which, for instance, someone claims that your work infringes their copyright, or is overly similar to their own work, or is based upon their true-life experiences. (The more successful your film, the more likely it becomes that such nuisance lawsuits will be filed, by those who actually believe their accusations—and by those looking for a quick buck at your, and/or the studio's, expense.)

Ideally, the language here will state that you are covered as a named insured on "an" E&O policy carried by the buyer, rather than by "any" E&O policy. This may seem an inconsequential distinction but, as with many contractual situations, it's not. If "any" is used, and there is no policy carried by the buyer—then you're not covered, because there isn't *any* policy. If "an" is used, you must be covered—and if there is no policy, the buyer must take one out or stand in breach of contract (either one of which leaves the buyer responsible for covering your expenses). WGA language does not adequately address this issue, so even Guild members can be tripped up here. (Now you see why you need an experienced entertainment attorney.)

The "warranties and indemnities" or "representations and warranties" section of the contract is a minefield; try to ensure that you are not liable for the actions of or material supplied by others (the buyer or anyone hired by the buyer) and that, in fact, the buyer indemnifies you (just as you indemnify them) against any liability arising out of any material they provide to you or cause to be incorporated into the work by someone else.

Without such a "reciprocal indemnity" provision, you could find yourself personally liable if, say, the buyer later hires someone else to rework the story, and that person (knowingly or unknowingly) adds something that infringes some third party's rights.

Find the phrase "breach or alleged breach" and see that it's changed to "willful and material breach" (or "material breach" or, if you can't get that, then "breach"), so you don't wind up punished, sued, or fired over something inadvertent or minor. If the contract says "alleged breach," the buyer can (for example) refuse to pay you because it alleges you've breached your representations or warranties. No proof is required, merely an allegation (hence, "alleged"). If the agreement says "breach," then there must be an actual, provable breach. A "material breach" is a higher standard (a breach that actually matters); "willful and material" higher still—meaning that you not only committed a serious breach, but did so knowingly.

You may see something saying that your original idea was actually the buyer's original idea, and that your creation of a preexisting project constitutes a "work-for-hire" (which means, essentially, that you are a hired employee with no ownership rights whatsoever). Try to eliminate this; a good attorney will help because he (or she) will point out that, technically speaking, signing any such statement constitutes fraud—and you cannot be contractually compelled to break the law.

Likewise, you'll see a provision requiring you to cooperate fully with the property's new owner in any legal action involving the property. While that may seem harmless at first glance, strictly speaking, it forces you to go along with whatever the buyer decides to do. How can that be bad? Suppose the buyer decides that the cheapest way out of a lawsuit is to agree to a settlement that says (or seems to say) that you did something wrong—stole some part of the work from someone else, for example. That, too, would be fraudulent. You need to get that clause changed to state that you cannot be compelled to admit to wrongdoing where none exists.

The plain truth of the matter is that, if the other side knows you have a serious entertainment attorney on your side (meaning they know the attorney or the firm, by reputation or experience), a lot of the usual bullshit won't even come up, because they know it's not going to fly—and any bullshit that does come up will be quickly shot down by your attorney.

When, on the other hand, your attorney is Uncle-Elmer-who-went-to-law-school, you'll find yourself buried so deep you need a snorkel to breathe. As Cathleen Blackburn notes, "the most important things in my view are understanding the value of what one has to sell to the people to whom you may be selling it, and having expert legal advice on how to sell it to best effect, both creatively and financially."

For more on rights, contracts, studio accounting practices, how to tell a good entertainment attorney from a bad one, what's negotiable and what isn't, war stories and more—see the author's online interviews with entertainment attorneys (including Bonnie Eskenazi) at http://makeyourstoryamovie.com/bookbonus.html.

CHAPTER 33
CREDITS

In Hollywood, credits are almost as important as money, and so—as with money—you want to make sure you (and not someone else) get your fair share. Credits add legitimacy, look good on the résumé, often mean additional payments, and let people who liked the movie know who they might want to option (or hire) for their next project. This applies even to rights owners who played no part in the actual production: if a fabulous movie was based on a story owned by a little-known author (or his estate), it's likely he (or the estate) will have other stories to sell.

Credits also come in handy when you begin approaching others about future projects; suddenly you're not just another wannabe—now you're part of the club. And while this doesn't guarantee that other members will like your next project, it does pretty much mean that you'll get your e-mail answered or your call returned. In short, people who may not have given you the time of day before, now will, because your credit marks you as a player.

When dealing with a non-Guild film (one that doesn't employ anyone belonging to one of the Guilds—Writers, Directors, Producers, etc.), the final credits can be spelled out in the contract. So if your contract says you will be (for example) the sole credited writer, that's it; you will be. Most such films are low-budget productions.

Once the Guilds become involved, though, things get complicated and in almost all cases it doesn't really matter what the contract says—the Guild is the final arbiter of onscreen credits within its jurisdiction.

Director credits are simple: if you direct the movie, you get the credit, and probably get to plaster the screen with some additional possessory nonsense like "A Joe Director Film." Unless you're codirecting with your brother, or you get fired and replaced in the middle of the shoot, that's about all there is to know. Director credits are determined by the Directors Guild of America.

PRODUCER CREDITS

Producer credits are a bit more complex. When it comes to feature films, the general pecking order is: producer, executive producer, coproducer, and associate producer. Most producers, even the household names, started out with one or several associate producer credits before moving up the ladder.

In television, the pecking order is somewhat different, with executive producer being the most prestigious, followed by coexecutive producer, supervising producer, producer, and coproducer.

The Producers Guild, oddly, does not have the authority to determine or enforce credits, making this area a bit like the Wild West of credits. So if your contract says you'll get a specific producer credit, *and* you're dealing with an independent production company, you should see your name on the screen.

Studios, on the other hand, are loathe to promise producer credits, and generally refuse to do so except when dealing with established producers who have previous credits behind them. They adopt this attitude because they want to keep the credits door open for other, more powerful producers who may come on board down the line. And every one of those guys winds up bumping your maybe-credit down the list, often to the point where it disappears completely. (Later on, if you pursue a successful producing career, you become one of those guys.)

If you're finding source material and are instrumental in getting it developed and/or made, there may be a producer credit in your future.

WRITING CREDITS

Writing credits and the rules used to determine them can be complex. For starters, there's "screenplay by" (the guy who wrote the screenplay) and "story by" (the guy who came up with the story told by the screenplay), but also "written by" (when the two are one and the same). The words "by Hot Writer and Hungry Writer" mean something different than "by Hot Writer & Hungry Writer" (in the first case, the writers worked the project sequentially; in the second, they worked as a team).

To get an original screenplay-by credit (not based on source material), the first writer must contribute more than 33 percent to the final script, regardless of whether the writer also directs or produces. Subsequent writers must contribute 50 percent or more, while subsequent writers who also produce or direct the project must contribute more than 50 percent to the shooting script. For non-original scripts, any writer must contribute more than 33 percent to the final script to be credited. In all cases, writing teams are treated (for purposes of credit determination) as a single writer.

There are other rules, and in the end it's all up to the Writers Guild, which can (and has) stripped credits from writers who not only wrote the first draft but originated the project—because it was so heavily rewritten that the first writer's contribution to the final script fell below the required percentage. Probably all of the screenwriters quoted in this book have done far more uncredited work than credited—sometimes because the project they worked or sold was never made, other times because their contribution fell below the Guild-mandated percentage.

The important thing to know is that, if you're looking for a writing or story credit on a Guild production, you want your name on the Notice of Tentative Writing Credits or NTWC, which is submitted to the Guild for final credits determination. Your contract should assign you a provisional credit (provisional because it's subject to WGA jurisdiction), and also state that your name will be on the NTWC. As well, it should cover your credit in the event the film never comes under WGA jurisdiction—either by stating what the credit will be, or providing that it will be determined using WGA rules and (if need be) WGA arbitrators.

SOURCE CREDIT

Now for some good news. Source credit exists only when a movie is based upon something else that came before it—book, comic, short story, play, true-life experience, etc. That something else is the source. Though it's not generally well known, this is the simplest credit of all, for a very simple and equally little-known reason: the Writers Guild—which has sole and exclusive authority over screenwriting credits on those projects under its purview—has no authority whatsoever over source credits, because they have nothing to do with screenwriting.

Therefore, if your contract flat-out states that you will receive source credit, you will, and there's pretty much not a damned thing anyone can do about it. And while the Writers Guild likes to say that any source material must have been "previously exploited" in some way, it's doubtful that would hold up if push came to shove. If the source material existed before the screenplay—*and* the contract obligates the buyer to provide a source credit—that should pretty much nail it down.

BAILOUT CLAUSE

Also, in the event that Hollywood really, really, *really* messes up your movie—it's nice to have a clause in your contract that says you can, at your option, remove your name from the project. And even then, you might want to weigh this option against the value of having an actual produced credit of any kind—which is (for reasons explained above) considerable.

After all, you can always blame someone else for the mess. (For more on the intricacies of credits, visit http://makeyourstory amovie.com/bookbonus.html.)

CHAPTER 34
THE DEATH (AND RESURRECTION) OF DEVELOPMENT

RISK AVERSION AT THE STUDIOS

Despite appearances and ever-larger grosses, Hollywood studios have, if not exactly taken a hit from the ongoing (let's call it what it is) Depression, then certainly become more cautious as a result. Part of this is that the studios themselves are owned by even larger companies, which have in some cases taken real (as opposed to imagined) hits from the economic downturn.

Another part of it is the studio system's longstanding and perpetual risk-avoidance mentality. This may seem odd for companies in the business of creating works whose success depends on public opinion, but it's been this way for a very long time.

Just as the studios feared that talking pictures, television, VCRs, DVDs, and the Internet would end the world as they knew it (when in fact each simply served to enrich them to the point where the studios now make more money from the media they tried to interfere with than they do from putting movies in theaters)—they now fear that the economy will keep people from spending money on movies. This despite the fact that, as the economy continues to tank, box office revenues continue to climb.

As mentioned previously, when you read dire headlines about box office declining, the statistics cited inevitably refer to domestic box office figures, which is misleading because, at the same time, foreign box office (which comprises 60 percent to 80 percent of the total) is climbing faster than domestic is declining—making for an overall gain. Rest assured, the studios are raking in more money than ever before. Any protestations to the contrary are based on the same sort of studio accounting practices that tell us (via a studio accounting statement leaked online) that *Harry Potter and the Order of the Phoenix* lost money. (Which is, of course, why the studio immediately produced three more Harry Potter movies, hoping to "lose" even more money.)

Paradoxically, it is this same aversion to risk that drives the studios to spend hundreds of millions of dollars on gargantuan "tentpole" movies that expose them to more risk than anything else.

The reasoning goes something like this: bigger movies are potentially more profitable (which is true in an absolute if not a relative-to-budget sense), and they have—in the case of adaptations based on already-popular works—a built-in audience (also true, though it doesn't guarantee existing fans will like the film, and if in fact those fans dislike the film it can tank more quickly than it otherwise might have). And perhaps most important of all, basing a movie on an already successful property tends to insulate decision makers from the fallout over a failed film: how could they have known? (This same reasoning applies to the use of large and costly stars, directors and, to a lesser extent, writers.)

Obviously, studios are still buying properties and screenplays—in some cases paying millions for scripts from unknown or unsold writers. And they're still making movies, many for previously unheard-of sums. So, if all of this is true—where have the studios become more cautious about spending money?

PRODUCTION SCHEDULES

First off, as producer Gail Lyon notes, "the studios are just flat-out making fewer movies on the whole. Some studios are making more,

some less, but on the whole there are fewer studio productions going on."

But, if overall revenues are going up (or even remaining anything close to level) while the number of releases is going down, it
would seem that business is good—and that making more movies
would mean making more money. Somehow, the studios don't see
it that way.

The practical upshot of this is that, with fewer production slots
available, the competition among projects hoping to win those slots
becomes more fierce. In short: it's not as easy as it used to be—and
it was never easy to begin with. Compounding this situation is . . .

THE NEAR-DEATH OF STUDIO DEVELOPMENT

"Development" is the process of taking something that's not yet
ready and *developing* it into something that is. The starting point
might be a finished screenplay, a book, play, true story, comic,
game, myth, even a bare-bones concept. Once upon a time, studios
would buy mere concepts, on the chance they might be developed
into films. Joe Eszterhas was famously paid nearly $4 million for the
Showgirls concept, which he'd sketched out on a cocktail napkin.
Those days are gone.

Time was, too, when studios had vast armies of development
people working hundreds if not thousands of projects, collaborating
with outside writers and producers to transform them into projects
the studios were willing to make. You may have heard this process
referred to as "screenwriting by committee" or (more likely) "development hell."

Sometimes the process worked brilliantly; most times it didn't.
In either event, it often dragged on for years, with an ever-rotating
cast of studio executives with different and often conflicting opinions on what the end result should be. Everyone involved drew
paychecks for seemingly endless rounds of notes and revisions. The
majority of projects that went into studio development died there,
never to be seen again. But for every hundred projects acquired and

developed, *x* number of those would pay off and become movies. The studios considered this a cost of doing business.

No longer.

Screenwriter/producer Leslie Dixon's career spans twenty-five years. "We're in a period now that's different from any I've known since I started in this business," she notes. "The studios finally seem to recognize that the way they've been doing development doesn't work very well. They're developing far less now, and spending their development dollars more wisely. It's not the same as it was five, six years ago. They're not really looking to make development deals anymore; they're looking for things that are ready to go."

Producer Michael Nozik recalls a project of his that made it to the screen when—and because—development was easier. "When I did *Motorcycle Diaries* (NFBs/TRU), my partner was Robert Redford. We really liked the project, obviously—but when you read that book, it's really a journal, a series of vignettes. There's no apparent narrative there that would drive a movie. It would have been very hard to sell that, even to independent studios, because it was a leap of faith, really, thinking we could turn it into a movie.

"We were able to do it because we had a deal with this European financing entity that provided a fund that we could use to develop projects at our discretion. So we didn't have to presell them, we didn't have to go in with the book and say, what do you think; will you finance this? We could say we want to access our money, develop this, and we'll bring you the script at the end, because we believe we can get there from here. Those kinds of deals are much harder to get these days.

"A few years ago, I was afforded a very inside look at the studio financing models and I realized that in fact, their profit center is in the distribution business. They wound up in the production and development business by necessity, in order to feed their distribution mechanism.

"There's a high risk associated with production, and especially with development. So if they can figure out a way to avoid that, they're happy. They used the economic crash of a few years ago as an excuse—which was a real excuse, but it was still an excuse—to downgrade their development and get out of that business. And to a large extent they have. I think this is a permanent shift. The world has been remade a little bit, and it's not going to come back, ever, in the way it was, regardless of how the economy fares."

As producer Gail Lyon observes, "what's happened is that much of the risk structure of moviemaking has shifted away from the studios. They're not willing to pay somebody a hundred thousand dollars to see if it's going to work out. They want you to write it, and then they'll let you know if it worked out by buying the script. For the writer, that may mean more speculative unpaid work, but a better chance at success, and probably a bigger payday at the end."

THE DOWNSIDE

The downside is the domino effect. With the studios looking for projects that are "ready to go" instead of merely "promising," all of the people and companies in the business of finding material and presenting it to the studios for consideration—which is just about everyone—must follow suit.

Agents, managers, and production companies can no longer afford to take on numerous projects requiring a significant amount of development work. Instead, they must concentrate almost exclusively on projects that are already "there," or very nearly so. With the studios no longer willing to pick up the development tab, development itself is on the wane. "And that," says screenwriter/producer Jonathan Hensleigh, "is a recent, sad and shitty development."

This has the effect of raising the bar at all levels, as material which might well have been taken on a few years back—and perhaps successfully developed—must now be turned away. Agents, managers, and production companies can't sell what no one's buying.

THE UPSIDE

"One of the very few good things about these hard economic times," says Leslie Dixon, "is that—once you have an agent—the major agencies will really work for you, the writer-client, to package a script you might write on spec.

"There are fewer movies being made and fewer jobs, so actors' agents will actually read the script that you wrote and think, hey this might be good for, say (*Limitless/Hangover* star) Bradley Cooper. You might even get Bradley Cooper to read it.

"Now if you're a good writer and you've written a good script, and you can go to a studio and say, 'Okay I've got David Fincher and Bradley Cooper attached and here's the script'—don't you think they'll give it an amazingly hard look? Whereas in better times, when jobs weren't so scarce, it was harder to get people's attention even with a good project.

"So that's the game right now, if you're willing to risk writing a script with no studio payment at all. You might be able to sell it outright. Or, depending on who you know, you might be able to get it packaged and sold and made by getting the right actor involved. That's the main trigger that gets movies made, as opposed to getting scripts bought—who's in it. That's the surest way to see it on the screen. But of course you need the script in order to interest and attach the actor or other element." (For more on packaging, see Chapter 27.)

The latter is, she adds, "advice for someone who already has their foot in the door." But a curious thing happened on the way to the development gallows. You might not need to have your own foot in the door—if you can hook up with someone whose foot is already there.

DEVELOPMENT RELOADED

The abandonment of studio development has quite recently spawned a new kind of entity: the development company. Their function is to identify promising properties, develop them into something with a reasonable shot at being sold—and then present them to industry players who can help sell, finance, or buy them. One of these—The Writers' Shop, founded in 2011 (http://thewritersshop.com/)— even specializes in adaptations. Their motto: "Adapt or Die."

"There are now a number of these non-studio entities," says Michael Nozik, "that are developing or financing development at a much lower cost than was possible at the studios. And then they go on to serve as producers on the movie, and sometimes as cofinanciers. They might develop a book, for example, a piece of literature that may be a drama or thriller, a midrange budget, maybe a project that falls between genres—in short, something that's not an obvious franchise and doesn't come in the door with a large star attached. Studios are loathe to finance development on something like that. They used to, but not now.

"So while the development game is getting tougher, there are a growing number of these new companies out there. And that's a good thing, because studio development—aside from development of branded names, meaning things that have already achieved some success as bestsellers, comic books, games, and so on—is certainly becoming an extinct beast."

Lacking the top-heavy staff and large budgets previously associated with studio development arms, these new dwellers in the Hollywood jungle must be everything their often lumbering predecessors were not: swift, efficient, and discerning. They can't be juggling a hundred different projects which might—and might not—pan out at some point in the next five or ten years. In a world too long ruled by dinosaurs, these are the early mammals.

Different companies pursue different strategies: some pay the project's owner and wind up with all rights to the developed or adapted version of the property; others charge for services and allow the project's creator-owner to retain ownership of the developed/ adapted versions, while helping to find an agent, manager, or buyer.

Some are tied to particular financiers or allied companies that have a say in which projects are pursued and/or get first dibs on all finished scripts; others operate independently and are free to pursue whatever they like, and take the finished projects to whatever people or companies seem the best fit.

Which of these and other strategies will ultimately prove successful, allowing their wielders to survive and evolve in a rapidly-changing environment, remains to be seen. Some of these players will learn to fly; others will be eaten.

Adapt or die, indeed.

CHAPTER 35
PASSION

You hear a lot of talk in Hollywood about "passion." The reason is simple: in a town where an ever-increasing number of people are all trying to get their projects made into movies, passion is often the tipping point that determines which projects move forward. And while it's true that all the passion in the world is unlikely to save an intrinsically flawed project—it's also true that when several projects of roughly equal merit are under consideration, passion can be your ace in the hole. This is true at every stage of the process, for the same reason that movies themselves affect us so deeply: we are emotional beings, driven by—and responding to—passion.

"With any project," says Oscar-nominated screenwriter Susannah Grant, "you look for something that gets you thinking about it when you're brushing your teeth and doing your grocery shopping. Where you're thinking about it all the time. Something that gets under your skin."

Producer Gail Lyon, who worked with Susannah on *Erin Brockovich* (TRU), says "it's unbelievably vague when you try to pin it down—a bit like the Supreme Court definition of pornography: I don't know exactly how to define it, but I know it when I see it. If something makes me laugh, makes me cry, makes me angry or uncomfortable; if it touches me on a human level and I'm thinking about it the next day, I pay attention. Even if it disturbed or upset me. Because anything that has the power to break through the clutter of our lives is something to pay attention to.

"And it has to be special, because you're going to be living with the material for a long time. So you need that passion to sustain you."

In the long run, it's passion—perhaps obsession might be a better word—that keeps you going in the face of adversity. Oscar-nominated writer/director/producer Lesli Linka Glatter stresses the importance of passion-driven tenacity. "Don't accept no. Just keep at it. You can have hundreds of no's, but all it takes is one person who says yes."

Producer Gale Anne Hurd's projects range from TV series and movies to big-screen blockbusters. "Work hard, be passionate about your projects, and persevere when the going gets tough," she counsels. "Jim [Cameron] and I had twelve passes on *The Terminator*. We were down to our very last pitch—and sold it on the thirteenth try."

"Write your passion," advises writer/director/producer Paul Haggis, who was nominated for five Oscars in three years (winning two). "I didn't do that for a long time. I didn't take the big risks. I always tried to do what my agent wanted or suggested, what he said the studios wanted. The only people who can truly hurt you in this business are the people who are trying to help you. And they'll do it with the best of intentions, because they want you to succeed. But you have to succeed on your own terms."

That's something Haggis is known for. His passion—and his talent—have allowed him to make (and inspire others to make) movies that break the rules. "*Crash* and *Million Dollar Baby* (STO)," he notes, "are not Hollywood studio movies. No one's going to make those. They're not even independent movies; every independent producer turned them down. *Million Dollar Baby* was a story about girl boxing and euthanasia, in which the hero kills the heroine in the end. I kept hearing, 'It's a really good movie, Paul, but no one's ever going to make it.' They said that about *Crash* as well.

"People wanted to change the ending, but I never considered it. I'm just glad I got Clint Eastwood to do it; someone who's not afraid to make a film with rough edges and really raw emotions. It ends in a very satisfying way, but it's not a happy way. You lead your characters toward their destiny, and that was her destiny. And if she'd suddenly gotten better and come back and won, it would be, 'Oh yeah, nice story.' No one would remember it.

"Both of those stories are in my heart, and that's the most important thing. The only rule one should never break is that you have to be passionate about what you're doing. That's it."

At the same time, it must be pointed out that *Crash* (Haggis' first film) was shot on a $6.5 million budget, while *Million Dollar Baby* (with its more substantial $30 million budget) had Clint Eastwood at the helm. Both films were raging successes.

Which brings up another issue: it's easier to break the rules when your project is (by Hollywood standards) inexpensive, or when someone with a solid track record and considerable industry influence becomes passionate about it. Neither of these particular movies was easy to put together. Several studios passed on *Million Dollar Baby* even after Eastwood signed on to star and direct, and his home studio refused to fully fund it, forcing Eastwood to find additional financing (and foreign distribution) on his own. The project was delayed for years. That's what you face when you break the rules. But, in the end, passion can—as it did here—carry the day.

When a producer, director, or star becomes truly passionate about a screenplay—falls in love with it—he (or she) will go to extraordinary lengths to make things happen. After producing the Tom Cruise/Jamie Foxx thriller *Collateral* (written by Stuart Beattie), producer Julie Richardson came across a romantic comedy script she couldn't live without. The only problem was—no one could find the writer.

"I wanted this script," Julie recalls, "and by God, I was going to get it." Unable to locate the vacationing writer on her own, she hired a private detective to track him down—and then optioned the script. I know this because I am that writer. (We're currently developing the script.) That's passion.

It's often said that Hollywood is more about who you know than what, and many writers spend vast amounts of time trying to connect with people in the industry. But if you can craft a screenplay that gets readers passionate about characters and story— Hollywood will want to know you.

And that, ultimately, is what you want.

PART VI

ADAPTATION ROUNDTABLE

When your project sells to Hollywood—it sells to Hollywood. "You put your stuff up for sale," says screenwriter and attorney Jonathan Hensleigh. "They offer you money for it. Once you accept the money, that's it. Unless you're a Michael Crichton type with a big fat name and come on as a producer. Otherwise you have no power, no rights, no nothin'."

Screenwriter Leslie Dixon concurs. "I can write a screenplay," she says, "but the minute I sell it, I no longer own it. Complaining about what the buyer does with it is like selling a house, and then getting upset because the buyer remodeled."

Or, as novelist and screenwriter Rita Mae Brown once put it, "You sell a screenplay like you sell a car. If somebody drives it off a cliff, that's it."

And of course, that's exactly what every author or rights-holder most fears. But how likely is that, really? Who exactly are these people who adapt other works into screenplays, and produce and direct them? What goes through their minds during the adaptation process? Are they looking to change everything they possibly can—or to preserve the essence of the original, insofar as that's possible?

This chapter presents a roundtable discussion featuring the thoughts of over two dozen authors, screenwriters, producers and directors on issues surrounding the central dilemma facing any adaptation: what stays, what goes, what changes—and why.

CHAPTER 36
KEEPING THE FAITH WHILE BEING DIFFERENT

The head of the screenwriting program at the world's best-known film school has flatly stated that the adapting screenwriter owes absolutely nothing to the source material or its author. Fortunately, those who actually perform adaptations—and do it best—feel differently.

"When I first met [screenwriter] Simon Beaufoy," recalls Vikas Swarup, whose novel *Q&A* became the movie *Slumdog Millionaire,* "he was very candid. He said, 'I've read your book; it's a fantastic novel, but the entire novel won't be made into a movie, because what you wrote is a book and what I am going to do is a screenplay, and the twain don't often completely meet, so to speak. But I promise you that I will remain faithful to the soul of your novel.'

"And although there are major deviations from the book, some of which I disagreed with, that's a promise he kept. So on the whole, I am satisfied with the final product. It's visually dazzling, emotionally appealing, and certainly packs a punch." *Slumdog Millionaire* became a worldwide sensation, earning nearly $400 million at the box office and winning eight Academy Awards, including Best Picture and Best Adapted Screenplay.

Mike Richardson is founder of Dark Horse Comics, a company whose titles have spawned over two dozen film adaptations including *300, Sin City, Alien vs. Predator, Timecop, R.I.P.D.,* and the *Mask* and *Hellboy* franchises. "Movies get developed in certain directions," he advises, "and it's just a fact of the process that changes from the underlying property will occur. At some point, films take on a life of their own."

Radical Publishing, a comic book company cofounded by Barry Levine in 2007, has already set up a dozen adaptation projects at Hollywood studios, including *Hercules: The Thracian Wars* (COM), *Oblivion* (COM), *Shrapnel* (COM), *The Last Days of American Crime* (COM), *Aladdin: Legacy of the Lost* (COM), *Hotwire* (COM), and *Earp: Saints for Sinners* (COM).

"I can sit here all day and say I want you to do this and this and this because I'm creative," he says, "but that and a cup of coffee will get me nowhere. The people who make movies are in a business, and I have to be collaborative and take that into consideration."

That doesn't mean, however, that the essence of the source material need be lost. "When adapting something," says Bill Marsilii, who is best known for *Déjà Vu,* but has adapted everything from children's books to comics to classic novels, "I think it's important to find that core of light at the heart of the original, the thing that makes it worth all the trouble you're going to go to in adapting it. And you build out from there. Different stories present different challenges. There's pulp fiction, which may have a fantastic plot but doesn't seem to have much of a soul. And there are beautiful, profoundly lyrical novels that have all the deep meaning in the world, but don't have a plot you can hang a movie on. In each case, it's up to you to provide what's missing.

"When I'm adapting someone else's work, I look at it as if they're the birth parents, and I've adopted their child. I feel a certain degree of fidelity and respect to them, and I certainly don't seek to deliberately do something with their work that is guaranteed to infuriate them for no better reason than my own ego. I don't blithely go in and change character names to something I like better, just because I can. As much as possible I try to use the original work.

"But also . . . I've never been an adoptive parent, but I imagine there comes a point fairly early on where you have to stop saying this is somebody else's child and I'm just looking after it. The story becomes, at least in your mind, your own—because if you don't bring the same degree of passion to this endeavor that you would with your own work, it's not going to be the best that you can do. And I say that without any disrespect to whoever originally created it.

"Ideally I want the creator of a work I'm adapting to look at what I've done with it and say, 'Wow, I never would have thought of that, but I like it.' I had exactly that happen on a comic I'm adapting, *Blood of the Innocent.* The creators of the comic (Mark Wheatley, Rickey Shanklin, and Marc Hempel) went out of their way to tell me how pleased they were with what I'd done. When I heard that, I thought, oh thank God. If they hadn't cared for it, I can't say that that would have stopped the whole thing in its tracks. But wherever possible, I'd certainly like to have the blessing of the person who started everything."

Screenwriter Terry Rossio's adaptations run the gamut from children's books to theme park rides, and have collectively earned billions at the box office. (In fact, some of them have earned billions all by themselves.) When asked about common problems with source material, his answer is swift. "Too much information. Too many scenes. Too many characters. Films are like songs or poetry; every scene, every line of dialogue counts toward the unified whole. Extraneous material can be distracting or boring in a movie, rather than immersive and deepening the theme, and characters, as in a book.

"Your first requirement in writing an adaptation is to *make an effective movie,* based upon the source material. Your goal absolutely cannot be to 'preserve the source material onto the screen.'

Whether the original source material was a novel, short story, play, comic book, television series or whatever, it has to now work, and be effective and powerful, on its own merits, in its new dramatic form.

"Make a good film and the die-hard fans may complain you took liberties with the source material, but ultimately respect you for it. Make a film that is ineffective, and you get no credit for the accurate translation of source material to the screen." As Terry's sometime cowriter Bill Marsilii notes, "A fairly faithful adaptation of an inherently noncinematic book helps no one."

Oscar-nominated producer Michael Nozik—best known for *The Next Three Days* (MOV), *Syriana* (NFB/TRU), *The Motorcycle Diaries* (NFBs/TRU) and *Quiz Show* (NFB/TRU)—agrees. "It's true that a book can support more characters than a movie. So what you often do is combine characters from the book into a single character, so that one character might serve multiple purposes. And you might invent new storylines—hopefully in the spirit of the source material—to bridge the things that were brought over from the book, and help get you from Place A to Place B.

"Everything is done on a case-by-case basis, but I don't think you can be doctrinaire or religious to the source material, because by doing that you may be hurting the movie. You try to honor the original, especially if there's an existing fan base because you don't want them to be pissed off. But at the same time you're creating something new, that must exist under a different set of rules.

"Whether you're a producer or a writer, the one thing that always applies is this: you have to be willing to kill your babies, to lose things you're fond of. You can't lose sight of the bigger picture. There may be things that you once needed in order to figure out the story, but they don't need to be in the finished screenplay. They were stepping stones along the way. And in order to get to the very essence of the story, they have to go. You have to do this without violating the spirit of the work that first attracted you to the source material—but it must be done."

John August has adapted children's books, TV series, and novels, and is perhaps best known for the *Big Fish* (NOV), *Charlie's Angels* (TVS), *Charlie and the Chocolate Factory* (NOV), and *Corpse Bride* movies. "The novelist can spend four pages describing the texture of a sheet," he observes. "The kinds of things you can do on the page are wonderful, but not all of them translate. The screenwriter only has sight and sound, and about two hours to tell everything, and that's very different.

"With a book, someone can stop and put it down, then pick it up later. If they miss something, they can flip back a few pages. Movies just keep trucking forward at twenty-four frames per second, and you can't hit the rewind button in the theater.

"A large part of the screenwriter's job is making sure that the reader, and ultimately the viewer, never becomes confused in a way that makes it impossible to follow the story. It's not just simplification, it's sort of predigesting the story so it can go down smoothly the first time through. The same thing is true in TV, which is very rewindable at this point: it has to make sense the first time. You have to moment by moment trust and understand what's happening in the story. And being able to model that in the reader and ultimately the viewer's head, in terms of what information they have at any given point, is a big focus for the screenwriter.

"A lot of times when people criticize movie adaptations of books, they seem to think that you should be able to just rip the pages out of the book and feed them one at a time into a machine and project them on the screen. And that never works well. Some of the projects I come into are so crammed with really good ideas that they'd make the movie a little bit overstuffed. I may need to simplify and winnow things down, or invent completely new characters and put them in new scenes and situations in order for the story to make sense.

"You have to approach the adaptation while asking yourself what is it about this idea that wants to be a movie, what parts of the underlying source material can translate well to a movie version, and what parts need to change in the transition? How will the audience know the information they need to know, when they need to know it? It's about taking something that you love and figuring out how to elevate it and make it rewarding on the screen. A lot of screenwriting is just setting your ego aside. It's trying to write the best version of the movie that you know how to write, so the people who need to make the movie will be able to do it.

"The book is already done, and it's always going to be exactly what the author wanted it to be. New people will discover it and love it through the movie, and they're going to discover that it's its own unique thing."

Terry Rossio comments on the perception that adaptations are easy. "If you're like me, when you first think about doing an adaptation, you're thrilled. Adapting a bestseller, say, is like having a brilliant, professional, award-winning writing partner who's willing to do all the work—characters, plot, the whole thing—but you get complete power to change any element you want. Sweet. And you think, 'Hey, these people are paying me to just sit down and retype that masterful prose into screenplay form!' That attitude doesn't last. Turns out doing adaptations is really hard.

"Plot and story are where most of the changes on a property will take place, as the original concepts find their form in the new medium of film. 'Plot' is defined here as the events that take place, and 'story' is the way in which you choose to present those events to an audience. It might not seem so at first, but plot is the least important element to retain from a property. The events which occur must remain malleable. This is where you bring all your knowledge of film structure, scene construction, visual storytelling, transitions, etc. to bear in order to tell the story on film. Yet scenes which are changed, and new scenes invented, must continue to feel as though they live in the world of the original property.

"In the end, when doing an adaptation, the true measure of success is whether you're able to duplicate in the film medium the experience the audience felt with the property in its original form. Simply, if they laughed during the play, or were inspired by the comic, or thrilled by the page-turner novel—those are the emotions they should feel when they see it on screen. Give them those same emotions on film, and your adaptation will be a success."

Jonathan Hensleigh's biggest film—*Armageddon*—was an original, but he's also written a number of adaptations, including *Die Hard with a Vengeance,* which was both a sequel to a book adaptation (because the first *Die Hard* movie was based on Roderick Thorp's novel *Nothing Lasts Forever*) and a screenplay adaptation (because the script that became *Die Hard with a Vengeance* was first written by Hensleigh as an original screenplay called *Simon Says,* and later adapted for the *Die Hard* franchise). He recently directed his second feature, *Kill the Irishman,* which is based on a true story.

"You see families of problems in source materials," he says. "Sometimes there are things there that shouldn't be there; other times things that should be there are not. I see both situations equally. The project I'm hoping to direct next is based on a high-concept graphic novel that has two wonderful characters but no plot. Well, it has a first act, but no middle and no end. So I have to add that.

"On the other hand, there's a lot of source material where you think, I don't know how the underlying rights author is going to react to this, but the final four hundred pages of his novel or whatever, I just don't need. Once you get to this point, this page, you can end it right there. And if you don't, the story—as a movie—is going to drag."

Leslie Dixon agrees, but points out that things can occasionally go the other way. "There might be something that has a great idea in it, but not a single scene that would translate to a cinematic experience," she notes. "While at the other extreme, there are books that are movies waiting to happen. You've got the characters, the story, the scenes are really dramatic, it's got action, and the author did the work for you in figuring out the action sequences. But for every hundred published novels, there's maybe only one that has a movie screaming to get out.

"In others, the story doesn't go where a movie audience would feel fulfilled and so you have to change it, or a character behaves in a way that is just so reprehensible—they kill a child or something— that it would throw you right out of the movie. There are some things that modern audiences for studio pictures—as opposed to art house pictures—simply won't accept.

"In the case of *Limitless,* somewhere around the halfway point in the novel, I just knew it was a movie. I felt this unbelievable gut surge that I had to get that book and it would become a movie. All told, the film's setup is identical and the character of Eddie is [novel author] Alan's character. That character and Alan's voice are what made me fall in love with the book. I felt a simpatico with him as a writer. He wrote the kind of prose that I would like to write if I wrote prose, and I knew that I could pick up his voice where he left off.

"At the same time, much as I respect Alan and the work, I knew this movie—unlike the book—was probably going to have to have some major action in it, or it would never be made. Also, I didn't think the audience wanted to see the movie end as the book does, with the hero in a motel room, waiting to come down from his last pill and die. I just didn't think that was going to work in a movie."

Alan Glynn wrote *The Dark Fields* novel on which *Limitless* is based. "The book is a morality tale, a Faustian pact where [main character] Eddie ultimately has to pay." The movie, though, had to be something else. Says Dixon: "It was always, always, always my intention to have him get away with it. The last thing anybody would want to see was some sort of moralistic comeuppance. I wanted this to be gleefully amoral."

Dixon made no secret of her intentions. "Just out of respect and liking for Alan, I kept him updated through the entire process. I always told him when I was changing something, I always told him why. He said that in the end there were a thousand emails between us."

"I knew Leslie 'got' the book," Alan recalls, "and wasn't going to turn it into a musical or a romantic comedy, so I wasn't worried in the slightest. I was very satisfied with the movie. In some respects it's very faithful to the book, and in other respects it goes its own way. The thing is, if you're saying something or making a point in a book you've written, you'd be foolish to expect a movie version to say exactly the same thing or make exactly the same point in the same way. My attitude has always been that it's my book, their movie."

Sideways author Rex Pickett had a similar experience. The whole middle of his novel—a lengthy hunting adventure gone awry—is absent from the movie. Character names and careers were altered, and the ending (ironically declared "too Hollywood" by the director) changed.

Nevertheless, says Pickett, "I was ecstatic, really, and thrilled with how faithful it was to my book. They were very generous to give me every draft of the script. I made very few comments, but [writer/director] Alexander Payne either incorporated them or met me halfway." Pickett's suggestions led to Maya's memorable wine dialogue on the porch, and also to Miles showing up at Maya's door in the final scene.

Oscar-nominated screenwriter Susannah Grant—whose credits include *Erin Brockovich* (TRU), *Pocahontas* (HIS), *The Soloist* (NFB/TRU), *Charlotte's Web* (NOV), *28 Days,* and *In Her Shoes* (NOV)—sees things from the other side of the fence, but winds up in pretty much the same place. "With an adaptation, you've got the start of a vocabulary that you're using, so you're starting with something as opposed to starting with nothing. That's both liberating and restricting. When adapting *In Her Shoes,* I took out, I think, a hundred page section of the book, and reduced it to two scenes. Because what happened to the character was very important, and it couldn't be left out, but the long journey that she went on, which was perfectly valid in novel form, couldn't possibly be done in a movie. It would have turned into a very meandering telling of the tale. And while that can be an effective way of telling a film story, it tends not to be effective in the marketplace, so that wasn't something my partners were terribly interested in.

"Still, there was something very truthful there that had to be included. And so I had to find a way to make it happen in a different way. I think it's a really faithful adaptation in spirit, and I know the novelist is really happy with it."

It should be said, however, that things don't always go so swimmingly. Screenwriter Jeb Stuart, best known for *The Fugitive* (TVS) and *Die Hard* (NOV), tells the story of his first meeting with the Big Producer on what would turn out to be Stuart's first produced film. The producer's words of greeting? "Hi. Nice to meet you. Great script. But I just want to tell you, you're fired." The same producer later rehired him—and then refired him. Such is life in Hollywood, the problem with professional courtesy being that it only applies to courteous professionals. Still, while it's always nice to find someone nice, it's not always necessary to find someone nice to get a great picture made. In Stuart's case, the resulting film was *Die Hard*.

"Every set of collaborators you have is totally different," says Leslie Dixon. "You can be on a lovely set with kind, delightful people and have a bomb of a movie. And you can have the most contentious pack of pit bulls tearing at each other for the entire shoot and have the movie turn out to be a hit. There is no one way that things happen."

Paul Haggis is one of the nice guys. He's been nominated for five Academy Awards, including Best Adapted Screenplay, Best Original Screenplay (twice), Best Director, and Best Picture—winning Best Picture and Best Original Screenplay for his first film, *Crash*. He's adapted source materials ranging from short stories and magazine articles to true-life dramas, other films, and James Bond novels. "It seems like adaptations should be easier," he finds, "but it's almost always harder to adapt. I thought adapting *Million Dollar Baby* (STO) would be simple, because I started with this great short story. But trying to figure out how to make it work as a movie involved many difficult decisions. *Flags of Our Fathers* (NFB) is this huge, wonderful, sprawling book that I never thought I would be able to adapt. I kept telling Clint [Eastwood, who directed] that someone else should do it, but he wouldn't let me give up. It wasn't possible to tell the whole story in two hours, so it became about which part of this big story to tell, and how best to tell it.

"What I do is, I read the book or other material once, and put it down. And then I create the story without referring to the book again. Because I find that if you keep refering to the book as you create the outline, there's so much to love in it, you get caught up and fall in love with every chapter and every character. And you can't do that, because your screen time is limited. You have to pick and choose.

"Go with your impressions, the things from the book that stick with you, and you can usually find a story there. Getting the structure down is the key. Each piece of work, each book or novel or piece of nonfiction or short story is its own distinct challenge, and you have to distance yourself a little to do it justice."

True stories present unique challenges. Real life seldom structures itself neatly into three acts, is sometimes repetitive, and can be boring for long stretches. The Big Important Stuff is invariably mixed in with mundane minutiae and maddening monotony. Real life can also seem, at times, random or pointless. None of which is acceptable onscreen. People can get that in their own lives; they don't need to go to the movies—much less pay for the experience.

The hardest thing to adapt is a true story," says Haggis. "I did that with *In the Valley of Elah* (ART/TRU). I wanted to base it on these horrific acts and this very real man who went in search of his dead son, but I also wanted to tell a more universal story. I needed to tell not just the father's story but, perhaps, a deeper truth. So I decided to fictionalize parts of the story. Because while the actual events were compelling, overall, it wasn't a movie story. I also had to fill in large parts of the story that were unknown to those who survived.

"Many of the specifics remain true. His search for his son is true, but took place over a period of eight months; I needed it to happen in a matter of weeks. I real life, every time the protagonist went back to the local police or military police or the FBI, he dealt with someone different; I constructed characters he'd deal with consistently, because you need continuity on the screen."

Early on, Haggis made a conscious decision to avoid meeting Lanny Davis, whose story he was writing. "I knew I'd fall in love with him, and I wouldn't be able to have any sort of distance from him. And I would tell his story, instead of the deeper, more universal truth. So I didn't meet with him until after I sent him the script. And Lanny was upset about it at first, saying this isn't true and that's not true.

"He wasn't talking about the facts—he was talking about what he believed to be true about the nature of his son, what he knew that he would and would not do, and what he suspected others of doing. He was talking about his truth. I had to tell the story based on what I believed to be true. And that hurt him. He wanted so desperately to think of his son as a hero. Which he was—but he was a very flawed human being as well. And the war and trying to be the hero his father was, had done that to him." Eventually, Lanny came to love the project, and helped promote the movie.

"But that was hard. You have to look at really painful truths. I have to hold my characters accountable, and to do that I may need to take a rusty butter knife and dig around in their hearts as well as my own. And with a true story, you've got someone else sitting there saying, 'Why are you doing this to me? Get the rusty butter knife out of my chest.' But I think in the end, if you trust the writer, it may be a better story than you thought it was going to be."

Susannah Grant, whose adaptations include true stories, children's books, and novels, took the opposite approach when writing *Erin Brockovich* (TRU), which was nominated for five Academy Awards, including Best Picture and Best Screenplay. "I know a lot of people come away from the movie with sort of this thematic idea that one person can make a difference," she says—which might be kin to Haggis' "deeper truth." But, says Grant, "that was never something that mattered that much to me.

"The thing that really attracted me to Erin was she was a person who had not fit well into a lot of situations in life, for reasons that were very particular to who she was as a person. And through the chain of events that you see in the movie, she found herself in a position where all of those aspects of her character that had made life difficult for her, and made her incompatible with many situations—were exactly the qualities that were needed in this situation.

"And to me that was beautiful; somebody finding their pocket in life and not barking up the wrong tree and being ineffective because they're not being true to who they are. She was incredibly true to who she was. And that was difficult for a lot of people, but that happens to anyone who is living really truthfully. And I was drawn to that. And also to the idea that she really believed that everybody deserves somebody there to hear their story."

Because she wanted to tell Erin's personal story, she decided to hang out with her before starting work on the screenplay. "You get their voice and their feel and their vibe in your system enough so that you feel like you can write with some semblance of confidence that you won't betray the truth of who they are—or a truth of who they are.

"I say, *a* truth rather than *the* truth because you can't possibly fit the totality of someone's life into a screenplay. Even if you take just one year of that life, you can't fit all of that human experience into a movie. Nor should you, because it would be stultifying and dreadful to watch. What I find most effective is to just figure out why you-the-writer have chosen this story to tell, and what the point is—why it's worth sharing. And for me, usually, that's about an idea the person represents. And then you think, okay, what parts of this story support that idea, and what parts of this person's story may be interesting but don't have anything to do with the point I'm trying to make in telling this story.

"And that becomes a way of figuring out which parts of their story to highlight and dramatize, and which to let fall by the wayside while knowing that those things may be part of their lives, but they're not part of this story. And obviously there are some things you just can't leave out, that you have to include to fall short of telling a fallacy."

Screenwriter Bill Marsilii holds to a similar standard. "The term that I've come up with for my own ethical satisfaction," he says, "is condensed truth. If I'm changing the order in which certain events happened, if I'm condensing certain characters, if I have no way of knowing what they said and I'm making it up, or if what they said isn't terrifically cinematic, or if it took them twenty minutes to say something that I know how to say in three lines—as long as I'm not twisting what really happened into a lie, I believe ethically that that's proper. In fact it's necessary. What I have a problem with is movies that present something as true when it isn't, or—far worse in my opinion—when they present something as true that is 180 degrees from what actually happened."

Adds producer Michael Nozik: "Anyone who's got a true story that they're trying to tell, they should be prepared for the reality that even in the best of circumstances, the story's going to get restructured and remade into something that works dramatically as a movie. In some cases, the real-life events are more inspiration than blueprint for the movie." Which is why you don't often see "This is a true story" come up on the screen.

"With fiction and nonfiction," Nozik continues, "the original author has to realize that someone is going to reinterpret what they've written, because it's now moving into another realm. Some of the most confident and experienced authors will be more comfortable with that, whereas younger authors who are more protective are going to have a hard time with it. But it's inevitable. There's always going to be some variance from what it was, and probably some significant variance, to make it work in a movie theater."

Producer Gail Lyon—whose credits include *Erin Brockovich* (TRU), *Gattaca, Edge of Darkness* (TVS) and *Stuart Little 2* (NOV)— says, "I always tell the people I'm getting involved with, when there's a book for instance, that they have to be willing to let go of the book, because film is a completely different medium with completely different accent points.

"You have to be emotionally prepared for the fact that your material has a life as a book, and it's now going to morph into a different entity. The movie and the book are not going to be the same, and if that disturbs you, you shouldn't do it. I try to deal with that very early on, because some people can accept it, and other's can't.

"Accepting it doesn't mean that we're going to denigrate your material, but it does mean it's going to be different. A lot of times, if we were to shoot even a fantastic book just the way it is— unchanged—it would be a fail as a movie. So let us help the story have its best life as a movie, just as it has a best life as a book."

Ed Solomon has adapted novels, novel series, movies, comics and TV series—including *Men in Black* (COM), *Charlie's Angels* (TVS), and the upcoming *How to Disappear Completely* (MOV) and *Tokyo Suckerpunch* (NOV). "The biggest lesson I've learned through all the different kinds of adaptations I've done," he counsels, "is that you have to ingest and digest the source material, so it's inside of you. Live with it until you feel like you know that world and those characters. But at the same time, try to treat it with the same deference and respect and arm's-length distance as your own ideas, so that you can then start to collaborate with the original piece in a non-attached and nonemotional way. So you're truly using what really works for the movie, but you're also free to not use those things that don't work for the movie. Because each individual movie is its own organic form that's going to need to exist separately from the original.

"Now, it also seriously depends on what your source material is, and where that source material lives in either cultural memory or current culture. If you're adapting *Harry Potter,* that's different from adapting an obscure Russian short story from the nineteenth century. There are legions of fans out there with certain expectations.

"I try to go with, what does this mean to me? What is this idea? And as you start to build the movie, certain things that you think you're going to keep start to fall away, and certain things that you thought would fall away maybe return. There's a lot of invention going on as the script starts to take on its own life.

"And in fact I've been in situations where the flaws of the first couple of drafts came about because I was holding on too tightly to things that already existed, and in their new incarnation they didn't feel real or true anymore. They were part of an older iteration of the story, and I had to be willing to let go of them in order to more truly hold onto the deeper spirit of the piece. It wasn't until I finally let go completely of what originally existed, that I was able to finish. Oddly, when I went back and looked at the original again, I realized how much of it I'd actually kept.

"I try really hard to honor not just the source material itself, but the spirit of what I perceived it could be, and what I found inspiring about it in the first place."

Terry Rossio seconds that. "In writing adaptations," he says, "we give ourselves an additional challenge: to preserve as much of the source material as possible, and write the new material in the voice of the source material as much as possible. In fact, adding to the story or complementing the story in the style and tone of the original writer is one of the main challenges of doing an adaptation."

He, too, takes a hard look at the original story's place in popular culture. "You need to consider the *prior* awareness of the property," he advises. "At the very start, you have to ask yourself some hard questions about what the general public knows about the material, and how widespread that awareness is. The answers can become a guide to what can be safely 'changed' and what needs to be protected at all costs. Audience expectations do affect the film-going experience.

"Disney Feature Animation is brilliant at understanding prior awareness of their properties. They pick high name-recognition material—such as *Aladdin* (MLF), or *The Little Mermaid* (MLF), or even *Hercules* (MLF). Then they figure out what the general public knows about them—with *Aladdin,* for example, people sort of expect a lamp, a genie, three wishes, and maybe a cave and a magic carpet. They don't exclude those elements, and then beyond them, they're free to change and invent as needed."

Isa Dick Hackett runs Electric Shepherd Productions, which administers the rights to the late Philip K. Dick's forty-five or so novels and 120-plus short stories. With a dozen films and TV series behind her—including *Blade Runner* (NOV), *Minority Report* (STO), *The Adjustment Bureau* (STO; she also executive produced the movie) and two *Total Recalls* (STO)—she's in a position to approve both the screenwriters and the directors who will bring her father's works to life onscreen. She could probably be dictatorial, if she thought that would make for better adaptations. But she doesn't.

"When I meet with someone about one of our stories," she relates, "I almost always say, 'Look, you need to know that I'm not so precious about the material that I think we should be watching the novel or the short story. I get that it has to be filmic, and sometimes there are great, fantastic films that keep only the core idea from the original. And that's fine, it's a different medium. So don't worry, we'll talk it through.' I don't ever want people to feel that somehow the goal here is to just have the novel on the screen. It doesn't work that way. I've seen adaptations that are so faithful it's remarkable. And that's admirable and wonderful and everything else, but you can wind up with less-than-stellar faithful films.

"Obviously, we want all good films. I'm not a writer, I'm not a director, and the best thing I can do is find the people who will do something terrific, put it in the right hands—and then say, 'Okay, go do your thing.' Because that's what they do." That strategy has paid off: at one time, most of her father's novels and stories were out of print; with the success of the movies propelling reader interest, U.S. publishers became confident enough to put the entire library back in print.

As one of those who does the doing, Bill Marsilii believes "the general challenge of it is to find those aspects of the book that are strongest, that are really the core of what it's about—even if it wasn't entirely successful at being about that. Then you jump in and try to make that as cinematic as possible. The late [screenwriter/producer] Jeffrey Boam had a phrase he used to refer to his writing, that I adopted very quickly. He said that at times his job as a writer was to come into an existing project and 'turn up the dials on everything.' If a scene is funny, try to make it gutbusting; if a scene is scary, try to make it terrifying; if uncomfortable, try to turn it all the way to incredibly creepy—and if it's something that's supposed to put a lump in the audience's throat, then try to make 'em bust out bawling.

"That doesn't mean there's no room for subtlety, and there are times when really all you want is a light moment, but often when one is adapting something, you take what the underlying material was doing well, and try to amplify it and deliver that in a movie. Of course if you're writing *Slinky: The Motion Picture,* then all bets are off and you have to invent virtually everything."

As a writer, director, and producer with heavy adaptation experience now writing a series of young adult novels he'd like to see made into movies, Jonathan Hensleigh finds himself in a fairly unique position. His knowledge of the film industry gives him the ability to render the books film-friendly from the start, by building cinematic appeal into the novels from page one.

"Everything that I like in a screenplay or movie," he says, "I also like in certain kinds of commercial literature, which is what I'm writing. And if you look at the things that have succeeded lately, blockbuster novels that have translated well regardless of age level—*The Girl with the Dragon Tattoo, Twilight, Harry Potter, Hunger Games*—I would venture vehemently that what made those things blockbuster novels is also what made them popular films. And that comes down to breakneck plotting and a very, very strong central character or core group of characters. That's it, that's what's powering those franchises.

"The world of Harry Potter, Hogwarts and all that, is lovely, it's wonderful, it's hugely inventive. But what powers those books, and Rowling has said this a number of times herself, is the breakneck plotting of the books. They're page-turners. It's the same with the others I've mentioned. They may be light-, middle-, or heavyweight in terms of violence and sex and other things, all of which can be dialed up or down for the movie. But they have jet fuel in them. The author keeps it moving, and that's the biggest translatable aspect, going from a novel to a film: you have to keep it moving. So that's what my emphasis is, and I'm constructing the plot of each novel as I would the plot of a screenplay."

A big part of that is—for want of a better word—simplification. "Simple is key," says Michael Nozik. "You have to be able to distill the dilemma, the crisis, the drama that the characters are going through down to something very simple and clear. That doesn't mean it has to be stupid simple, but we have to understand it.

"So many times you read a script that's very convoluted, and the drama is diffuse because of that. It doesn't work, because it could be distilled down to essential things. That's why a lot of movies that are strong emotionally are about things like family; we all have brothers and mothers and sisters and fathers, and those dynamics are always available to be shorthand for drama, because we all share that same shorthand."

Walter Kirn agrees. His *Up in the Air* novel underwent truly massive changes on its journey to the screen. Lead character Ryan Bingham now loves his job rather than hates it, bit player Alex (who had a drug habit) has been elevated to a story-spanning (and drug-free) romantic interest, and would-be nemesis Natalie Keener is almost a complete fabrication (one can sort of see where she came from, but the character just doesn't exist in the book). The film did over $160 million in box office, and was nominated for six Academy Awards, including Best Picture and Best Adapted Screenplay.

"Finally," says Kirn, "Hollywood movies—except for the very very greatest—are a lot simpler than even simple novels. They can accommodate so little. One love affair. One thing not working out and then getting repaired. One moment of disaffection where someone realizes their life is not what they thought it would be, or can even stand it to be. You have such a richer object in the book, really, especially for readers who want to dramatize it in their mind and illuminate it.

"But when you realize this, you then appreciate the genius of the screenwriter who knows that movies for the most part can't be as interior as books, and knows how to solve the problem by coming up with a solution that not only doesn't feel like problem-solving but lifts the whole thing into a whole different sort of tale, and gives the character a chance to show sides of himself, and interior patterns and thoughts and feelings that you the novelist would have loved to have shown too, but never figured out a way to.

"In the end, my experience of the whole adaptation was positive. Firstly because there's something in the artistry, to see all these beautiful, visual, technical and artistic resources applied to the poor skeletal structure of words where it began. Oh wow, they got casting, they got great singers to sing about the themes of my book, and people to make sure that the rooms in my book were the best-lit rooms, or the worst-lit but in a perfect way.

"It sort of feels like you're one of those struggling unemployed people on a home makeover show, and you drag back in from the payday check-cashing place where you just lost your last thirteen bucks to interest, and you walk into your house and a whole crew of smiling girls in hot pants and tool belts has fixed the place up, and even put a Jacuzzi in every bathroom. And you ask, 'is this mine?'

"In my case, I have put back on my artist's hat, and coolly ap-
praised the product of the adaptation process. And when I do that,
I guess I can imagine a different movie. But I can't imagine the
movie that got made being any better. And the movie that got made
was so very very good, I think, that I won't mind being associated
with it henceforth. I'm thrilled that it is as sharp and as adept as it is
at doing the things Hollywood does really right. That it has a kind
of integrity as an object and is incredibly watchable and means
something too I think. I admire people who do something I can't,
and do it extremely well. And in this case I got to see that.

"To be sure, the movie is a peculiar and loose adaptation of my
novel, with a great many changes. But I think to do anything less
than fall on my bare knees onto gravel in ecstatic appreciation of
how gloriously much better it turned out than it might have, would
be kind of unlucky, ungrateful, and unappreciative. That you can
somehow, from something you created, cause another work of art
to be born into the world, that has a kinship relationship to yours,
and which you are delighted to be seen and associated with—and to
actually enjoy sitting by yourself watching—is something of a triple
play experience for an artist.

"So, I loved it would be the easiest way to put it."

Every author and rights-holder's nightmare, of course, is that
the opposite will happen: that Hollywood will screw up their story,
that it won't be what it could or should have been or—in the case of
true-life stories—won't bear any resemblance to what really took
place. And, to be sure, sometimes that happens.

But a pack of idiots getting hold of your story and running it
into the ground remains the exception, and people don't get into
this business to make bad movies. As screenwriter/producer Leslie
Dixon points out, "writers of books and other nonfilm formats always have the option of pulling a Salinger and just not selling the
rights, so that a crappy movie won't be made."

But stories are meant to be told, not squirreled away in steamer
trunks in the basement. And the way to get your story told to the

greatest number of people is to get it made into a movie. If we as storytellers are going to cower in the corner for fear that someone, somewhere, somewhen might possibly mess up the film version of our story—then we might as well never walk out the front door, either, for fear of being run over. Which, statistically speaking, is a lot more likely than having your book turned into a bad movie. "You can't live your life thinking about worst-case scenarios," says Susannah Grant. "That's no way to live."

John August offers this advice: "Your book is finished, it's published, and it sits on a shelf. The screenwriter's never going to rip your pages off the shelf and change your book. It's still there, it's still yours, and it's still exactly what you wanted it to be."

Finally, as Walter Kirn observes, "The thing about movies, from the author's point of view, is this: if you want to claim the movie, you can. You're free to say yep, that's my movie, or the movie of my book. So you can get all the credit for the good sexy part of it. And if you want to disavow it, you can do that, too, and have no responsibility at all. It goes both ways."

And so, really, you can't lose.

For extreme-depth interviews with the people quoted here (and others), visit:

http://makeyourstoryamovie.com/bookbonus.html.

PART VII

BONUS MATERIAL

Movies aren't the only things going digital—and this book is more than what you hold in your hands. Although I've done my best to squeeze in as much useful information and as many insightful quotes as possible, there's just too much to fit—and I'm not done yet. I needed a way to make this book like Dr. Who's pad: bigger on the inside than the outside. And so you'll find a wealth of additional material on the book's companion Web site at:

http://makeyourstoryamovie.com.

CHAPTER 37
BONUS CHAPTERS AND MORE

Because the online content of the companion Web site is constantly being expanded, there's no way to list it all here. So what follows is just a sampling of what you'll find there now or in the reasonably near future . . .

BONUS CHAPTERS (now live or coming soon)

The Pitch Pack: Pitching the Screenplay—Without the Screenplay

How I Got an Agent in 48 Hours, Over the Christmas Holiday, Without Asking to Be Represented

Logline Workshop: *Titanic*

Structure Workshop: *Harry Potter* (Book and Film)

Story Map Workshop: *Harry Potter* (Book and Film)

Structure Workshop: *Jurassic Park* (Book and Film)

From Story to Screen: *Erin Brockovich*

From Story to Screen: *Limitless*

Going Rogue: Make Your Own Damned Movie

Copyright: Who Needs It?

INTERVIEWS (now live or coming soon)

Alan Glynn (author)

Barry Levine (comic book publisher)

Bill Marsilii (screenwriter)

Bonnie Eskenazi (entertainment attorney)

Christopher Lockhart (story editor)

Ed Solomon (screenwriter)

Ehren Kruger (screenwriter)

Evan Daugherty (screenwriter)

Gail Lyon (producer)

Gale Anne Hurd (producer)

Isa Dick Hackett (producer and administrator, Philip K. Dick Estate)

Jay Simpson (screenwriter)

John August (screenwriter)

Jonathan Hensleigh (screenwriter/producer/director)

Julie Richardson (producer)

Leslie Dixon (screenwriter/producer)

Michael Nozik (producer)

Mike Richardson (comic book publisher/producer)

Paul Haggis (screenwriter/producer/director)

Rex Pickett (author/playwright)

Ryan Condal (screenwriter)

Steve Niles (screenwriter/comic book writer)

Susannah Grant (screenwriter)

Terry Rossio (screenwriter)

Vikas Swarup (author)

Walter Kirn (author)

OTHER (now live)

Updated information on the highest-grossing film adaptations of all time, record-breaking sales, and more.

For a shortcut to all of this, visit:

http://makeyourstoryamovie.com/bookbonus.html.

PART VIII

CONTRIBUTORS

CONTRIBUTORS INTERVIEWED FOR THIS BOOK

The following is a quick-reference guide to the authors, comic creators and publishers, screenwriters, producers, directors, entertainment attorneys and others whose advice appears in these pages. (More complete details can be found online at http://makeyourstoryamovie.com/bookbonus.html.)

ALAN GLYNN is author of the novels *The Dark Fields* (rereleased as *Limitless*), *Winterland*, *Bloodland* (winner of the 2011 Irish Book Award for Crime Fiction), and *Graveland*. The *Limitless* movie earned over $150 million in theaters.

BARRY LEVINE cofounded comic book company Radical Publishing in 2007, and has already set up a dozen adaptation projects in Hollywood, including *Hercules: The Thracian Wars* (COM), *Oblivion* (COM), *Shrapnel* (COM), *The Last Days of American Crime* (COM), *Aladdin: Legacy of the Lost* (COM), *Hotwire* (COM), and *Earp: Saints for Sinners* (COM).

BILL MARSILII's first script sale (*Déjà Vu*, cowritten with Terry Rossio) was a record-breaker, selling in a deal worth $5.6 million. His other credits include *The Wind in the Willows* (NOV), the television series *The Wubbulous World of Dr. Seuss* (NOVs), and *Lightspeed* (also cowritten with Terry Rossio)—which recently sold for $3.5 million.

BONNIE ESKENAZI is a partner at Greenberg Glusker, which is perhaps Hollywood's most respected entertainment law firm. Clients have included such luminaries as James Cameron, Steven Spielberg, Jerry Bruckheimer, Tom Clancy, the estate of J. R. R. Tolkien, and The Beatles. The firm handles both contracts and litigation; Eskenazi is one of their top litigators, and also lectures on entertainment law at Harvard and Stanford universities.

CATHLEEN BLACKBURN is a founding partner of UK law firm Maier Blackburn, and the principal attorney for the estate of J. R. R. Tolkien, advising on matters of copyright, publishing, and contracts.

CHRISTOPHER LOCKHART is executive story editor at reigning Hollywood superagency WME, and formerly held the same position at ICM, where he was also in charge of the agent trainee program. His job is to read and consult on scripts for top-end clients, which have included Nicolas Cage, Russell Crowe, Robert Downey Jr., Richard Gere, Mel Gibson, Jennifer Lopez, Steve Martin, Matthew McConaughey, Liam Neeson, Ed Norton, Michelle Pfeiffer, Winona Ryder, Sylvester Stallone, Sharon Stone, and Denzel Washington, among others. Chris is also a producer; his first documentary, *Most Valuable Players,* was selected by Oprah Winfrey for her Documentary Film Club, and aired on the Oprah Winfrey Network. He produces the *Collector* franchise as well.

ED SOLOMON's writing credits include *Men In Black* (COM), *Charlie's Angels* (TVS), *The In-Laws* (MOV), *Levity, Super Mario Bros.* (GAM), *Bill & Ted's Excellent Adventure, Bill & Ted's Bogus Journey, How to Disappear Completely* (MOV), *Tokyo Suckerpunch* (NOV), and a number of series TV episodes (including *Bill & Ted's Excellent Adven-*

tures (MOV). He's also directed and produced for film and television.

EHREN KRUGER began his career by winning a Nicholl Fellowship for his *Arlington Road* screenplay. His writing credits include the *Transformers* (GAM), *Ring* (NOV), and *Scream* franchises, *Blood and Chocolate* (NOV), *Reindeer Games*, *The Brothers Grimm*, *Skeleton Key,* and *The Talisman* TV series (NOV). He's also produced for film and television.

EVAN DAUGHERTY's first script sale was *Snow White and the Huntsman* (MLF)—which brought $3.2 million in a 2010 studio bidding war. His second film, *Killing Season,* is already in production.

GAIL LYON is a producer whose credits include the Oscar-nominated *Erin Brockovich* (TRU), *Gattaca, Edge of Darkness* (TVS), *Peter Pan* (NOV/PLY), *Stuart Little 2* (NOV), and *Win a Date with Tad Hamilton!* She has also produced for television.

GALE ANNE HURD's producing credits include *The Terminator, Hulk* (COM), and *Punisher* (COM) franchises, *Armageddon, Aliens, The Abyss, Safe Passage* (NOV), *Aeon Flux* (TVS), *The Waterdance, The Wronged Man* (ART/TRU), and *The Walking Dead* TV series (COM). She's also produced several documentaries, and cowrote *The Terminator* with James Cameron. She chairs the Academy's Nicholl Fellowships Committee.

ISA DICK HACKETT oversees the rights to the works of her father, the late Philip K. Dick, whose novels and short stories have been adapted into films including *Blade Runner* (NOV), *Minority Report* (STO), two *Total Recalls* (STO), *The Adjustment Bureau* (STO), *Through a Scanner Darkly* (NOV), *Next* (STO), *Paycheck* (STO), and others.

JOHN AUGUST's writing credits include *Charlie's Angels* and *Charlie's Angels: Full Throttle* (both TVS), *Charlie and the Chocolate Factory* (NOV), *Big Fish* (NOV), *Corpse Bride, Titan A.E., Dark Shadows* (TVS), *Tarzan* (NOV), *Frankenweenie, Preacher* (COM), and the *D.C.* TV series. He directed *The Nines,* and also produced *Prince of Persia: The Sands of Time* (GAM) and the *D.C.* television series. His first adaptation was a children's book with the unlikely title *How To Eat Fried Worms* (NOV).

JONATHAN HENSLEIGH's writing credits include *Armageddon*, *Die Hard with a Vengeance* (NOV/SCR), *Jumanji* (NOV), *Next* (STO), *The Punisher* (COM), *The Saint* (NOVs/TVS), *Kill the Irishman* (TRU), *A Far-Off Place* (NOVs), and *The Young Indiana Jones Chronicles* TV series (MOV). He directed *Kill the Irishman* (TRU) and *The Punisher* (COM), and produced *Armageddon, Con Air,* and *Gone in Sixty Seconds* (MOV).

JULIE RICHARDSON's producing credits include *Collateral, Nice Girls Don't Get the Corner Office* (NFB), and *The Collector* franchise.

LESLI LINKA GLATTER wrote and directed her first film, *Tales of Meeting and Parting* (TRU), which earned an Oscar nomination for Best Live Action Short. She has directed feature and television movies and dozens of episodes for series TV, and recently won the Director's Guild Award for Best Director of Dramatic Series (Night). She currently has several adaptations in development.

LESLIE DIXON is one of Hollywood's few female A-list writers. Her credits include *Mrs. Doubtfire* (NOV), *Freaky Friday* (NOV/ MOV), *Hairspray* (PLY/MOV), *The Thomas Crown Affair* (MOV), *Pay It Forward* (NOV), *Look Who's Talking Now, The Heartbreak Kid* (STO/ MOV), *Just Like Heaven* (NOV), *Overboard,* and *Outrageous Fortune*. She's also produced several features, including *Limitless* (NOV).

MICHAEL NOZIK is an Oscar-nominated producer with over two dozen movies, including *The Next Three Days* (MOV), *Love in the*

Time of Cholera (NOV), *Syriana* (NFB), *The Motorcycle Diaries* (NFBs), *The Legend of Bagger Vance* (NOV), and *Quiz Show* (NFB/HIS). He's also produced several movies for television.

MIKE RICHARDSON is founder and publisher of Dark Horse Comics. As a producer, he's been instrumental in bringing about such adaptations as *300* (COM/HIS), *Sin City* (COM), *The Mask* and *Timecop* (both COM, and both of which he cowrote), *30 Days of Night* (COM), *Alien vs. Predator* (COM/MOVs), the *Hellboy* franchise (COM), and *R.I.P.D.* (COM). All told, he's optioned or sold close to 100 projects, produced 28 films (including TV), has another two dozen in development, and won an Emmy for the television documentary *Mr. Warmth: The Don Rickles Project*.

PAUL HAGGIS was nominated for an unprecedented five Academy Awards in three years—one for directing, one for producing, and three for writing (original and adapted)—winning two. His writing credits include *The Next Three Days* (MOV), *Casino Royale* (NOV/MOV), *Quantum of Solace* (NOVs), *Million Dollar Baby* (STO), *Crash, In the Valley of Elah* (ART/TRU), *Flags of Our Fathers* (NFB/HIS), *Letters from Iwo Jima* (NFBs/HIS), and episodes for over a dozen different television series. He directed and produced *Crash, The Next Three Days* (MOV), and *In the Valley of Elah* (ART/TRU), produced *Million Dollar Baby* (STO) and the *Crash* TV series (MOV) and dozens of episodes of other series, and wrote and directed *Third Person*.

REX PICKETT is author of the novel *Sideways* and its sequel, *Vertical*. The *Sideways* movie grossed $109 million at the box office and drew five Academy Award nominations, including Best Picture and Best Adapted Screenplay (winning the latter). A film called *My Mother Dreams the Satan's Disciples in New York*—written by Rex—won an Academy Award for Best Live Action Short. He's also adapted his *Sideways* novel into a play.

290

RYAN CONDAL sold his first script, *Galahad,* for $500,000, and has since been hired to adapt several works for the screen—including *Hercules: The Thracian Wars* (COM).

STEVE NILES is a comic writer whose graphic novel *30 Days of Night* was adapted for the screen (he cowrote the screenplay as well) and also spawned a television miniseries, which he produced. Other adapted works include *Steve Niles' Remains* (COM) and *Wake the Dead* (COM).

SUSANNAH GRANT began her screenwriting career by winning a Nicholl Fellowship for her script *Island Girl,* and has since gone on to write films like *Pocahontas* (HIS), *The Soloist* (NFB/TRU), *Charlotte's Web* (NOV), *In Her Shoes* (NOV), *28 Days,* and *Erin Brockovich* (TRU)—for which she received an Academy Award nomination. She's also written, produced, and directed for television, and is the former chair of the Academy's Nicholl Fellowships Committee.

TERRY ROSSIO's writing credits include the *Pirates of the Caribbean* (THM), *Shrek* (NOV), *Zorro* (STO/MOV/RAD/TVS), and *National Treasure* franchises, *The Lone Ranger* (RAD/MOV/TVS), *Treasure Planet, Small Soldiers, Godzilla* (MOV), *Aladdin* (MLF), *Little Monsters,* and *Déjà Vu*—a spec screenplay that sold in a record-breaking deal worth $5.6 million. He's also written and directed for TV, and produced features including *Shrek, Déjà Vu, G-Force,* and *Pirates of the Caribbean: On Stranger Tides.* His *Lightspeed* project (co-written with Bill Marsilii) recently sold for $3.5 million.

VIKAS SWARUP is author of the novel *Q&A,* which was adapted and retitled *Slumdog Millionaire.* The film made nearly $400 million at the box office and won eight of the ten Academy Awards for which it was nominated, including Best Picture and Best Adapted Screenplay. His latest novel is called *Six Suspects.* Swarup has written for *Time, The Guardian, The Telegraph, The Financial Times,* and *DNA* (India), among others, and serves as Consul General of India in Osaka-Kobe, Japan.

WALTER KIRN's novel *Up in the Air* was made into a movie starring George Clooney, which grossed over $160 million at the box office and earned six Academy Award nominations (including Best Adapted Screenplay and Best Picture). Kirn is the author of several other novels, including *Thumbsucker* and *The Unbinding* (which is online-only), and a nonfiction book titled *Lost in the Meritocracy: The Undereducation of an Overachiever.* He's also written for *New York Magazine, The New York Times Book Review,* and *New York Times Sunday Magazine,* and is a contributing editor for *Time.*

ABOUT THE AUTHOR

JOHN ROBERT MARLOW is a novelist, screenwriter, producer, and adaptation specialist and consultant.

NOVELS AND SCREENPLAYS

His first tech-thriller novel, *Nano,* was published in hardcover by Forge/St. Martin's Press in 2004, and was immediately recognized as inherently cinematic ("Marlow's debut is a real page-turner"— *Kirkus Reviews*; "Reads like a big-budget summer blockbuster"— *Booklist*).

The adapted *Nano* screenplay John wrote recently went into development with producer/director Jan de Bont (*Speed, Twister, Minority Report*), and has drawn mention in *Variety, The Hollywood Reporter,* and *The Los Angeles Times.*

Collateral producer Julie Richardson liked John's romantic adventure-comedy screenplay *Snowjob* so much she hired a private detective to track him down on vacation, so she could option it before anyone else. In 2012, John closed a deal on another adapted screenplay (*War Gods,* based on his own sci-fi comic script), which he will also executive produce on an estimated $60 million budget.

Before making his first deal, John was twice a finalist (top 10 of over 5,000 entries) in the Nicholl Fellowships in Screenwriting

Program of the Academy of Motion Picture Arts & Sciences (the same organization that awards the Oscars). Over the course of the program's 25-year history, over 50,000 screenwriters have competed for top honors. John is one of only seven to reach the top 10 twice, and the only one to do so with adaptations.

NONFICTION

John's nonfiction articles and photography have appeared in numerous print and online publications, with circulations of up to 30 million. His articles on writing have been published in the *Screenwriter's & Playwright's Market* and the *Novel and Short Story Writer's Market* (both from *Writer's Digest Books*), *The Writer, Writers' Journal*, and *Fellow Script*, and online at *Backspace, Women On Writing, Writing-World*, and his own *Self Editing Blog* (which offers free advice to authors and screenwriters).

EDITING, CONSULTING, AND ADAPTATIONS

John has worked as a developmental editor since 2001, upgrading the screenplays, novel and book manuscripts of others to the point where they can be offered for sale.

In 2011, he launched the Make Your Story a Movie blog to offer free advice and fee-based services to those wishing to turn their books and other stories into movies. This book is an adaptation/expansion of the blog. John's Web site and e-mail address appear below.

Make Your Story a Movie blog:
http://makeyourstoryamovie.com

Contact John at:
mysam@makeyourstoryamovie.com

INDEX